D0214716

Through Other Continents

Through Other Continents

AMERICAN LITERATURE ACROSS DEEP TIME

Wai Chee Dimock

PRINCETON UNIVERSITY PRESS

PRINCETON AND OXFORD

Copyright © 2006 by Princeton University Press
Published by Princeton University Press, 41 William Street, Princeton, New Jersey 08540
In the United Kingdom: Princeton University Press, 3 Market Place, Woodstock,
Oxfordshire OX20 1SY

Library of Congress Cataloging-in-Publication Data
Dimock, Wai-chee, 1953–
Through other continents: American literature across deep time / Wai Chee Dimock.
p.   cm.
Includes bibliographical references and index.
ISBN-13: 978-0-691-11449-1 (cloth: alk. paper)
ISBN-10: 0-691-11449-8 (cloth: alk. paper)
1. American literature—History and criticism.   2. American literature—Foreign
influences.   3. Globalization in literature.   4. Literature, Comparative—American and
Ancient.   5. Literature, Comparative—Ancient and American.   6. Influence (Literary,
artistic, etc.)   I. Title.
PS157 .D56 2006
810.9—dc22   2005057723

British Library Cataloging-in-Publication Data is available

This book has been composed in Sabon.

Printed on acid-free paper. ∞

pup.princeton.edu

Printed in the United States of America

10 9 8 7 6 5 4 3 2 1

For GD and Beatrice

Contents

Illustrations

Acknowledgments

THIS BOOK would not have been possible without the incisive—and some-times infuriating—questions from students and colleagues. I am especially grateful to Jonathan Arac and Dominick LaCapra for the remarkable ex-changes at the Lionel Trilling Seminar at Columbia and the School of Criticism and Theory at Cornell. For their toughness and generosity, I thank David Palumbo-Liu, Don Pease, Bruce Robbins, Gayatri Spivak, Mary Louise Pratt, Russ Castronovo, Susan Friedman, Gordon Hunter, Brian Edwards, Dilip Gaonkar, Jonathan Freedman, Sara Blair, Patsy Yae-gar, Susan Griffin, Lawrence Buell, Priscilla Wald, Michael Denning, and Lloyd Pratt. I am also fortunate to find myself among so many formidable linguists: Ben Foster, Haun Saussy, Giuseppe Mazzotta, and Andrew Co-hen provided invaluable help with the Near Eastern languages and with Greek, Latin, and Italian. Roger Blandford inspired thoughts of "deep time" from the scale of astronomy. Doris Sommer brain-stormed in the Boston subway and came up with the title. Tim Powell, David Greven, Radi Clytus, Louise Bernard, Jennifer Greeson, Mark Greif, Rebecca Berne, Lara Cohen, Leslie Eckel, and Jeff Glover show me a future I look forward to.

At Princeton University Press, Hanne Winarsky, Adithi Kasturirangan, and Ellen Foos make up a great team. Cindy Crumrine not only im-proved my prose but actually heard live a song that I discuss, "Deep Elem Blues," performed by the Grateful Dead at Harpur College on May 2, 1970.

Through Other Continents

Introduction:
Planet as Duration and Extension

ON APRIL 14, 2003, the Iraqi National Library and the Islamic library in the Religious Ministry were burned to the ground. For months before this happened, archaeologists had been warning the United States government that an invasion of Iraq would pose the gravest threat to legacies from the Sumerian, Babylonian, and Assyrian civilizations, going back ten thousand years. After the invasion, the same archaeologists urged the U.S.-led coalition to observe the "international law of belligerent occupation" and protect the artifacts and archives left vulnerable by the conduct of war.[1] The coalition forces had in fact been protecting a number of selective sites, notably the oilfields. But buildings housing ancient manuscripts were not on that valued list. No military personnel was present when the looters and arsonists came. When a journalist, Robert Fisk of the *London Independent*, ran over to report the attack to the U.S. Marines Civil Affairs Bureau, mentioning that the buildings were only five minutes away, easily identifiable by the hundred-foot flames leaping from the windows and the smoke visible from a distance of three miles, still no action was taken.[2]

The entire contents of the two libraries were reduced to ashes. According to the Associated Press, these included one of the oldest surviving copies of the Qur'an, ancient Arabic linguistic treatises, records from the caliphate when Iraq was part of the Ottoman Empire, as well as records from the Abbasid period, an archive "dating back a millennium." These documents, produced when Baghdad was the cultural center of the Arab world, had survived by sheer luck for a length of time that said something about the human species as a whole: its extended sojourn on this earth, its ability to care for objects in its safekeeping. The destruction of these records in 2003 says something about the human species as well, in ways we might not care to think about.

The marines certainly did not think about it. Operating under a military timetable, and under the short chronology of a young nation, they were largely indifferent to the history of the world. That history, in existence long before the United States came into being, has an uncanny way of multiplying references for current events. For the archives of Baghdad had in fact been destroyed once before. In 1258, the Mongols, led by Genghis

Khan's grandson Hulegu, had sacked the city and emptied the contents of its libraries into the Tigris River, so much so that the water turned black. Modern Iraqis see the actions of the United States as yet another installment of that long-running saga: "The modern Mongols, the new Mongols did that. The Americans did that."[3] All of these made no sense to the marines. The year 1258 was long ago and far away. It is separated by 745 years from 2003. The United States has nothing to do with it.

This book is an extended argument against that view, and against the all-too-common image of time underwriting it. This is a spatialized image: time here looks a bit like a measuring tape, with fixed segments, fixed unit lengths, each assignable to a number. The distance between any two events is measured by the distance between these numbers, telling us whether they are remote or proximate, pertinent or not pertinent. Standardization reigns. Benedict Anderson and Anthony Giddens see this as the mark of modernity, linked to the rise of the nation-state and the rule of the mechanical clock. These two, the nation and the clock, not only unify time but also "dis-embed" it, removing it from local contexts, local irregularities, and abstracting it into a metric, at once "empty and homogeneous."[4] The guiding spirit is serial numbers, doubling here as chronological dates.[5] On the strength of these dates, the ancient and the modern can be certified to be worlds apart, never to be in contact. An immutable gulf separates them, as immutable as, say, the gulf between 1258 and 2003.

Is this always the case? Are the properties of time truly identical to the properties of number?[6] And do modern human beings always experience time as a measuring tape, uniform and abstract, untouched by locality, and untouched by the differential weight of the past? I would like to argue not. The uneven pace of modernity suggests that standardization is not everywhere the rule. In many parts of the non-Western world, a very different ontology of time prevails.[7] And since, thanks to global military ventures, this non-Western world is now inexorably present to the West, these alternate durations are inexorably present as well. For an Iraqi, the distance between 1258 and 2003 is nothing like the distance between these dates for an American. There is nothing empty about this stretch of time. It cannot be rationalized and fitted into the semantic scope of American English. The dates are not just numbers; they are bound up with Arabic, with the long history of a turbulent locale, and saturated by its passions. The short chronology of the United States is not adequate to that history, just as its numerical order is not adequate to those passions.

It is in this context, against the glaring inadequacy of a nation-based model in world politics, that I would like to point to its parallel inadequacy in literary studies. For too long, American literature has been seen as a world apart, sufficient unto itself, not burdened by the chronology and geography outside the nation, and not making any intellectual demands on that score. An Americanist hardly needs any knowledge of English literature, let alone Persian literature, Hindu literature, Chinese literature. It is as if the borders of knowledge were simply the replicas of national borders. And yet, what does it mean to set aside a body of writing as "American"? What assumptions enable us to take an adjective derived from a territorial jurisdiction and turn it into a mode of literary causality, making the latter reflexive of and indeed coincidental with the former?

Nationhood, on this view, is endlessly reproduced in all spheres of life. This reproductive logic assumes that there is a seamless correspondence between the temporal and spatial boundaries of the nation and the boundaries of all other expressive domains. And, because this correspondence takes the form of a strict entailment—because its causality goes all the way up and all the way down—it is also assumed that there is a literary domain lining up in just the same way. This is why the adjective "American" can serve as a literary epithet. Using it, we limit ourselves, with or without explicit acknowledgment, to an analytic domain foreclosed by definition, a kind of scholarly unilateralism. Literature here is the product of one nation and one nation alone, analyzable within its confines.

American literary studies as a discipline began with this premise. And yet, as witnessed by the recent outpouring of work aspiring to the "transnational" and the "postnational," the analytic adequacy of the sovereign state has been increasingly called into question.[8] *Through Other Continents* reflects this sea change. The preposition "through" is especially important to my argument. I have in mind a form of indebtedness: what we called "American" literature is quite often a shorthand, a simplified name for a much more complex tangle of relations. Rather than being a discrete entity, it is better seen as a crisscrossing set of pathways, open-ended and ever multiplying, weaving in and out of other geographies, other languages and cultures. These are input channels, kinship networks, routes of transit, and forms of attachment—connective tissues binding America to the rest of the world. Active on both ends, they thread America texts into the topical events of other cultures, while also threading the long durations of those cultures into the short chronology of the United States. This double threading thickens time, lengthens it, shadowing in its midst the abiding traces of the planet's multitudinous life.

I would like to propose a new term—"deep time"—to capture this phenomenon. What this highlights is a set of longitudinal frames, at once projective and recessional, with input going both ways, and binding continents and millennia into many loops of relations, a densely interactive fabric. Restored to this, American literature emerges with a much longer history than one might think. This elongation is effected partly through its off-center circulation in the world and partly through the presence of alternate measures—African, Asian, and European—unfolding in its midst. Literature is the home of nonstandard space and time. Against the official borders of the nation and against the fixed intervals of the clock, what flourishes here is irregular duration and extension, some extending for thousands of years or thousands of miles, each occasioned by a different tie and varying with that tie, and each loosening up the chronology and geography of the nation.

Dates such as 1776 are misleading for just reason, for the temporal duration for American literature surely did not begin at just that point, that upper limit. Nor did it begin at 1620, when the Plymouth Colony was settled. These putative beginnings, monumentalized and held up like so many bulwarks against the long histories of other continents and the long history of America as a Native American habitat, cannot in fact fulfill their insulating function. The continuum of historical life does not grant the privilege of autonomy to any spatial locale; it does not grant the privilege of autonomy to any temporal segment. The nation, as a segmenting device, is vulnerable for just that reason. It is constantly stretched, punctured, and infiltrated. Territorial sovereignty is poor prophylactic.

This book explores some of the consequences of this breakdown in sovereignty. As an associative form, the nation-state is a late arrival in human history; it had a finite beginning and, just conceivably, it might also have a finite end. Rather than naturalizing its clock and its border, I try to loosen up both. What would happen if we go beyond 1776 and 1620, if we trace threads of relation to the world that antedate these allegedly founding moments? What would American literature look like then, restored to a *longue durée*, a scale enlargement along the temporal axis that also enlarges its spatial compass?

Scale enlargement is, of course, most eloquently proposed by Fernand Braudel and by historians of the *Annales* school, as an alternative to standard national histories, organized by dates and periodized by decades, if not by years. Against such thin slices of time, Braudel proposes "a history to be measured in centuries this time: the history of the long, even of the very long time span, of the *longue durée*."[9] This *longue durée* yields a different archive, data of different nature and scope. It also brings to light a different analytic fabric, throwing into relief trajectories and connections that might otherwise have been obscured:

For the historian, accepting the *longue durée* entails a readiness to change his style, his attitudes, a whole reversal in his thinking, a whole new way of conceiving of social affairs. It means becoming used to a

slower tempo, which sometimes almost borders on the motionless . . .
[I]t is in relation to these expanses of slow-moving history that the
whole of history is to be rethought, as if on the basis of an infrastruc-
ture. All the stages, all the thousands of stages, all the thousand explo-
sions of historical time can be understood on the basis of these depths,
this semistillness.[10]

For Braudel, it is the slow tempo of time that gives a true sense of history: a structure of evolving relations, a structure of everyday ties, rather
than a few executive dates. Scale enlargement along the temporal axis
changes our very sense of the connectedness among human beings. It
also suggests that different investigative contexts might need different
time frames, with no single one serving as an all-purpose metric. Some
historical phenomena need large-scale analysis. They need hundreds,
thousands, or even billions of years to be recognized for what they are:
phenomena constituted by their temporal extension, with a genealogy
much longer than the life span of any biological individual, and interesting for just that reason.[11] A shorter time frame would have cut them off
in midstream, would have obscured the fact of their cumulation.

In the hands of Immanuel Wallerstein, the *longue durée* has served as
a pivot to lay bare the folly of shoehorning large-scale developments
into the chronology of a single nation. Only a "world-system" can bear
the explanatory weight of deep structural transformations. Of course,
for Wallerstein, the emergence of capitalism is the prime example of
such deep structural transformations; his large-scale model is geared
specifically toward this analytic object.[12] Without disagreeing with him,
I would like to suggest, nonetheless, that there are other phenomena,
not reducible to capitalism, that also unfold against long durations, requiring scale enlargement for their analysis. World religions, for one, in-
vite us to think of the world's populations as a locally inflected and yet
globally connected unit. The morphology of language, especially a language as diverse and dispersed as English, likewise presents us with an
array of vernaculars, creolized forms developed through centuries and
spread across continents. Then there are categories of experience, such
as beauty or death, that seem not entirely predicated on the temporal
and spatial boundaries of the nation-state. This is also the case with
long-lasting genres, such as epic and novel, with thousands of years behind them, and demanding analytic frames of comparable magnitude.
Finally, the concept of a global civil society, by its very nature, invites us
to think of the planet as a plausible whole, a whole that, I suggest,
needs to be mapped along the temporal axis as well as the spatial, its
membership open not only to contemporaries but also to those centuries apart.

The question is very much a question of scale. Gayatri Spivak speaks of "planetarity" as a never-to-be-realized horizon, a "catachresis for inscribing collective responsibility."[13] She urges us to hazard it for just that reason. This book takes that risk. It is an attempt to rethink the shape of literature against the history and habitat of the human species, against the "deep time" of the planet Earth, as described by two scientific disciplines, geology and astronomy.[14] The former works with a geological record of some 600 million years, and the latter with a record still more staggering, 14 billion light-years. The humanities have no time frame of comparable length. What we do have are written records going back five or six thousand years, and oral, musical, and visual material going back further. Since American authors have made a point of engaging this material, drawing on it and incorporating it in their own writings, the least we can do, as scholars and readers, is to do likewise. These old records and their modern transpositions give us a "deep time" in human terms. They alert us to our long sojourn on this planet, a sojourn marked by layers of relations, weaving our history into our dwelling place, and making us what we are, a species with a sedimented imprint. Honoring that imprint, and honoring also the imprints of other creatures evolving as we do, we take our place as one species among others, inhabiting a shared ecology, a shared continuum.

CHAPTER ONE

Global Civil Society:
Thoreau on Three Continents

HOW PERMANENT is the nation as an associative form? Do human beings congregate naturally as sovereign states, defining themselves naturally by their membership in nations? Or are there other ties, other loyalties and commitments, based on non-national ideals and flourishing on non-national platforms? Bruce Ackerman speaks of a "world constitutionalism,"[1] creating a rule of law across national boundaries. Jürgen Habermas argues for a "postnational constellation," made up of a broad array of nongovernmental forms, an integrated network reflecting the planet as an integrated environment. Such a network casts doubt not only on the primacy but on the very rationality of the nation-state, with its necessarily exclusive citizenship, necessarily "circumscribed within a determinate national territory."[2]

This chapter explores the nature and efficacy of one such nongovernmental form, as it emerges and bears critically on the claims of the nation-state. To give this form an argumentative edge, I invoke a phrase much used these days, perhaps overused—"global civil society." An entire program has been set up at the London School of Economics under this heading; it is also the stated goal of the United Nations, appearing often on the lips of Kofi Annan.[3] The broad appeal of this phrase probably began in the late 1980s, in Eastern Europe, in the aftermath of the crushing of the Prague Spring. That show of military force gave rise to a contrary hope, the hope for a domain opposed to the military, a domain purposely and unyieldingly civilian. Michael Walzer, one of the earliest theorists to take note of this new development, points out that the concept is in fact not new, but descended from the eighteenth century. It is an idea of the Enlightenment, a name given to a sphere of life "outside of, prior to, or in the shadow of state and citizenship."[4] And it is crucial that this name should be in place, Walzer says, for democracy suffers "when the state takes up all the available room,"[5] when there is no definitional counterpoint, no theorized limits to its sovereignty. Civil society might indeed be one of the side effects of the nation-state, but it is not coincidental with it, for, as a side effect, "it must also be *another place*,"[6] a place not territorial but associative, and extending as far as those associations extend.

SUBNATIONAL AND TRANSNATIONAL

What is especially interesting about Walzer's formulation is that global civil society, as he envisions it, is a sphere of life that is both smaller and larger than the territorial regime: it is subnational in one sense, transnational in another. This duality of scale means that its sphere of action is on either side of the state apparatus. On the one hand, it is a low-skill, low-stakes, low-level playing field, where people of no particular consequence can become momentarily consequential, can have some say, can take it upon themselves to step forward and "propose, debate, and decide."[7] On the other hand, because these players are such low-level players, there is also nothing to stop them from sliding under and spreading out, in a sort of rhizomatic fashion.[8] They are below the jurisdictional plane, below the militarized infrastructures where state sovereignty comes into play. Walzer's example is an NGO (nongovernmental organization) such as Amnesty International, a civilian network that can afford to be international precisely it is a grassroots organization, because its platform is a nonstate platform, made up of small working groups all over the world.

This is an interesting paradox, definitely worth pursuing. In this chapter I will do some on-site exploration, focusing on one sphere of life that is constituted by just this duality of scale, though not discussed by Walzer. What I have in mind is the playing field called "literary culture," brought into being by that most minute, most intimate of acts, the act of reading. This act, pursued within the compass of a word, a phrase, a sentence, generates relational ties that can nonetheless extend for thousands of miles and thousand of years. It is an NGO of sorts, an NGO *avant la lettre*, an unusually fine-grained as well as long-lasting one, operating on a scale both too small and too large to be fully policed by the nation-state.

Robert Pogue Harrison proposes that we think of literary culture in just this way, as a "lexical" civil society, made up of strings of words, nuances, and etymologies reflecting the long histories of linguistic usage, and weaving our lives into a semantic network, at once endlessly localized and endlessly extended:

> It allows the past to reach out to us from the future and the future to meet us from out of the past, transforming human finitude into a field of historical relations rather than a flow of chronological moments. . . . As it binds the living to the ever-receding priority of the dead and the eventuality of the unborn, it is the true "synthetic a priori" of civil society.[9]

What would world governance look like if this civil society were given a voice? In what follows I test that possibility.

SEMANTIC NETWORKS

I begin with a single reader, doing his reading in one particular locale, Concord, Massachusetts. To what extent is this a national locale, American in its dispensation? The robustness of its literary culture suggests that we cannot be entirely sure. Other continents seem to be intervening, and other time frames seem to be activated by that intervention. That, in any case, is the story told by *Walden*. In "The Pond in Winter," Thoreau writes:

> In the morning I bathe my intellect in the stupendous and cosmogonal philosophy of the Bhagvat-Geeta, since whose composition years of the gods have elapsed, and in comparison with which our modern world and its literature seem puny and trivial. . . . I lay down the book and go to my well, and lo! There I meet the servant of the Brahmin, priest of Brahma and Vishnu and Indra, who still sits in his temple on the Ganges reading the Vedas, or dwells at the foot of a tree with his crust and water jug. I meet his servant come to draw water for his master, and our buckets as it were grate together in the same well. The pure Walden water is mingled with the sacred water of the Ganges.[10]

The map of the world that Thoreau lives in is probably not one that we recognize. As far as he is concerned, the Ganges River is in direct contact with Walden Pond; he owes his intellectual genesis to the mixing of the two.[11] Concord, Massachusetts, might be an American locale, but it is irrigated by an ancient text from Asia. Swept by that text and its torrents of time, *Walden* in turn flows outward, circumnavigating the globe, gliding past Europe and Africa on its way back to India.

WAR AND PEACE IN ANCIENT INDIA

Thoreau gives this ancient text, the *Bhagavad Gita*, an honored place not only in *Walden* but, even more emphatically, in the "Monday" chapter of *A Week on the Concord and Merrimack Rivers*. There, he says that it is "as wide as the world, and as unwearied as time; preserving the universe with Asiatic anxiety."[12] The *Bhagavad Gita*, the most sacred text in the Hindu religion, is not an integral poem by a single hand, but a composite work, layered over and written over a long period of time. Parts of it were taken from the *Katha and Svetasvatara Upanishads*, dating from about 400 BCE. The bulk of it was probably written two centuries after that.[13] Written in Sanskrit, it was translated by Sir Charles Wilkins into English in 1784, by Schlegel into Latin in 1823, and by Humboldt into German in 1826.[14] The Wilkins translation was the one Thoreau read.

The poem is structured as a dialogue between two people: Krishna, Hindu god incarnated as a charioteer, and Arjuna, the great warrior. It begins with a call to battle, a fratricidal battle between the Kurus and the Pandavas. A heated dispute then ensues between Krishna and Arjuna about the nature and justification for war. Arjuna has a hereditary obligation to fight, but he is repelled by that thought, repelled by the elevation of war into an arbitrating vehicle, a way to bring human beings to order. Any shedding of blood, he says, is unjustifiable:

> When I shall have destroyed my kindred, shall I longer look for happiness? I wish not for victory, Krishna; I want not dominion; I want not pleasure; for what is dominion, and the enjoyment of life, or even life itself, when those, for whom dominion, pleasure, and enjoyment were to be coveted, have abandoned life and fortune, and stand here in the field ready for the battle? . . . Should we destroy them, tyrants as they are, sin would take refuge with us. . . . How, O Krishna, can we be happy hereafter, when we have been the murderers of our race?[15]

For Arjuna, war and happiness are antithetical. Not only is happiness not achievable through war, it is not even repairable once war has done its damage. For any shedding of blood has lasting emotional consequences. Even the blood of tyrants, once shed, will reproduce itself in the veins of the shedders, making them tyrants in turn. Between those who initiate violence and those who respond in kind, there is a kind of doubling, a burden of guilt passed back and forth, sparing no one. Any use of force, however ethical to begin with, must sooner or later find its ethical ground in ruins. It is a too-deadly price to pay even when we need it for survival. Survival, the mere preservation of life and limb, loses its sweetness when it is at someone else's expense. Rather than returning blow for blow, Arjuna says, it is far better to throw away all protective armor, to disarm oneself through an act of the will: "I would rather patiently suffer that the sons of Dhreetarashtra, with their weapons in their hands, should come upon me, and, unopposed, kill me unguarded in the field" (1:46).

The *Bhagavad Gita* has a pacifist beginning. It opens with an agonized cry against the necessity of war, the irreparability of what it destroys. Its emotional intensity makes it unique in world literature. There is nothing in the Western canon remotely like it, not even the *Iliad* and *Odyssey*, texts most familiar to Thoreau.[16] But, emotional intensity notwithstanding, pacifism represents only one side of the debate. It is eventually overruled by a contrary argument, one that makes an even more powerful case for military action.

Krishna has no patience with what he judges to be Arjuna's squeamishness, a "despicable weakness of thy heart" (2:3). He then goes on,

with far greater force and in far greater detail, to lay down a set of philosophical justifications for war. He argues, first, that Arjuna is wrong to
be fixated on the idea of death, as if it were the absolute end, the unan-
swerable rebuke to all those who would kill. Death is not the end, Krishna
says. Being is more permanent than nonbeing, and the permanence of
being is vested in the soul, which is different from the body precisely because it will never cease to be. Immortality, in other words, is truer and
higher than mortality, and, from this perspective, death is not final, not
even real:

> The wise neither grieve for the dead nor for the living. I myself never
> *was not*, nor thou, nor all the princes of the earth; nor shall we ever
> hereafter cease to be. . . . The man who believed that it is the soul
> which killeth, and he who thinketh that the soul may be destroyed, are
> both alike deceived; for it neither killeth, nor is it killed. It is not a
> thing of which a man may say, it hath been, it is about to be, or is to
> be hereafter: for it is a thing without birth; it is ancient, constant, and
> eternal, and is not to be destroyed in this its mortal frame. How can
> the man, who believeth that this thing is incorruptible, eternal, inex-
> haustible, and without birth, think that he can either kill or cause it to
> be killed? (2:19–21)

Since the soul will never die, since there is an all-encompassing and
never-perishing foundation to the world, the physical death of the body
is largely deceptive, a mirage perpetrated by the senses. It is a short-term,
low-level phenomenon, and can be pegged to one specific locale, a secondary tier of human existence. Any sorrow it occasions is misplaced;
we feel it only because we do not know any better.

Krishna's justification for war is based on the *containability* of
death. To erase its accusing finger, he has to banish it from the eternity
of the soul. He then goes on and banishes it yet again, this time from
the behavioral psychology of human beings. That psychology is dominated not by a proleptic mourning for the death of oneself or the death
of other people, but by a drive forgetful of death, a drive to act in the
here and now, and a corresponding reluctance to sit still. Action is an
instinct, an imperative, the temporal form by which we prove ourselves. It is the form by which we give definition to our humanity, give
definition to what it means to be more than an animal, more than a
vegetable. We are not free to reject it, because without action we are
not even human:

> Man enjoyeth not freedom from action, from the non-commencement
> of that which he hath to do; nor doth he obtain happiness from a to-
> tal inactivity. No one ever resteth a moment inactive. Every man is

involuntarily urged to act by those principles which are inherent in his nature. (2:4–5)

According to Krishna, action, including military action, is what constitutes our humanity in the first place, what links us in kinship to every other human being. It is more powerful than anything we wish or not wish to do, more powerful than the volition of any single individual, because this is the existential cloth out of which the species is cut.

As a justification for war, Krishna's argument is also more deeply grounded than anything in Western literature. Thoreau, as we know, is an admirer of the Sanskrit poem—in *A Week* he quotes this particular passage on action as the key embodiment of humanity (*Week* 139)—but there is a limit to his admiration. "Kreeshna's argument, it must be allowed, is defective. No sufficient reason is given why Arjoon should fight. Arjoon may be convinced, but the reader is not" (*Week* 140).

DEATH REPRODUCED

Why isn't Thoreau convinced? We can only speculate, of course, but there is, first, the question of death and Krishna's attempt to make light of it, to show that it touches only the body but not the soul. That argument—especially in the context of *A Week*—must have seemed so wrong as to be eerie. That book is, after all, not just a record of some casual vacation but a record of probably the most important journey in Thoreau's life, taken with a companion so intimately a part of him that he uses the pronoun "we" throughout, not seeing much need for the first person singular. But, even as he continues to speak of "we," even as he commits it to paper, the pronoun has already become a memory, a mockery.[17] Thoreau's brother, John, his companion on that trip, had died in the interval, on January 11, 1842, a sudden, agonizing death from lockjaw. Ten days later, Thoreau himself displayed the same symptoms. These were psychosomatic symptoms, and they made a logical if miserable kind of sense. In a journal entry on January 8, 1842, Thoreau had written: "Am I so like thee my brother that the cadence of two notes affects us alike?"[18] If the living sounds of music have exactly the same effect on these two, it is fitting that the terminal sounds of death should as well. Even as it kills off the body of one, it tears apart the soul of the other. And it is because the soul of the other is torn apart that further symptoms open up in *his* body, a dialectical continuum of wounds. It is a travesty, then, to speak of the body and soul as separate, as if something could happen to one without happening to the other, as if the soul could be safely tucked away while the body comes undone.

On February 21, 1842, Thoreau wrote in his journal: "My soul and body have tottered along together of late tripping and hindering oneanother [*sic*] like unpractised Siamese twins."[19] Body and soul are Siamese twins because a single human being houses both. And they are Siamese twins in a different sense as well: not just within the compass of one person but, even more strikingly, across the relational fabric of more than one, dramatized (perhaps unconsciously) by Thoreau's peculiar spelling of "oneanother." With that spelling, body and soul are also united, but transversely, against the grain of individuation. The physical death of one person binds the stricken soul of someone else to an analogous state, dissolving the boundaries between them, in a faithful memorializing of the physical by the nonphysical.

Krishna has nothing to say to this. He has nothing to say when death is seen as permanent rather than ephemeral: not contained inside the skin of one person, but seeping through that skin, raging through the souls of all those around. Death, in that sense, is without terminus: it is endlessly fertile and reproductive. Krishna's defense of war, based on the containability of death, must flounder on that fact. It must flounder on all those "twinnings" across mortality, as unwilled as they are unstoppable.

Those twinnings have a further implication, less lethal, if equally wayward. While it is true that the symptoms of the dead are reproduced among the living, the explosiveness of that reproduction also suggests that not all the symptoms are pathological or malignant. The spilling over of death is a form of "life" after all, however odd it might seem. And while it lasts, densely exfoliated, it brings with it a corresponding luxuriance of outcome, erupting on many different levels and not pinned down to one. Unlike the taut line that marks our physiological end, the death that inundates life is a wavering shadow, fuzzy and indeterminate. Thoreau writes:

> To die is not to begin to die—and *continue*—it is not a state of continuance but of transientness—but to live is a condition of continuance and does not mean to be born merely.[20]

This journal entry was written on March 12, 1842, two months after the death of John, when the psychosomatic symptoms were still lingering, not fully abated, in the living Henry. And that is perhaps the point. John is dead, period. This physiological event is as clean as can be. We can date it down to the hour, the minute, the second. This is not true of the seepage across the line of mortality. *That*, as Thoreau says, is a "state of continuance."

LONG-DISTANCE SURVIVAL

This state of continuance has a direct bearing on the debate between Arjuna and Krishna about the nature and justification of war. Krishna has defended war (this is his second defense) on the grounds that action is an imperative, that human beings are hardwired for it. Thoreau does not disagree. He does not believe, however, that there is just one kind of action, the kind that leads to a quick result, instantly adducible and demonstrable. To define action in this way is to subject it to a built-in bias. It is to put a premium on military action, where victories can indeed be won with the speed of lightning. This is not a protocol Thoreau will consent to. "What is that which a man 'hath to do'? What is 'action'?" (*Week* 140), he asks. He is not convinced it must take a swift, instantaneous form. Krishna has unduly narrowed our choices because "his active faculties are paralyzed by the idea of cast[e], of impassable limits, of destiny and tyranny of time." His criterion is bluntly instrumental because his time frame is bluntly truncated. But not everyone has to accept this shotgun regime. "[T]hey who are unconcerned about the consequences of their actions, are not therefore unconcerned about their actions" (*Week* 141).

Just how far can deed and consequence by strung out? Across what distance can this relation be maintained? Is an action still meaningful if the outcome transpires far beyond the life span of the actor? If Thoreau is right—if the criterion of instant demonstrability is to be resisted—words and actions would seem to need the largest possible scope both in their backward extension and in their forward reach. They must be recognized as the long-distance survivors that they are, their agency residing in their unfolding lives.

The *Bhagavad Gita* is a case in point. In Thoreau it finds an unexpected reader, a dedicated reader, but a skeptical one, not won over. Still, this skeptic says in tribute:

> The reader is nowhere raised into and sustained in a higher, purer, or rarer region than in the Bhagvat-Geeta. Warren Hastings, in his sensible letter recommending the translation of this book to the Chairman of the East India Company, declares the original to be "of a sublimity of conception, reasoning, and diction, almost unequalled," and that the writings of the Indian philosophers "will survive when the British dominion in India shall have long ceased to exist, and when the sources which it once yielded of wealth and power are lost to remembrance." (*Week* 137)

When Warren Hastings was writing those words—when Thoreau was quoting them—British dominion in India was yet on the rise, with no end in sight. Thanks to a sense of *longue durée*, however, these two veterans of time were able to look forward to a future when the British Empire would be no more. And the *Bhagavad Gita*, outlasting the British Empire as it outlasted other empires in the past, amply affirms that *longue durée* in its two-thousand-year history.

What then is the legacy of this ancient text? What literary culture does it promote and sustain? This must be traced as a dialectic, I think, which is to say, in terms of the misreadings it inspires. If literary culture represents a form of civil society, the civility that it puts into circulation would seem to be based on a provision for skepticism, a provision for inversion. Thoreau might be a fan of the Sanskrit poem, but he is also a resisting reader every step of the way. Not persuaded by the *Bhagavad Gita*'s justification of war, he has this to say about the U.S. military in his classic essay "Resistance to Civil Government":

> a file of soldiers, colonel, captain, corporal, privates, powder-monkeys, and all, marching in admirable order over hill and dale to the wars, against their wills, ay, against their common sense and consciences. . . . Now, what are they? Men at all? Or small movable forts and magazines, at the service of some unscrupulous man in power? Visit the Navy-Yard, and behold a marine, such a man as an American government can make, or such as it can make a man with its black arts,—a mere shadow and reminiscence of humanity, a man laid out alive and standing, and already, as one may say, buried under arms with funeral accompaniments.[21]

Krishna sees war as a humanizing gesture; Thoreau sees it as a monstrosity: "black arts." These black arts preserve the outward form of humanity only to instrumentalize it, only to reduce it to a "mere shadow and reminiscence" of what it was. Human beings who have been turned into "small movable forts and magazines" are so much military equipment, assembled for a strategic purpose, a quick fix. They march not only to martial drumbeats but also to "funeral accompaniments" because their allotted time has been abbreviated to the point of instantaneity.

SLOW TRANSLATION

What does it mean not to move with that kind of speed? Thoreau does not need to look very far for an answer. Just as his own brother John has dragged on for months, surviving as psychosomatic symptoms beyond his allotted end, the same capacity for lingering would seem to be within the reach of every dead body. Certainly the legendary John Brown's:

On the day of his translation, I heard, to be sure, that he was *hung*, but I did not know what that meant; I felt no sorrow on that account; but not for a day or two did I even *hear* that he was *dead*, and not after any number of days shall I believe it. Of all the men who were said to be my contemporaries, it seemed to me that John Brown was the only one who *had not died*.[22]

The physiological fact of death is razor sharp. Its mode of being in the world, however, is oblique, prolonged, lengthened by its slow passage from one recipient to another. The key words here are *heard* and *hear*. Thoreau hears that the hanging has taken place, he hears that John Brown is dead, and the report remains just that: hearsay. It circulates, it finds its way to his ears, but it grants no closure, it does not shut up: a not-shutting-up that persists, for "not after any number of days shall I believe it."

The death of John Brown does not shut up because it is not experienced as the last word, just as, years ago, the death of John Thoreau was also not experienced as the last word. In both cases, to put death through a loop—through a recipient with a persevering and often perverse soul of his own—is to feed it into the fabric of life itself, giving it license to spill over into a reproductive cycle. That spilling over now has a name. The day of John Brown's hanging is the "day of his translation." This is the day on which his "horizontal body"[23] is borne by a freight train across distances not traveled by human feet. It is also the day on which the burden of his life is given over to the care of others, across distances equally wide, people including Thoreau but not limited to him, who will go on to write such things as "The Martyrdom of John Brown" and "The Last Days of John Brown."

Translation—the movement of a corpse by a vehicle driven by something other than himself, and the movement of a text by a vehicle driven by something similarly alien—unites the living and the dead in a gesture steeped in mortality and inverting it, carrying it on. Rather than banishing the body of the deceased from the eternity of the soul, as Krishna does, translation restores it and turns it over to as many receiving hands as the history and habitat of the species will allow. This is the civility that Thoreau extends to the *Bhagavad Gita*. It is his way of being a "reproductive" reader: reproductive, in the sense of rewriting the text, updating it, giving it a new context of action. He is probably not thinking of the Sanskrit poem when he writes these lines in *Walden*, but they speak directly to it: "The volatile truth of our words should continually betray the inadequacy of the residual statement. Their truth is instantly *translated*; its literal monument alone remains."[24]

FLEET OF CARRIERS

Translated in just this way, its volatile truth betraying its literal monument, the *Bhagavad Gita* is threaded into an American context unthinkable at its moment of genesis. This sort of threading requires the deepest of time. It requires the gathering of many hands, none of which has exclusive say over the civil society that issues from their commingling. For to every act there is always a sequel, rejoinders that extend what they receive and literally pick it up, carrying it forward.[25] This fleet of carriers is rooted in the etymology of the word *action* itself, as Hannah Arendt reminds us:

> Greek and Latin, unlike the modern languages, contain two altogether different and yet interrelated words with which to designate the verb "to act." To the two Greek verbs *archein* ("to begin," "to lead," finally, "to rule,") and *prattein* ("to pass through," "to achieve," "to finish") correspond the two Latin verbs *agere* ("to set into motion," "to lead") and *gerere* (whose original meaning is "to bear"). Here it seems as though each action were divided into two parts, the beginning made by a single person and the achievement in which many join by "bearing" and "finishing" the enterprise, by seeing it through.[26]

In the case of the *Bhagavad Gita*, the beginning was never made by a single person: it was a composite vehicle from the outset. Is there a unified vision governing the entire work? Scholars disagree.[27] Thoreau seems to have wondered about this as well. As he notes, the *Bhagavad Gita* is riven with "Asiatic anxiety,"[28] more conflicted than it would let on at any given point. Even though military action is clearly and unhesitatingly recommended by Krishna, there are also passages such as this, racked by other thoughts:

> The learned even are puzzled to determine what is work, and what is not. I will tell thee what that work is, by knowing which thou wilt be delivered from misfortune. It may be defined—action, improper action, and inaction. The path of action is full of darkness. He who may behold, as it were, inaction in action, and action in inaction, is wise amongst mankind. (4:16–18)

To the apparent dichotomy between action and inaction, a third term is now added: improper action. This newcomer—highlighting a potential negativity in every chosen deed—alters the relation between the two initial terms, making them not so much the positive and negative of an antithesis as vexed partners, with a space intervening in between. There is such a thing as inaction in action, and action in inaction, Krishna now says. The recipe is too complicated for all-out warfare. It is too complicated even for the sort of armed insurgence practiced by, say, John Brown. Such logic suggests, if anything, passive resistance, a gesture sinuous and contrarian in thought as in deed. It is this sinuous logic that speaks more directly to Thoreau, that he would carry forward most directly to the burning question of the day, the question of violence and nonviolence—an impossible question in the nineteenth century, given the conflicting claims of its two major social movements: abolitionism on the one hand, pacifism on the other.

PACIFISM AND ABOLITIONISM

Pacifism had grown sharply with the Mexican War of 1846, a use of force illegitimate in the eyes of many. Should this pacifist philosophy be extended and generalized? Should it serve as the cornerstone for all other reform efforts? Could slavery itself be opposed without recourse to violence? Pacifism and abolitionism were uneasy bedfellows within the antislavery movement, a tension that predated even the Mexican War. The Non-Resistance Society, founded by Adin Ballou in September 1839, gave visible shape to a split that had been brewing for years.[29] The Concord Lyceum itself held three successive meetings in January 1841 to debate "Is it ever proper to offer forcible resistance?" Thoreau and his brother John took an active part in these debates, arguing for the affirmative at the second meeting.[30] They thus found themselves on the opposite side from William Lloyd Garrison, the most powerful figure in the nonresistance movement.[31] Garrison had authored "The Declaration of Sentiments" at the Peace Convention held in Boston on September 20, 1838, and printed it the following week in the *Liberator*:

> We love the land of our nativity, only as we love all other lands. The interests, rights, and liberties of American citizens are no more dear to us, than are those of the whole human race. Hence, we can allow no appeal to patriotism, to revenge any national insult or injury. . . . We register our testimony, not only against all wars, whether offensive or defensive, but all preparations for war; against every naval ship, every arsenal, every fortification; against the militia system and a standing army; against all military chieftains and soldiers; against all monuments commemorative of victory over a foreign foe, all trophies won in battle, all celebrations in honor of military or naval exploits; against all appropriations for the defence of a nation by force and arms on the part of any legislative body; against every edict of government, requiring of its subjects military service.[32]

In its fiery condemnation of military action, military buildup, military monument—its condemnation of patriotism itself—the "Declaration of Sentiments" is as astonishing today as it was in the nineteenth century. There is no question that, for Garrison, any use of force was unjustifiable. Pacifism took precedence over everything else, took precedence even over the fight against slavery: "We cannot acknowledge allegiance to any human government; neither can we oppose any such government, by a resort to physical force."[33]

Garrison had many supporters in Concord. Bronson Alcott was one. So were Thoreau's mother and sisters; they were avid readers of Garrison; the *Liberator* came regularly to the house.[34] Thoreau, however, was of two minds. When it came to the abolition of slavery, he was much less of a pacifist, perhaps not a pacifist at all. He had made no bones about it in an early essay, "The Service," where he wrote: "To the brave soldier the rust and leisure of peace are harder than the fatigues of war."[35] In "A Plea for Captain John Brown," he was even more empathic: "It was his [Brown's] peculiar doctrine that a man has a perfect right to interfere by force with the slaveholder, in order to rescue the slave. I agree with him."[36] And, in his journal, he was most emphatic of all: "Rather than thus consent to establish hell upon earth—to be a party to this establishment—I would touch a match to blow up earth and hell together."[37]

Pacifism, as expounded by Garrison, was too single-minded, too lucid and undeviating in its forward momentum. Thoreau's action, on the other hand, had to have a certain curvature, a few more twists and turns, as in this account of the night he spent in jail for failing to pay the poll tax:

> Under a government which imprisons any unjustly, the true place for a just man is also a prison . . . on that separate, and more free and honorable ground, where the State places those who are not *with* her but *against* her—the only house in a slave-state in which a free man can abide with honor.[38]

Prison, the house of incarceration, is the only place that confers freedom on those who voluntarily enter its doors. It is the only unenslaved place in a nation chained to slavery. And it is the only place in that nation where sitting still is tantamount to bearing arms. With these twisted paradoxes, Thoreau slows down the accelerating speed of Garrison's rhetoric, bending it to his own idiom. For he has help from another quarter. A more sinuous logic—the logic of the *Bhagavad Gita*—guides him here, though not straightforwardly either, not without some reversals in its turn.

It is not Krishna's defense of the use of force, but Arjuna's protest against it, that now shapes the contents and constraints of action. With

Garrisonian pacifism thrown into the mix, it is now possible for Thoreau to think of action not as a feat of the body, proven on the battlefield, but as a feat of the soul, proven by the will to disarm and to suffer the bodily consequences of that disarming. Uniting body and soul in this way, and making the finitude of the former the condition of freedom for the latter, Thoreau creates a political philosophy indebted to the *Bhagavad Gita* and opposed to it.[39] The syntax of thought is preserved, but subject to the contrary demands of pacifism and abolitionism in the nineteenth century.

GANDHI'S *SATYAGRAHA*

This is what it means to be a civil reader, an inspired reader, of the *Bhagavad Gita*, what it means to have a nontrivial relation to the poem. The literary culture that it generates is indeed a dialectic, based on a structure of point and counterpoint, extension and inversion. And, because it is based on these things, it is also a literary culture that goes in both directions, backward as well as forward, east as well as west. These are the space and time coordinates of a global civil society. Thoreau is a conduit here, a carrier. Through him, the inverted meanings of the *Bhagavad Gita* would turn into a form of action, sweeping into the United States, into the Civil Rights Movement of the 1960s. "During my early college days I read Thoreau's essay on civil disobedience for the first time," Martin Luther King writes:

> I was so deeply moved that I re-read the work several times. I became convinced then that non-cooperation with evil is as much a moral obligation as is cooperation with good. No other person has been more eloquent and passionate in getting this idea across than Henry David Thoreau. As a result of his writings and personal witness we are the heirs of a legacy of creative protest. It goes without saying that the teachings of Thoreau are alive today, indeed, they are more alive today than ever before. Whether expressed in a sit-in at lunch counters, a freedom ride into Mississippi, a peaceful protest in Albany, Georgia, a bus boycott in Montgomery, Alabama, it is an outgrowth of Thoreau's insistence that evil must be resisted.[40]

That insistence would flow in the other direction as well, from America back to Asia. And it brings with it an older text, a Sanskrit text, one that needs to be carried to be read at all. This is how the *Bhagavad Gita* makes its way back to India. Traveling through other continents and other languages, it would end up becoming an Indian philosophy one more time, taking the form of *Satyagraha*, Gandhi's philosophy of nonviolent resistance.

Gandhi, a native speaker of Gujarati, his knowledge of Sanskrit "limited," did not read the *Bhagavad Gita* till the age of twenty. He first read it in English—Sir Edwin Arnold's translation—when he was a second-year law student in London.[41] He then went back to the Sanskrit and translated it into Gujarati, adding commentaries and annotations of his own.[42] "When doubts haunt me, when disappointments stare me in the face, and I see not one ray of light on the horizon, I turn to the *Bhagavad Gita*," Gandhi wrote in the August 6, 1925, issue of the *Young India* weekly.[43] Even so, he could not bring himself to accept this poem's justification for war. In the introduction to his Gujarati translation, Gandhi writes: "After 40 years' unremitting endeavor fully to enforce the teaching of the *Gita* in my own life, I have, in all humility, felt that perfect renunciation is impossible without perfect observance of *ahimsa* [nonviolence] in every shape and form."[44]

What does *ahimsa* mean in logistical terms? The answer would come to Gandhi, not from the *Bhagavad Gita* itself, but obliquely, through its American counterpoint. It is Thoreau's "Resistance to Civil Government" (better known to the world as "Civil Disobedience") that would give a tangible shape to *ahimsa*, the shape of a law-defying and freedom-conferring prison sentence:

> I know this well, that if one thousand, if one hundred, if ten men whom I could name—if ten honest men only—aye, if *one* honest man, in this State of Massachusetts, ceasing to hold slaves, were actually to withdraw from this copartnership, and be locked up in the county jail therefor, it would be the abolition of slavery in America. For it matters not how small the beginning may seem to be: what is once well done is done for ever.[45]

Thoreau is right. His small beginning matters not, for its subsequent translation is such as to give it an afterlife exceeding even its most broadly stated goal, exceeding the jurisdictional boundaries of the nation-state. In response to the question of an American reporter, Webb Miller, whether he had read Thoreau, Gandhi's "eyes brightened and he chuckled":

> Why, of course, I read Thoreau. I read *Walden* first in Johannesburg in South Africa in 1906 and his ideas influenced me greatly. I adopted some of them and recommended the study of Thoreau to all my friends who were helping me in the cause of Indian independence. Why, I actually took the name of my movement from Thoreau's essay, "On the duty of Civil Disobedience," written about eighty years ago. Until I read that essay I never found a suitable English translation for my Indian word, *Satyagraha*.[46]

That translation is, of course, bilateral. The phrase "civil disobedience" takes the Indian words, *ahimsa* and *Satyagraha*, into the English-speaking world; at the same time, the Indian Independence Movement also takes the English words, coined with the help of William Lloyd Garrison, into the heat and dust of South Asia. In fact, this bilateral process does not even fully capture the complexity of this global circuit. Gandhi was in fact reading Thoreau, not in India but in South Africa, where he lived for twenty-one years, from 1893 to 1914, practicing law and editing a weekly, *Indian Opinion*. After reading Thoreau in 1906, he published long extracts in *Indian Opinion* the following year.[47] Civil disobedience was quickened to life in South Africa before it was transported back east. It was in South Africa that it took the form that it did—as a voluntary sojourn in the county jail—a sojourn Gandhi himself practiced three times, twice in 1908 and once in 1909, for his resistance to the Asiatic Registration Act.[48] *Satyagraha*, Gandhi writes, "is for all practical purposes a history of the remainder of my life in South Africa, and especially of my experiments with truth in that sub-continent. I wrote the major portion of this history in Yeravda jail."[49]

Asia, America, Africa—these continents make up the spatial width of one community of readers, at once nonmilitary and nongovernmental. This spatial width brings with it a corresponding temporal length, extending slowly from the fourth century BCE, passing through the nineteenth century, passing through the twentieth, and always updating the meaning of some long-lasting words. This is a duality of scale fit both for literary culture and for world governance. It is a duality that enables us to see not only the sinuous logic of each of Thoreau's sentences, but also the threads of deep time that string them together, giving us a civil society woven of continents and millennia.

CHAPTER TWO

World Religions:
Emerson, Hafiz, Christianity, Islam

DEEP TIME, understood as temporal length added to the spatial width of the planet, gives us a set of coordinates at once extended and embedded, as fine-grained as it is long-lasting, operating both above and below the plane of the nation. The subnational and the transnational come together here in a loop, intertwined in a way that speaks as much to local circumstances as it does to global circuits.

In this chapter I take the subnational and the transnational into a different sphere of relations. As before, my starting point is a far-flung literary culture, spanning many centuries, threaded through many linguistic environments, and requiring translation on many fronts. Rather than seeing this as the template for a global civil society, a utopian ideal that has yet to come to pass, I explore its intersections with a well-established phenomenon, one of the most durable and extensive on earth: world religions.

Literary cultures and world religions are, of course, very different enterprises. There is an obvious asymmetry between the two, reflected in the strict membership of one versus the loose membership of the other. Religions are strict. To be a Christian is, by definition, not to be a Muslim, a Buddhist, an observing Jew. Filiation here is clear-cut, and historically sharpened by well-staffed ecclesiastical structures, with an interest in drawing a sharp line between the true faith and others correspondingly discredited.[1] The muddled landscape called "literary culture" has no such sharp line. As we have already seen in the case of Thoreau, there is nothing to stop a Hindu sacred text, the *Bhagavad Gita*, from being read side by side with the Christian Bible. And there is nothing to stop these two from getting further tangled up with the *Oracles of Zoroaster,*[2] *Alwakidis' Arabian Chronicles,*[3] or Eugene Burnouf's *Introduction a l'histoire du Buddhisme indien,* which Thoreau edited (and probably translated) for *The Dial.*[4] As literary diet, these become matters of affinity rather than matters of dogma. One gravitates to the texts one likes; one mixes them up in one's head. Attachment here is idiosyncratic, and nonsectarian by default. As Thoreau says: "The reading which I love best is the scriptures of the several nations, though it happens that

I am better acquainted with those of the Hindoos, the Chinese, and the Persians, than of the Hebrews, which I have come to last. Give me one of these Bibles and you have silenced me for a while."[5]

Only in a literary culture can one speak casually—and fondly—of "one of these Bibles," without any intended insult. Nothing seems more different from a religious sensibility. And yet, in spite of this difference, the overlap between the two is perhaps even more significant. Literary culture and world religion each represents a form of attachment tangential to the nation-state. Each defines its membership by something other than national citizenship. And each becomes consequential when it is seen on a large scale, mapped against the length and width of the world's populations, rather than the geography and chronology of one sovereign state. This large-scale mapping makes it possible to speak of *variation*, the particular inflections wrought by particular locales. Literary cultures and world religions are "dialects" in this sense: they spread across the planet primarily as vernacular forms, not only transnational but also subnational, a web of folk variants.

Hemispheric Islam

All of these suggest that the literary and the religious might be fruitfully studied together. As forms of cultural contact, they have done much to integrate the globe, breaking down the separation of periods as well as the isolation of regions, making long-term, long-distance kinship possible. This is as true of Islam as of Christianity. Robert Irwin speaks of the emergence of an "Islamic world system" between the years 1000 and 1500.[6] Of hemispheric proportion, this extended at one time from Sumatra to Spain, from the Nile to the Volga, spilling over from its "classical borders" into Asia Minor, eastern Europe, sub-Saharan Africa, much of India, and further on to southeastern and central Asia, and even parts of China.[7] The travels of the fourteenth-century scholar Ibn Buttuta, from Morocco to the Moluccas, dramatized just what it meant to be part of this world system.[8] Spanning three continents, it was "Afro-Eurasian" in a way we might not fully understand.[9] This geographical vastness meant that Islam was multilingual from the first, becoming a "civilization" (and not just a religion) through the mixing of these tongues, and through the mixing of the Islamic faith with a wealth of secular forms, from poetry and philosophy to law, architecture, the visual arts, medicine, mathematics, and the natural sciences.[10] Against such magnificence, Europe can only be called an intellectual backwater for hundreds of years, its centrality on the world stage a late development. The map that aligns the "West" with literate progress and the

"East" with brute tyranny is a recent invention. Deep time reveals a very different map.

That map was not solely Arabic. Islam achieved its military dominance largely because of the input from a group of foreigners: the steppe "barbarians," the Turks. As William McNeill points out, by "1000 AD the steppe gradient had been in full operation for thirteen or fourteen centuries, sporadically impelling one tribe after another to seek better pastures in more favorable western environments."[11] This influx of Turkish-speakers transformed Islam, for while "these Turks accepted the Moslem faith and took on something of Islamic manners . . . , they did not entirely lose themselves in the Moslem world. A sense of superiority, based upon pride in their military prowess, kept them from full assimilation; and they retained their own language, together with much of the warlike ethos of the steppe."[12] This warlike ethos found a responsive chord in the Islamic concept of *jihad*. And so it was that the "Turks provided a majority of the Moslem rulers and soldiers from the eleventh century onward and constituted the cutting edge of Islamic expansion into both Christendom and Hindustan."[13]

Even before these military triumphs, Islam had already been expanding steadily in its religious base. Spearheading this expansion was Sufi mysticism, a popular form of Islam emerging around the eighth century and emphasizing the direct experience of God outside the *Ulama* (the state-sponsored clerical orthodoxy). By the middle of the ninth century, it was publicly taught in Baghdad and elsewhere. The Sufi followers—*faqirs* in Arabic and *darwish* in Persian—organized themselves into small groups led by a spiritual leader, called *Shaykh* in Syria and Iraq, *pir* or *murshid* in Persia and India, and *muqaddam* in Africa.[14] As is clear from these diverging tongues, Sufism was at once transnational and subnational, with many local names. Operating well below the power of the state, it spread rapidly for just that reason, assimilating easily, blending with folk practices and beliefs. According to Fazlur Rahman, the "popular preachers, also known as *qussas* or 'storytellers,' exerted a powerful influence on the masses by enlarging Qur'anic stories with the aid of materials borrowed from all kinds of sources, Christian, Jewish, Gnostic, and even Buddhist and Zoroastrian, indeed, anything that would make their sermons persuasive and effective."[15] Local cults from "animism in Africa to pantheism in India" all found a home in Sufism, which, thanks to its spread, was much less a religion of the zealous than of "the half-converted and even nominally converted."[16]

The very word "Sufism" itself seems to have been of non-Islamic origin. The name referred to the coarse woolen attire worn by the *faqirs*, rather than more expensive silks and cottons. These clothes looked much like those worn by Christian monks and ascetics, and were frowned upon by the Muslim clerics. Still, the fashion caught on. And, by "metonomy, the name of the material was transferred onto those who made the habit of wearing it. Originally used by itinerant outsiders (possibly in a derogatory sense), by the end of the eighth century CE, in the central lands of Islam the nick-name *sufiyya* ('wool people' or 'wool-wearers') became a self-designation of those given to ascetic life and mystical contemplation."[17] This was not the only instance of the "folk" mixing of Christianity and Islam. In some Sufi orders in Africa, the Islamic practice of *dhikr* (gathering to recite the Qur'an aloud) turned into the practice of *wird*. This "came to mean not the recitation of the Holy Book but short religious formulas, usually containing the ninety-nine 'beautiful names' of God, and repeated on a chain of beads." The resemblance to Christian practice was uncanny. Again, mundane matters, suspiciously un-Islamic, seemed to have fueled the spread of Sufism from the first.[18]

In fact, even its vaunted asceticism was not altogether pure. Sufism (like Islam itself) is largely a "dialectical theology," as Rahman points out, with a knack for "spiritual jugglery."[19] It affirms a polarity of terms, believed to be inversely conjoined, the prime example being "annihilation" and "subsistence": it is only when one's selfhood is annihilated that one can subsist in God. Another pair of polar opposites, the ascetic and the ecstatic, turn out also to be bound by the same inverse logic. For the Sufis, these are embodied by two contrary states, sobriety and intoxication, equally honored. It is not a contradiction for ascetics to sing, dance, and twirl the body around—a sensuous abandon that irked the orthodox, especially because its demographics were so hard to ignore. From the twelfth century on, then, a "rising tide" of fringe activities began to wash over Islam, so much so that "the original stamp—of which the carriers were the *Ulama*—became submerged if not entirely suppressed."[20]

Marshall Hodgson has proposed a neologism—"Islamicate"—to describe just this phenomenon. Rather than using "Islamic" as a blanket term to refer to everything that comes into the orbit of Islam, he proposes to use it only in a strict sense, to designate a sphere of conduct corresponding directly to the doctrinal faith. Everything else, a broad swath of phenomena entering the paths of this world religion, can only loosely be called "Islamicate." These two are by no means the same, Hodgson argues, for "not only have the groups of people involved in the two cases not always been co-extensive (the culture has not been simply a 'Muslim' culture, a culture of Muslims)—much of what even Muslims have done as a part of the 'Islamic' civilization can only be characterized as 'un-Islamic' in the first, the religious sense of the word. One can speak of 'Islamic literature,' of 'Islamic art,' of 'Islamic philosophy,' even of 'Islamic despotism,' but in such a sequence one is speaking less and less of something that expresses Islam as a faith."[21]

"Islamic" philosophy is a case in point. Its chief inspiration was Greek, coming from Aristotle, Galen, Euclid, and Ptolemy, whose writings had been translated into Arabic since the ninth century. This produced a "rationalist" philosophy, an attempt to reconcile the Prophetic Revelation of Islam with a Hellenistic model of human cognition.[22] Expounded by such figures as Ibn Sina (known to the West as Avicenna, 980–1037, a doctor and theologian), al-Biruni (Alberuni, 973–1046, a polymath and student of Indian thought), and Ibn Rushd (Averroës, 1126–98, an Aristotelian and a major influence on Christian theologians), this Islamic philosophy clashed not only with the Muslim clerics but also with the mystical populism of the Sufis. This was its "brilliant originality and its tragic fate," Rahman says, for in the end, failing to appease the orthodox, "it was denied the passport to survival."[23] The dismantling of philosophy began early in the twelfth century, with *Incoherence of the Philosophers*, a scathing attack by the leading theologian Al-Ghazali (1058–1111).[24] As the century came to an end, a bonfire in 1197 destroyed the books of Ibn Rushd, a dramatic occurrence, though hardly the first instance of book burning in Islamic history.[25] From the first, Islam was a hotbed of internal strife, fueled by deep disagreement and periodic repression. This, no less than its scope, makes Islam an important record keeper for the species.

WORLD HISTORY

Historians such as William McNeill and Marshall Hodgson see the world through just this lens. The method they expound, traversing continents and millennia, puts Islam at the center of the map.[26] Generally called by its umbrella term, world history, this scholarship remains housed within a traditional discipline while working steadily to revise its protocol. Once dismissed as amateurish, this subfield of history has burst into fresh vitality in recent years. A new *Journal of World History* began publication in 1990.[27] McNeill's *The Rise of the West*, first published in 1963, was reissued by the University of Chicago Press in 1991. As the first date suggests, world history is not exactly a recent development. It has many early advocates: UNESCO's *History of Mankind* (now renamed *History of Humanity*), *Destins du monde* edited by Lucien Lebvre and Fernand Braudel, and, in the United States, an internationalist high school curriculum proposed by Leften Stavrianos.[28] History, Stavrianos says, is "no longer simply West versus non-West, or a Toynbeean assessment of the meaning of the rise and fall of civilizations."[29] Rather, the more crucial question has to do with "ourselves as a species," for "no longer can we avoid asking why this age of unprecedented human dominance and achievement is also the age when the possibility of species extinction for the first time is a sober possibility."[30] The species is an integral unit of analysis whether or not we like it. We stand or fall as one. This is the starting point of world history: its subject is the collective life of humans, beginning with "the first emergence of civilization—and writing—in Mesopotamia less than six thousand years ago," and tracing these "lifelines from our past" backward, to the prehistory of *Homo sapiens*, as well as forward, to the precarious future of an endangered planet. History of this sort needs to take stock of the world as a whole; it must be studied "over a span of tens of thousands of years rather than over a few short centuries."[31]

Students of literature have much to learn from this sense of duration. To take it seriously is to challenge the short, sharp, executive thrust of dates: 1776, or 1620, when the Mayflower arrived. Such dates (and the periodization based upon them) assume that there can be a discrete, bounded unit of time coinciding with a discrete, bounded unit of space: a chronology coinciding with a territory. Such coincidence is surely a fiction. Rather than taking it for granted—rather than taking our measure of time from the stipulated beginning of a territorial regime—I propose a more extended (and seemingly off-center) duration to rethink the scope of American literature. This produces a map that, thanks to its receding horizons, must depart significantly from a map based on the short life of the United States. It takes us to a time when this nation was nowhere in sight, though the world was already fully in existence. What is the relation of American literature to that world? It is helpful to begin with this question, opening up the borders of American literature to a temporal continuum that disabuses it of any fancied centrality. A backward extension has spatial consequences. Deep time is denationalized space.

What would American literature look like then? Can we transpose some familiar figures onto this broadened and deepened landscape? I would like to test that possibility. Using Islam as one of the lifelines of the world, I trace a thread spun of its migration, dissemination, and vernacularization. Running through the terrain usually called "American," this thread will knit together kinships no doubt surprising to many. These kinships would not have registered in a period-based paradigm. They owe their legibility to the deep field of time: its scope, its tangled antecedents, and its ability to record far-flung and mediated ties. Scale enlargement, I argue, enlarges our sense of complex kinship.

My paradigm is, in this sense, the obverse of Edward Said's *Orientalism*, his account of images of the East (primarily Islam) in post-Enlightenment Europe.[32] "Taking the late eighteenth century as a very roughly defined starting point," Said writes, "Orientalism can be discussed and analyzed as the corporate institution for dealing with the Orient—dealing with it by making statements about it, authorizing views of it, describing it, by teaching it, settling it, ruling over it."[33] This corporate institution was clearly of European vintage. "To speak of Orientalism therefore is to speak mainly, although not exclusively, of a British and French cultural enterprise."[34] Started in England and France, and never leaving these nations far behind, Orientalism was less an homage to an alien world than a symptom of Western domination. As a regime of expert knowledge, it helped forge "the idea of European identity as a superior one in comparison with all the non-European peoples and cultures."[35] For Said, Orientalism is ideological through and through, and Eurocentric through and through. This is what he unmasks. And yet, in scaling the problem as he does—scaling it to put Eurocentrism at front and center—he ends up reproducing the very map he sets out to scrutinize. On this map, the West is once again the principal actor, the seat of agency. The Orient is no more than a figment of its ideological projection, brought "home" to serve the needs of imperial rule. As Said himself says, his study is "based more or less exclusively upon a sovereign Western consciousness out of whose unchallenged centrality an Oriental world emerged." His analytic domain is strictly "within the umbrella of Western hegemony over the Orient."[36]

That umbrella gives rise to an odd paradigm, oddly hierarchical and segregated: West versus East, the dominating versus the dominated. The latter exists only as clay molded by Western hands. The Orient is a fabrication, an artifact. As such, it has no agency of its own, no life apart from the ideological constructions foisted upon it, no ability to generate a web of significant and durable relations. The historical sequence that Said narrates is a sequence that begins in the West and rarely strays from that genetic locale. This is not so much a history of the world as a history of a gigantic ideological factory, a Western factory. Not surprisingly, Islam can show up here only as a product, not the maker but the made. To put agency and causality all on one side, as Said does, is to reaffirm an all-too-familiar map, scaled to fit the outlines of Western nations, scaled to highlight their input as dominant.[37]

Can we draw a different input map of the world? A sequence that begins at an earlier point in history, that goes back to other parts of the globe? Off-center duration is especially helpful here. Extending much further back than the late-eighteenth century that is Said's starting point, it also predates the "umbrella of Western hegemony" institutionalized during that period. What this *longue durée* allows us to see is an Afro-Eurasian civilization, much more interesting and consequential than it would appear when the analytic field is no more than a couple of hundred years.

This civilization is not fully describable under the stamp, the scope, and the chronology of European nations. Its long life demands a different time frame. Given that, it will in turn yield a genealogy more surprising and certainly more militant: one that challenges the jurisdiction of nations, of periods, and of the taxonomic divide between "East" and "West."

BLACK MUSLIMS

This Afro-Eurasian civilization would soon spread to the Americas. Muslim slaves from West Africa had been brought to New World since the seventeenth century.[38] The legacy from this group is not entirely clear, but immigration from the Middle East, beginning in the 1870s, gave the United States a solid Muslim presence. By the early 1900s, Muslim communities were well established in the Midwest.[39] The Nation of Islam came into being in 1930, beginning with W. D. Fard's preaching in Detroit, followed by the establishment of its headquarters in Chicago in 1932, under Elijah Muhammad. It is interesting to think of this "Nation" as another instance of vernacular Islam, a folk variant of a world religion. Black Muslims are not usually called "Orientalists," but that is what they are: a new twist on that word, the latest and most controversial incarnation. As a separatist group, the Nation of Islam was specially emphatic about its eastward orientation. Its members were taught that they "were not Americans but Asiatics," that their homeland was elsewhere, on other continents.[40] According to Elijah Muhammad, the planet began 66 trillion years ago, when an explosion separated the moon from the earth, populating the latter with the black tribe of Shabazz, the earth's first inhabitants. This original nation, ruled by twenty-four scientists, spoke Arabic and practiced Islam. Unfortunately, 6,600 years ago, this paradise was subverted by a mad scientist, Yacub, who schemed to create a new race of devils, whites, out of the original humans. After trying for 600 years, he succeeded (Muhammad based these calculations on Qur'an 49:15 and 76:2). For 6,000 years, the white devils would be allowed to reign supreme on earth.[41]

Mythology of this sort was meant to maximize enemies, not only among whites, but also among the black Christian churches and among other Muslim groups. In 1959, after WNTA-TV in New York aired a five-part series on the Nation of Islam entitled "The Hate That Hate Produced," articles began to appear in the *Reader's Digest*, *U.S. News and World Report*, and the *New York Times*, charging the NOI with racism in reverse. Civil rights leaders, including the NAACP Executive Director Roy Wilkins and Martin Luther King, Jr., also distanced themselves from the movement, which they denounced as "one of the hate groups arising in our midst which would preach a doctrine of black supremacy."[42] If the legacy of Islam was a divided spectrum—torn between the latitude of a worldwide brotherhood and the clannishness of a tribe—Black Muslims would seem to rehearse that spectrum to the full.[43]

MALCOLM X AND JAMES BALDWIN

At the two poles stand Malcolm X and James Baldwin. What these two eloquent—and antithetical—voices represent is nothing less than the antithetical scope claimable by Islam. For Malcolm X, Islam is very capacious indeed; it belongs to the whole world; nothing is broader, nothing falls outside its rubric. This religion can accommodate every branch of the human family, as the American nation cannot:

> I only knew what I had left in America, and how it contrasted with what I had found in the Muslim world. . . . Never have I witnessed such sincere hospitality and the overwhelming spirit of true brotherhood as is practiced by people of all colors and races here in this Ancient Holy Land, the home of Abraham, Muhammad, and all the other prophets of the Holy Scriptures. . . . I have been blessed to visit the Holy City of Mecca. I have made my seven circuits around the Kaba, led by a young *Mutawaf* named Muhammad. I drank water from the well of Zem Zem. I ran seven times back and forth between the hills of Mt. Al-Safa and Al-Marwah. I have prayed in the ancient city of Mina, and I have prayed on Mt. Arafat.
>
> There were tens and thousands of pilgrims, from all over the world. They were of all colors, from blue-eyed blonds to black-skinned Africans. But we were all participating in the same ritual, displaying a spirit of unity and brotherhood that my experiences in America had led me to believe never could exist between the white and the nonwhite.[44]

Malcolm X is not wrong to credit Islam with a "spirit of unity and brotherhood," for this is the specific injunction in Qur'an 49:13: "Mankind! We created you from a single (pair) of a male and a female, and made you into nations and tribes, that ye may know each other (not that ye may despise each other)."[45] For Malcolm X, the weight of that injunction is backed by the long history of Islam. Here is a religion that goes back to Abraham and Muhammad; its scriptures and rituals are ancient; it is almost as old as the primordial landscape of Al-Safa, Al-Marwah, and Mt. Arafat. This *longue durée* is not a just a matter of time past; it is also a matter of time present. This temporal continuum means that Islam is coextensive with the history of the world. It is mappable onto the entire species, not exclusive to one racial group. That is why it can take in the blue eyed and the black skinned and have room to spare. To become a Muslim is to undergo a scale enlargement in every sense.

This is, of course, the very opposite of what strikes James Baldwin. *The Fire Next Time* (1962) is a passionate dissent from the Nation of Islam precisely because of the scale reduction Baldwin experiences in its midst. Where Malcolm X sees an expanse of time going back to the seventh-century prophet Muhammad, Baldwin feels suffocated by a small and contracting circle gathered around Elijah Muhammad, the current prophet, a noose very much in the present:

> I had the stifling feeling that *they* knew I belonged to them but knew that I did not know it yet, that I remained unready, and that they were simply waiting, patiently, and with assurance, for me to discover the truth for myself. For where else, after all, could I go? I was black, and therefore a part of Islam, and would be saved from the holocaust awaiting the white world whether I would or no. My weak, deluded scruples could avail nothing against the iron word of the prophet.[46]

Is Islam capacious or is it stifling? Is its radius coextensive with the species, or is it locked into one particular race, its membership automatically decided by identity politics? Can it encompass the life of someone who sees himself primarily as a writer? These antithetical questions, put forth by Malcolm X and James Baldwin, yield some of the terms on which American literature bursts out of the confines of the nation-state, becoming a thread in the fabric of a world religion.

WHITE PROTESTANT ISLAM

It would be a mistake, however, to see this as a strictly twentieth-century phenomenon, affecting only African-American authors. Indeed, the importance of Islam lies precisely in its ability to break down some of the standard dividing lines, turning them into unexpected lines of kinship. For the scope of this world system weaves it not only into African-American history but also into the history of other groups. James Baldwin and Malcolm X have company in the nineteenth century.

Washington Irving, for one, was just as struck by the splendor of Islam. Fluent in Spanish, he was in Spain for a total of seven years,[47] writing *Columbus* (1828), *The Conquest of Granada* (1828), and *The Alhambra* (1832), dealing with the many layers of Spanish history. In 1829 he was in Granada for four months, living in the Alhambra, monument both to the glories of Muslims and to their brutal expulsion in 1492. Of the Court of Lions, Irving writes: "Earthquakes have shaken the foundations of this pile," yet "not one of these slender columns has been displaced, not an arch of that light and fragile colonnade given way, not all the fairy fretwork of these domes, apparently as unsubstantial as the crystal fabrics of a morning frost."[48] Tenacity is especially impressive when it seems so slight. It is this combination that makes Irving think that Islam is at the beginning rather than the end of its career, that its history is far from finished:

> Such is the general aspiration and belief among the Moors of Barbary; who consider Spain, or Andaluz, as it was anciently called, their rightful heritage, of which they have been despoiled by treachery and violence. . . . These families, it is said, continue to sigh after the terrestrial paradise of their ancestors, and to put up prayers in their mosques on Fridays, imploring Allah to hasten the time when Granada shall be restored to the faithful: an event to which they look forward as fondly and confidently as did the Christian crusaders to the recovery of the Holy Sepulchre. Nay, it is added, that some of them retain the ancient maps and deeds of the estates and gardens of their ancestors at Granada, and even the keys of the houses; holding them as evidences of their hereditary claims, to be produced at the anticipated day of restoration.[49]

1492 was not only the year when Columbus discovered America; it was also the year when Andalusia was lost to Islam, leaving a bitter aftertaste for centuries to come. Irving, indefatigable traveler, learned about that bitterness on site, amidst the tangled history of Christians and Muslims on the Iberian Peninsula. But travel was by no means a prerequisite. Other nineteenth-century authors, somewhat more sedentary, also had a keen sense of that tangled history, attested to by many works of literature. These were the Transcendentalists: avid readers, commentators, and translators, importing books from abroad and filling local libraries with them, making these their regular diet.[50] Comparative philology and comparative religion—two newly minted disciplines of the nineteenth century—were high on their reading lists. The relative claims of civilizations were hot topics for them. Bronson Alcott was doing nothing special when he tried to borrow these books from the Boston Athenaeum on March 24, 1849:

Collier's Four Books of Confucius
History of China (by the Jesuit)
The Kings of Confucius

The Vedas
The Saama Vedas
Vishnu Parana
Saadi
Firdusi
The Zendavesta
The Koran.[51]

Nor was this only a masculine pursuit. Margaret Fuller was an early and enthusiastic reader of Persian poetry, and was rueful about her lack of competence in the Asian languages: "Gentle Sanscrit I cannot write. My Persian and Arabic you love not."[52] Meanwhile, linguistic competence or not, Lydia Maria Child was able to write a three-volume treatise called *The Progress of Religious Ideas through Successive Ages* (1855), beginning with "Hindostan," followed by "Egypt," "China," "Thibet and Tartary," "Chaldea," and "Persia," and ending with a sixty-eight-page chapter, "Mohammedanism."[53] This religion and Christianity had long been at each other's throat, she concedes, but of late, "[a] more kindly state of feeling begins to manifest itself," which gives one hope, for

> they both derive so much from Jewish foundations, that Lessing calls them "Two litigating sons of the same father."
>
> The extension of Mohammedanism, though occasionally checked, has gradually increased ever since the Hegira. Its professors are now estimated at one hundred and eighty millions; nearly one-fifth of the whole human race.[54]

MONGREL RELIGIONS

The "human race" was an important idea for the Transcendentalists, and Islam—one of its principal bearers—was important for that reason. So with Lydia Maria Child, and so with Emerson. Emerson's introduction to Islam began as early as 1819, when he was sixteen. He seemed to have read the Qur'an on his own: a journal entry in October 1819 featured this quotation from George Sale's translation: "In aforetime I created *Jan* from out of a scorching fire."[55] In 1822, Emerson read Gibbon's *Decline and Fall of the Roman Empire*;[56] Chapters 50 to 52 of that book are devoted to Arabic culture, with high praise for its language and poetry.[57] His subsequent readings included *Oriental Geography* (1800) by Ibn Haukal; the *Annales Muslemici Arabice et Latine* (1837) by Abulfeda; Simon Ockley's *Conquest of Syria, Persia, and Egypt by the Saracens* (1708–18),[58] not to say Carlyle's admiring chapter on Mahomet in *Heroes and Hero Worship*.[59]

What impressed Emerson about Islam (and world religions in general) was what would later impress Malcolm X: the scope, the long duration, the ability to bind people across space and time, a point he made as early as 1822, in one of his first journal entries:

> The History of Religion involves circumstances of remarkable interest and it is almost all that we are able to trace in the passage of the remote ages of the world. . . . Indeed the only record by which the early ages of any nation are remembered is their religion. We know nothing of the first empires which grasped the sceptre of the earth in Egypt, Assyria, or Persia, but their modes of worship. And this fact forcibly suggests the idea that the only true and legitimate vehicle of immortality, the only bond of connection which can traverse the long duration which separates the ends of the world and unites the first people to the knowledge and sympathy of the last people, is religion. (*JMN* 1:62)

World religions are probably the most durable diachronic axes known to the human species. This is their strength. But this longevity suggests something else as well. Phenomena that last a long time are likely to change, to disperse, to become mongrelized by many new contacts. A book that exemplified all of these was the *Akhlak-I-Jalaly*, translated from the Persian by W. F. Thompson as *The Practical Philosophy of the Muhammedan People* (London, 1839). This came into Emerson's hands in 1845, giving him some fifty quotations for his journals.[60] Thompson was quite clear about why he was moved to become a translator. His hope, announced in the preface, was that the "depreciation of the Muhammedan system should now be at an end."[61] For that purpose he picked the *Akhlak-I-Jalaly*—a text showing Islam at its most compelling, though hardly its purest. Cobbled together in the fifteenth century by a worldly philosopher, Molla Jaladeddin Davani (1410–88), the *Akhlak* was anything but Islamic dogma. Mixing the Qur'an with Sufi mysticism as well as the ethics and politics of Plato and Aristotle, it was a mutt, a linguistic and philosophical hybrid, with Arabic, Persian, Greek, and now English in its veins.[62]

This did not bother Emerson in the least. Nor was he bothered by counterfeit texts, such as the Desatir or the Zoroastrian Oracles.[63] In a journal entry in 1832 he wrote: "Do we not feel in reading these elemental theories that these grotesque fictions are globes and diagrams on which the laws of living nature are explained? Do we not seem nearer to divine truth in these fictions than in less pretending prose?" (*JMN* 4:12). Like Thoreau, with his equal attachment to the "bibles" of the Hindoos, the Chinese, and the Persians, Emerson saw different scriptures (even counterfeit ones) as parallel descriptions of the planet—"globes and diagrams" each and every of them. In a late essay, "Books," he lumps all of them together in "a class of books which are the best":

> I mean the Bibles of the world, or the sacred books of each nation, which express for each the supreme result of their experience. After the Hebrew and Greek Scriptures, which constitute the sacred books of Christendom, these are, the Desatir of the Persians, and the Zoroastrian Oracles; the Vedas and Laws of Menu; the Upanishads, the Vishnu Purana, the Bhagvat Geeta of the Hindoos; the books of the Buddhists; the Chinese classic, of four books, containing the wisdom of Confucius and Mencius. . . . They are not to be held by letters printed on a page, but are living characters translatable into every tongue and form of life. . . . Is there any geography in these things? We call them Asiatic, we call them primeval; but perhaps that is only optical.[64]

BIBLICAL SCHOLARSHIP

Emerson's literary atlas might come as a surprise to us. What does it mean to put the Bible in the company of all these other texts, with such strange names? Is the Bible just like them? And is Christianity itself on the same footing as these religions, and indeed nonreligions? Emerson seems to think that sectarian divisions—like continental divisions—are just "optical," not real. An earlier journal entry in April 1838 was even more emphatic. "It is idle to represent the historical glories of Christianity as we do," Emerson said. "The heart of Christianity is the heart of all philosophy. It is the sentiment of piety which Stoic & Chinese [,] Mahometan & Hindoo labor to awaken" (*JMN* 5:478). Christianity is not unique, but one variant of a truth of which other religions are also variants. It is "idle" to single it out as the one true faith, for at heart it is no different from the other religions: no different in its essence, and no different even in its lengthy duration, its "historical glories."

"Historical" was of course a loaded term for Emerson, as for the literate circle around him. This was a code word for the historical reconstruction of the Bible—the "higher criticism"—practiced by Johann Gottfried Eichhorn, Johann David Michaelis, and Johann Griesbach at German universities, especially Göttingen.[65] As Jerry Wayne Brown points out, this historical (rather than theological) approach to the Bible had been making an inroad in New England since the early-nineteenth century. Joseph Stevens Buckminster, pastor at the Brattle Street Church in Cambridge and the first appointed Dexter Lecturer at Harvard, was the initial force behind this mode of scholarship. Buckminster's interest was sparked by Michaelis's *Einleitung in die göttlichen Schriften des Neuen Bundes* (1750), translated into English by Herbert Marsh and accompanied by Marsh's own critical account of the New Testament, "Dissertation on the Origin and Composition of the First Three Gospels" (1802). He turned next to Griesbach's edition of the Greek New Testament, promoting it, getting it reprinted in America and adopted as a textbook at Harvard.[66] When Buckminster went to Europe in 1806–7, he used the legacy from his grandfather to acquire a library of three thousand volumes. These were sold at an auction after his sudden death in 1812, with the New England reading public—President Kirkland of Harvard, Moses Stuart of the Andover Seminary, William Ellery Channing, and Edward Everett—all assembled for two days bidding for the books. Eichhorn's *Einleitung ins Alte Testament* was the prize acquisition, and even his edited numbers, the *Allgemeine Bibliothek der Biblischen Litteratur*, originally set at twenty-five cents, sold for over two dollars each.[67]

The central premise of the higher criticism was that the Bible was a "historical" document, its evidence to be weighed just as any other ancient text. Eichhorn's focus was initially on the Old Testament,[68] but the polemical thrust of the field had always been with the New Testament, beginning with Michaelis's *Einleitung in die göttlichen Schriften des Neuen Bundes*. That book (along with Marsh's "Dissertation") put forth the bold hypothesis that the unity of the New Testament was not to be taken for granted, that some books were more reliable than others, some being only "historical" artifacts, reflecting the circumstances of their writing rather than divine revelation. For Michaelis, only those books written by the Apostles were trustworthy. Mark, Luke, and Acts were not.[69] This hypothesis was further extended by Eichhorn, who argued in his *Einleitung in das Neue Testament* that the four synoptic Gospels were second-century recensions of one original Gospel, and should not be relied upon as accurate historical accounts of Jesus.[70]

For the theologically minded, and for Christians in general, no question could have been more momentous. Edward Everett, later Emerson's teacher at Harvard, went to Göttingen expressly to study with Eichhorn, as did George Ticknor and George Bancroft.[71] When William Emerson, Waldo's brother, in turn went to Göttingen in 1824, there was nothing unusual about that destination. Waldo, staying at home, wrote a series of letters, half envious and half curious, about William's privileged attendance at the source. "I can never go to Germany," he wrote on November 1, 1824; and "[i]f you could in a letter designate in what particulars consist the superior advantages of Göttingen you would convey much desired information into your poor dear country who wants booklearning."[72] On November 18, 1824 he wrote again: "You had better get us some Theol Interpretation books, for if we do not want them others will."[73] William did send two books of Eichhorn's: *Einleitung ins Alte Testament* (1780), and *Die hebräischen Propheten* (1816). These came into Emerson's hand on October 17, 1828.[74] However, the Old Testament did not seem to have been his primary interest. On April 5, 1830 he wrote to William again: "It w'd be a very great obligation to me if you w'd in some hour at leisure put into a synopsis tangible to me th leading objections to th Evidence of Xty [Christianity] as they strike yr mind—just mark th books of Eichhorn or others & chap. & verse as near as may be that ought to have weight with a seeker of truth to remove his belief in th divine authority of th New Testament."[75]

The New Testament is, of course, that half of the Bible that separates Christianity from Judaism and Islam. German higher criticism was especially effective in dismantling it, casting doubt not only on the "divine authority" of the Gospels but on the divinity of Jesus himself.[76] Emerson's 1831 Vestry Lectures were devoted to this body of scholarship.[77] "It is my object this evening to show you the evidence upon which we know our four Evangelists to be what they pretend to be," he said. "Our Bible [is] so familiar to the eye in a single volume that many are apt to forget that it was ever a multitude of separable compositions. And it is important to a Christian that he should know (since this is not the original work but for the most part a translation of a translation) the means through which it came to him, that he may be sure it was really written by those to whom it is ascribed."[78]

HISTORICAL JESUS

From this scholarly scrutiny of the historical Bible, it is a short step to Emerson's famously scandalous Divinity School "Address" of 1838. As is well known, Emerson here chides Christians for being bad readers, taking the Gospels as a collection of words literally rather than figuratively true. When Jesus said, "I am divine," he was only waxing metaphoric, speaking in hyperbole about the divine nature of human beings. That hyperbole is unfortunately rigidified into dogma: "the idioms of his language and the figures of his rhetoric have usurped the place of his truth; and churches are not built on his principles, but on his tropes." This, Emerson said, was "the first defect of historical Christianity. Historical Christianity has fallen into the error that corrupts all attempts to communicate religion. As it appears to us, and as it has appeared for ages, it is not the doctrine of the soul, but an exaggeration of the personal, the positive, the ritual. It has dwelt, it dwells, with noxious exaggeration about the *person* of Jesus."[79]

That noxious exaggeration had irritated Emerson before. In 1832, when he gave up his ministry at the Second Church of Boston, he had singled out one particular ritual centered on the person of Jesus—the "Lord's Supper"—as one to which he could not be reconciled. His ally here, not surprisingly, is that tried and tested technique of higher criticism, textual scholarship.[80] Pointing out that there is a discrepancy among the four synoptic Gospels—Matthew, Mark, Luke, and John—he notes that it is only "St. Luke, after relating the breaking of the bread, [that] has these words: 'This do in remembrance of me' (22:15)."[81] On the basis of this one account, a perfectly mundane act—the eating of bread and the drinking of wine—gets turned into an institutional allegory, an allegory of our soul receiving God. This is ludicrous. "Now observe the facts. Two of the evangelists (namely, Matthew and John) were of the twelve disciples and were present on that occasion. Neither of them drops the slightest intimation of any intention on the part of Jesus to set up any thing permanent. John especially, the beloved disciple, who has recorded with minuteness the conversation and the transactions of that memorable evening, has quite omitted such a notice." These two apostles said nothing about a "permanent" ritual because it was not meant to be. On the contrary, Jesus was just doing "with his disciples exactly what every master of a family in Jerusalem was doing at the same hour with his household. It appears that the Jews ate the lamb and the unleavened bread and drank wine after a prescribed manner."[82] The Lord's Supper was nothing more than that: a regular Passover. But what about those famous words, "This is my body, this is my blood?" Well, Emerson says, these were just "parables and symbols. It was the national way of teaching and was largely used by him."[83]

The historical Jesus was "national" in the sense he was Jewish, acting like everybody else in the city of Jerusalem. This means that the Lord's Supper is really "a local custom and unsuitable in western countries."[84] It was all right that the Apostles, "Jews like Jesus, should adopt his expression and his type."[85] But not everyone else should. "Admitting that the disciples kept it and admitting Paul's feeling of its perpetuity, that does not settle the question for us. I think it was good for them. I think it is not suited to this day. We do not take them for guides in other things. They were, as we know, obstinately attached to their Jewish prejudices."[86]

One has to wince at this. Still, in being openly anti-Semitic, casting aspersion on the historical Jesus as a "national," a Jew, Emerson is also making a point that perhaps needs to be made, namely, that the religion of this one person is not applicable to everyone else. For the historical Jesus cannot in fact claim to speak for the whole of humanity. In a later letter to Elizabeth Peabody, Emerson is explicit on this point:

You have studied much the character of Jesus & I read with pleasure every considered expression of praise of him. But perfect in the sense of complete man he seems not to me to be, but a very exclusive & partial development of the moral element such as the great Compensation that balances the universe provides to repair accumulated depravity. The weight of his ethical sentences deserves more than all the consideration they have, & his life is one original pure beam of truth, but a perfect man should exhibit all the traits of humanity & should expressly recognize the intellectual nature.[87]

For Emerson, Jesus lacks the intellectual brilliance that the German scholars (say) exhibit in such abundance. He cannot be said to represent all humankind, and there is no reason why he should be singled out for universal remembrance in the sacrament of the Eucharist. For though this "mode of commemoration [was] every way agreeable to an Eastern mind, and yet on trial it was disagreeable to my own feelings, I should not adopt it." Jesus was a local figure; he should not be made out to be more than what he was. Our memory of him should be kept within limits: "For what could he wish to be commemorated for? Only that men might be filled with his spirit. I find that other modes comport with my education and habits of thought. For I chuse that my remembrances of him should be pleasing, affecting, religious. . . . A passage read from his discourses, the provoking each other to works like his, any act of meeting which tends to awaken a pure thought, a glow of love, an original design of virtue I call a worthy, a true commemoration."[88]

GOETHE

After delivering the Lord's Supper sermon, Emerson resigned as pastor of the Second Church. Henceforth, he would try to commemorate not just a single historical figure, Jesus, but many figures from many locales, so that "all the traits of humanity" would indeed be represented. What languages would he need? A letter to his aunt, Mary Moody Emerson, on August 19, 1832, three weeks before his resignation, gives some sense of the task ahead:

I apprehend a separation. . . . The farthing candle was not made for nothing—the least leaf must ope & grow after the fashion of its own lobes & veins & not after that of the oak or the rose, and I can only do my work well by abjuring the opinions & customs of all others & adhering strictly to the divine plan a few dim inches of whose outline I faintly discern in my breast. Is that not German enow? It is true. . . . I am entering into acquaintance with Goethe who has just died. The

Germans think there have been but three men of genius—Homer, Shakespear, & Goethe. If I go into the country to books, I shall know him well, & you will come & board with Mother & me, & we will try him whether he deserves his niche.[89]

German, the language that has done so much to sever Emerson's ties to the Christian church, will make up for that loss by offering him a different set of ties, with their own "lobes & veins" of remembrance. Goethe, "who has just died," has a claim on Emerson, rivaling and indeed outstripping that of the historical Jesus. Even before Emerson's resignation becomes official, Goethe is already taking over the field, turning the theological crisis into a literary beginning.

Emerson is right, though, to wonder whether he has "German enow." This was not a language he was initially equipped to read. In college, he had been taught the classical languages, and seemed to read Latin with ease.[90] His borrowed books from the Boston Athenaeum and the Harvard College Library included many texts in French.[91] German and Italian were languages that he had to learn on his own.[92] William's trip to Göttingen had, of course, given him a boost. On November 20, 1824, Emerson wrote: "If you think it every way advisable, indisputably, absolutely important that I shd do as you have done and go to G—& you can easily decide—why say it distinctly & I will make the sacrifice of time & take the risk of expense, immediately. So of studying German."[93] By 1828 he apparently knew enough of the language to check out from the Harvard College Library volume 3 of Goethe's *Werke*, the beginning of a lifelong relation to that author, carried out at least partly in German.[94]

Twenty years down the road, Goethe would be featured as the concluding figure in Emerson's *Representative Men* (1850). He receives high praise:

Goethe was the philosopher of this multiplicity; hundred-handed, Argus-eyed, able and happy to cope with this rolling miscellany of facts and sciences, and, by his own versatility, to dispose of them with ease. . . . What is strange, too, he lived in a small town, in a petty state, in a defeated state, and in a time when Germany played no such leading part in the world's affairs as to swell the bosom of her sons with any metropolitan pride, such as might have cheered a French, or English, or once, a Roman or Attic genius. Yet there is no trace of provincial limitation in his muse. He is not a debtor to his position, but was born with a free and controlling genius.[95]

Goethe is the opposite of the "national" Jesus. Though he is a dweller in a petty Germany, a petty Weimar, his horizons are not the same as the horizons of either place. On the contrary, with hundreds of hands and eyes, he is able to set his sights on distant things, capturing the "rolling miscellany" of the planet. When it comes to representing the world, there is no contest.

Still, high praise notwithstanding, this does not strike one as an entirely fond portrait. And the fondness seems to lessen as the chapter progresses. "I dare not say that Goethe ascended to the highest grounds from which genius has spoken. He has not worshipped the highest unity; he is incapable of a self-surrender to the moral sentiment," Emerson writes. And he adds, "Goethe can never be dear to men."[96] Something vital seems to be missing in this author. He has not given himself over to the "highest unity," and, perhaps for that reason, he will never be loved. Part of the problem, Emerson suggests in a 1834 journal entry, is that one "cannot read of the jubilee of Goethe, & of such a velvet life without a sense of incongruity. Genius is out of place when it reposes fifty years on chairs of state & breathes/inhales a continual incense of adulation" (*JMN* 4:258). A velvet life is a velvet prison: "Goethe & Carlyle & perhaps Novalis have an undisguised dislike or contempt for common virtue standing on common principles. . . . Praise Socrates to them, or Fenelon, much more any inferior contemporary good man & they freeze at once into silence. It is to them sheer prose" (*JMN* 4:301). Goethe has such an exalted definition of poetry that much of the world is indeed "prose" to him, an alien and inferior genre. This is why he and his "Weimarish Art friends . . . are contemptuous. They fail in sympathy with humanity. The voice of Nature they bring me to hear is not divine, but ghastly hard & ironical" (*JMN* 6:306). Poetry of this sort speaks to but a few, for "[t]he roots of what is great & high must still be in the common life" (*JMN* 6:306).

German Translations

The "highest unity" turns out to reside in the lowest common denominator. Goethe can offer no guidance here. In the end, "common life," as Emerson understands it, would have to come not from this author but from the German tongue itself: an unglamorous vernacular in the pantheon of languages, and very much a low common denominator as measured by Emerson's competence. Barely able to read the language, he nonetheless had access through it to a world of translations not available to an English-speaking world. As a medium, a conduit, German is indispensable, as we might glimpse from these lines by Goethe, which Emerson copies into his journal:

The Koran says, "God has given every people a prophet in its own speech." So is every translator a prophet to his people. Luther's translation of the Bible produced the greatest influence, if the critics up to this day continually stipulate and cavil thereon.[97] (*JMN* 6:292)

German scholarship had not only vernacularized the Christian Bible, it had made available other bibles and nonbibles. To Goethe, the Qur'an was a familiar text, to be quoted offhandedly. Likewise, Persian poetry, especially the work of the fourteenth-century poet Hafiz (1320–90), became known to the German-speaking world with two translations by the Austrian scholar Joseph von Hammer: *Der Diwan von Mohammed Schemsed-din Hafis* (1812–13) and *Geschichte der schönen redekünste Persiens* (1818).[98]

Goethe was an early reader of these anthologies. Bowled over, he in turn paid his homage to the Persian poets in the form of a cycle of poems, the *West-östlicher Divan*, followed by a series of explanatory essays, the *Noten und Abhandlungen zu besserem Verständnis des West-Östlichen Divans*.[99] This lyrical and highly erotic outburst was quite a surprise. Goethe was then in his sixties; his return to the lyric form was sparked, it would seem, by his encounter with the Persian lyric, the *ghazal*, unlike anything he had seen before.[100] Hafiz, prince of the *ghazal*, was thus the central presence for Goethe, not only in book 2, "Buch Hafis," but throughout the entire poem cycle, directly named in no fewer than nineteen poems.[101] Goethe saw the Persian poet as his twin: "Lust und Pein / Sei uns den Zwillingen gemein!"[102] This "twin" lived a long time ago, but temporal distance poses no problem, for a few hundred years mean nothing to Hafiz. The duration activated by this poet is of a different order of magnitude from the length of the human life span:

Daß du nicht enden kannst, das macht dich groß,
Und daß du nie beginnst, das ist dein Los.
Dein Lied ist drehend wie das Sterngewolbe,
Anfang und ende immerfort dasselbe,
Und was die Mitte bringt, ist offenbar
Das, was zu Ende bleibt und Anfangs war.

That you cannot end, that makes you great,
And that you never begin, that is your fate.
Your song revolves as does the starry dome,
Beginning and ending for evermore the same,
And what the middle brings is the open truth
that what stays in the end is what was in the beginning.[103]

The title of the poem is "unbegrenzt"—unbounded—and Hafiz is just that. He is off the human scale altogether, which is why there are no human figures at all in this tableau. Astronomical time is what it takes to measure the beginning and end of this poet, since the span of his poetry is not the span of a biological organism, but that of the cosmos itself. His grandeur is the grandeur of the firmament, of stars and galaxies in their everlasting orbits. For Goethe, Hafiz stands as empirical proof of the duration achievable by poetry, a superhuman duration, having nothing in common with the petty lengths of ordinary mortals.

Emerson had in his library all four German books: the two anthologies by von Hammer and both Goethe texts.[104] It was these German works that he owned and read, rather than Sir William Jones's Latin translation.[105] He quoted them for the rest of his life. The *West-östlicher Divan* first appeared in his journals in 1834; it made its last appearance in 1872 (*JMN* 4:271, 16:276). Likewise, he would go back to the *Noten und Abhandlungen* again and again, reading them sometimes on odd occasions, as attested by this journal entry from 1851: "Goethe's 'Notes to W. O. Divan,'—I read them in bed for I was very ill today. I can always understand anything better when I am ill" (*JMN* 11:485).

Emerson was not just a reader. He also translated. He had always been in the habit of rendering for himself bits and pieces of foreign texts and including them in his journals. He now tried his hand on Goethe. The earliest lines that he translated from the *West-östlicher Divan* were these from March 29, 1834:

> My Heritage how (far) long & wide
> Time is my heritage my field is Time.[106]
> (*JMN* 4:271)

For Emerson too, time is the province of poetry: a heritage, a field. This field, though, is not likely to show up on any official map, for its extended network flies in the face of any standard measurement. In the motto to his late essay, "Poetry and Imagination," Emerson writes: "The muse can knit / What is past, what is done, / With the web that's just begun; / Making free with time and size."[107] The metric of poetry is a nonstandard metric. That is why the Persian poets—the fourteenth-century Hafiz and the thirteenth-century Saadi (1213–92)—are not thousands of miles away but hauntingly here, not ancient but contemporary.

They made their way into Emerson's journals in 1841 (*JMN* 8:67).[108] In 1842 he published his own poem "Saadi" in *The Dial*.[109] And, just as he had been translating Goethe for himself, he now did the same for Hafiz. Working from von Hammer's German texts, he included his first translation as a journal entry in 1846, and kept up the practice for the rest of his life. Over the course of the next thirty years, Emerson produced at least sixty-four translations, a total of seven hundred lines of Persian poetry.[110] Some of these were included in his long essay, "Persian Poetry," first published in the *Atlantic* in 1858, later collected in his *Letters and Social Aims* (1875).[111] When Ticknor and Fields brought out the first American edition of Saadi's *Gulistan* in 1865, it was Emerson who was called on to write the preface.[112] And finally, toward the end of his life, he paid yet another tribute to these beloved poets in a long poem of his own, entitled "Fragments on the Poet and the Poetic Gift."[113] Hafiz was one of the last names to appear in Emerson's Pocket Diary. From 1841 to 1879 he was never absent from the journals.[114]

Low Hafiz

> O Hafiz, give me thought,
> In fiery figures cast,
> For all beside is naught,
> All else is din & blast.
>   (*JMN* 14:120)

Emerson would go over the translations again and again, filling many notebooks with many drafts. This one, turned back into a tribute to the Persian poet, came in at least three other versions.[115] Unlike the serene and majestic poet celebrated by Goethe, however, Emerson's Hafiz is not only fiery, but downright riotous, at once ill-favored and ill-used. This might be closer to the historical fact, for Hafiz was known to be an unattractive man, short and ugly, and not always well behaved.[116] This was how he chose to portray himself in one of his *ghazals*, one that Emerson in turn chose to translate:

> My crooked ↑old body↓ bent [form] ↑forlorn↓
> Seems ↑to you↓ to merit [only] scorn;
> [Yet] ↑look again↓ it is [only] a bow
> Whose [arrows] ↑shafts shall↓ strike many ↑a↓ foe[s].

> Does my old body bent forlorn
> Seem to you to merit scorn?
> Look again, it is a bow
> Whose shaft shall strike all [rival/gazers] ↑gazers↓ low.[117]
>   (*TN* 2:129)

Here then is "low" poetry, in quite a literal sense. It does make free with time and size, as Emerson says, for it retools our yardstick, giving us a different scale on which to measure beauty. Any true poetry must be able to do this: it must confer beauty on the old, the decrepit, those who are bowed down. Its emblem is not the timeless orbits of the stars, but the time-disfigured human body. This is the geometry of our common life. And, just as it gives voice to the common failings of the misshapen body, it also gives voice to the common failings of the misshapen will. Many of Hafiz's poems are devoted to the taverngoers of Shiraz, people not exactly upstanding. "I side with the [open] drunkards," he says (*PN* 287).[118] He seems to be one himself, as in this poem that Emerson also translates:

> So long as there's a trace
> Of wine & banquet house
> My head will lie in the dust
> Of the threshold of the winehouse
> Ask thou for grace [one day] ↑hereafter↓
> At my gravestone
> [Since] that will be the pilgrim city
> Of all the drinkers of wine
> The ring of the [landlord] mine host hangs
> Forever in my ear.
> I am; what I was
> My dust will be again.
>
> (*PN* 310–11)

Common life, to be common, cannot be on the moral high ground. Its appropriate place is "in the dust," where the head of the inebriated is, and where his dust will commingle presently. This is Mecca, the "pilgrim city," where future lovers of poetry will have to look for him.

What is the relation between this Mecca in the dust and the Mecca of Islam? And can we call Hafiz an "Islamic" poet? Emerson was struck by the name Hafiz. The Persian word, he noted, "signifies one gifted with so good a memory that he knows the whole Koran by heart" (*JMN* 10:17). Knowing the Qur'an by heart, however, does not make one an orthodox Muslim. Quite the contrary. Persian poetry—with antecedents both rich and ancient, dating back to the Achaemenian dynasty of 600 BCE—had never been unduly deferential toward the Arabic language.[119] The Persian *ghazal* especially, though based on Arabic prosody (it is composed on a single rhyme, like the Arabic *qasida*), is supple in a way as to constitute a separate genre.[120] It is made up of a series of couplets, with no enjambment, so that each couplet is autonomous: one might be comic, another tragic, another whimsical, and so on. The mono-rhyming form is a harsh constraint, however. It gives the *ghazal* an emotional rawness, dramatized, Agha Shahid Ali says, by "one definition of the word *ghazal*: It is the cry of the gazelle when it is cornered in a hunt and knows it will die."[121]

The *ghazal* is a cry of finitude that refuses to be comforted, refuses to look the other way. Its ability to face death is much more austere—and in some sense much more reliable—than the solace of religion. In the hands of Hafiz, it becomes a kind of negative extension of the Qur'an, an extension sometimes dejected, sometimes reckless and flaunting, but always giving the poet a path oblique and tangential to Islam. It is possible, of course, to read Hafiz as a Sufi mystic and to allegorize his poems, so that wine "does not mean an alcoholic beverage (forbidden in Islam) but has a wealth of spiritual meanings, such as the drunken bliss of Love that comes from the grace of God."[122] Such high-minded readings have no appeal for Emerson. Just as he has once refused to allegorize the wine in the Eucharist, he now refuses to allegorize the wine imbibed by this scandalous Islamic poet. We need not "strew sugar on bottled spiders," Emerson says, "or try to make mystical divinity out of the Song of Solomon, much less out of the erotic and bacchanalian songs of Hafiz. Hafiz himself is determined to defy all such hypocritical interpretation."[123] These poems should be taken as they are: wine-soaked and death-fronting. And, if they emerge as a snide reflection on Christianity, that makes them even more compelling:

Cheer thy heart with wine:
The earth is only
A house to which our bones
Give the mortar.

Seek not in thy friend, truth;
Truth is dead;
Holy fire comes not
Out of Church lamps.

Blacken thou not my name
For my riot;
Who knows what the lot
Inscribed on the brow?

Turn not thy steps
From the grave of Hafiz,
Since though in sins sunken
He waits for/ expects Heaven.
                    (PN 315–16)

Hafiz's poetry is stubbornly earthbound, precisely because he knows the Qur'an so well, because he knows it by heart. Knowing the Qur'an by heart, and knowing that the earth is no more than "A house to which our bones / Give the mortar," he nonetheless has every expectation of

"Heaven." It is not entirely clear what Hafiz means by this word, but Emerson, his translator, seems to have a pretty good idea of what this entails. In a poem that is as much a tribute to Hafiz as an imitation of him—not published, but carefully written down in the notebooks—Emerson has his own version of a drinking song, one that does in fact turn the dust of the finite into more volatile material:

> Pour the wine, pour the wine;
> As it changes to foam[s],
> So the Creator,
> New & unlooked for,
> Rushing abroad,
> In farthest & smallest
> Comes royally home.
>
> In spider wise
> Will again geometrize,
> Will in bee & gnat keep time
> With the annual solar chime.
> Aphides, like emperors,
> Sprawl & creep their pair of hours.
> (PN 332)

Living six hundred years after Hafiz, Emerson knows (as perhaps the Persian poet did not) that the "wine" of his poetry is effervescent, that it can rise from the earth as well as sink into it. Turning into foam, it can stream out in laces and eddies, like a spider "geometrizing" the world with its web. The work of human hands is indeed like "the house of the spider," as the Qur'an warns us. In the George Sale translation, Emerson would have come across these lines in the celebrated 29th sura, entitled "The Spider": "The likeness of those who take other patrons besides God is as the likeness of the spider, which maketh herself a house; but the weakest of all houses surely is the house of the spider."[124] He seems to have memorized these words, only to have inverted their meaning. His spider, with its rickety house, will persevere. It does not bow its head before the Qur'an, or, for that matter, before a "God that holds you over the pit of hell, much as one holds a spider."[125]

The spider does not bow its head, for when it dies, its house will remain, "Will in bee & gnat keep time" and will further "sprawl & creep" with the aphides. Who are these creatures? Emerson might have counted himself among their numbers, since Hafiz's foaming poetry does travel "abroad," and "In farthest and smallest / Come royally home." New England is as good a place as any for that homecoming. But it is not the only place. For if it is a question of the "farthest and smallest," there are others who will answer to that description, bees and gnats and aphides who, in one guise or another, will serve as carriers for the likes of Hafiz. "A good scholar will find Aristophanes & Hafiz & Rabelais full of American history," Emerson says (*JMN* 10:35).

BLUES FOR ALLAH

What American history would Hafiz be "full of" in the twentieth century? Emerson would not live to see it, but his translations, as always incomplete, offer a proleptic clue:

> The very wind pipes rowdy songs,
> [Drives sober people mad] ↑Makes saints and patriarchs bad↓
> [Should] ↑Shall↓ we [suffer] ↑tolerate↓ such wrongs
> And not [give the alarm] ↑cry out like mad↓
> Makes saints perverse [&] ↑makes↓ angels bad
>
> (*TN* 2:46)

What did Emerson mean by "bad"? The word has a rich vernacular sound in the twentieth century, a sound that, surprisingly, it was already beginning to acquire in the nineteenth. Emerson knew this. In the same notebooks in which he translated Hafiz, he also kept a list of "street speech":

> Gimcracks,
> Kecksies, plainly derived from *qu'est ce que c'est?*
> Chickenhearted
> jawing
> Mamma, I love you very bad (*TN* 2:152)

Hafiz's is "bad" in just that way. This is how he comes home to Emerson. And it is in that spirit that I would like to propose another homecoming, a twentieth-century replay of his fourteenth-century "badness":

> Once I knew a preacher, preached the Bible thru and thru
> He went down to Deep Elem, now his preaching days are thru
> Oh, Sweet Mama, your Daddy's got them Deep Elem Blues
> Oh, Sweet Mama, your Daddy's got them Deep Elem Blues[126]

It is the blues, the "low" poetry of the United States, that will carry on the badness of Hafiz, speaking now as he once did to the down and out, those whose heads are in the dust. Common life is never more common than in this musical genre, one that spills out, energizing and "vernacularizing" the English tongue. It is in the blues that the word "Mama" would be whispered and crooned and grunted, one of the primal words in the language. This particular number, "Deep Elem Blues," first sung by the Shelton Brothers in the early 1930s, was featured by the Grateful Dead in their acoustic album *Reckoning* (1978). For many Dead Heads, the more satisfying performance is probably the one at Harpur College on May 2, 1970, captured in *Dick's Picks*, volume 8.

The Dead not only sang about badness in others; its fallen band members—Jerry Garcia, Ron McKernan, Keith Godchaux, Brent Mydland—seem to personify the word "bad" themselves, lyrically and terminally.[127] Hafiz would have understood this, just as he understood, from the first, that there is a heaven even for those brought low. For many of us, this is probably the only heaven that is not a caricature. Not "ghastly & hard & ironical," it has to be reedy, wishful, precarious and yet persevering: the sound of the blues-rock. This vernacular form, once African-American, is now the common tongue of the whole world, one that makes song out of being "in sin sunken." Weak but tenacious, a spider's house, it speaks as much to Islam as to Christianity. It carries on the work of Hafiz and Emerson both.

It should not come as too much of a surprise, then, that the Grateful Dead should happen to have another song, "Blues for Allah." This is a "requiem for King Faisal of Saudi Arabia, a progressive and democratically inclined ruler (incidentally, a fan of the Grateful Dead) whose assassination in 1975 shocked us personally," Robert Hunter tells us.[128] The song was performed live only five times, all in 1975. Perhaps it needs to be heard again:

> Arabian wind
> The needle's eye is thin
> The ships of state sail on mirage
> and drown in sand
> Out in no man's land
> Where Allah does command
>
> What good is spilling blood
> It will not grow a thing
> "Taste eternity," the swords sing
> Blues for Allah
> In 'sh'Allah
> They lie where they fall
> There is nothing more to say
> The desert stars are bright tonight
> Let's meet as friends

The flower of Islam
The fruit of Abraham

The thousand stories have
come around to one again
Arabian night
Our gods pursue their fight
What fatal flowers of darkness
Bloom from seeds of light

CHAPTER THREE

The Planetary Dead:
Margaret Fuller, Ancient Egypt,
Italian Revolution

Do the dead remain "human"? Does their membership in the species persist beyond their biological end? Or does that membership cease the moment their breath ceases? What is the principle that aggregates them, that makes us speak of them as one, a collective unit, "the dead"? And how does this oneness of the dead reflect on humans in general, currently not one but perhaps needing to be? What does it mean to belong to a species made up of two populations: those who are physically present and those who are not, no longer full-fledged members but also not quite nonmembers?

This chapter ponders these questions by way of *Woman in the Nineteenth Century*, a text that, at first blush, might seem far removed from such concerns. Its no-nonsense title gives the impression that this is a book on a contemporary subject, clearly defined, clearly periodized. The actual text, of course, is nothing like that. Talking about nineteenth-century women, Fuller goes back to the dead, to the ancient civilizations: Egypt, Greece, Mesopotamia. She includes, among her roster of names, figures who would seem to have no truck with the nineteenth century—figures such as Isis and Panthea—before moving on to the ususal suspects, the likes of Madame De Staël, Mary Wollstonecraft, and George Sand.

LARGE-SCALE CAUSATION

It is instructive to take a look first at Fuller's discussion of someone belonging squarely to the nineteenth century, Madame De Staël:

> De Stael's name was not so clear of offence; she could not forget the Woman in the thought; while she was instructing you as a mind, she wished to be admired as Woman; sentimental tears often dimmed the eagle glance. Her intellect, too, with all its splendor, trained in a drawing room, fed on flattery, was tainted and flawed; yet its beams make the obscurest school-house in New England warmer and lighter to the little rugged girls who are gathered together on its wooden

bench. They may never through life hear her name, but she is not the less their benefactress.[1]

Fuller begins by listing De Staël's faults, and they are numerous. But, as the syntax makes clear, these faults are only half the story; the paragraph is literally split down the middle, giving tangible shape to De Staël's split career. Halfway through, it relocates itself, leaving Europe behind, crossing the Atlantic, winding up on a different continent. Even though De Staël, a pampered aristocrat, has a somewhat spotty record herself, the "beams" of her intellect nonetheless travel far, casting their light on schoolgirls in New England. She is the "benefactress" of these schoolgirls. Something has been passed on.

How that passing on takes place—and what it does to the benefactress as well as to the beneficiaries—is the central argument of *Woman in the Nineteenth Century*. What Fuller is developing here is a model of large-scale causation, based on remote agency, unforeseen effects, action at a distance. A light beams out from a remote source; it is picked up by faraway receptors. This long-distance exchange means that causation cannot be limited to the boundaries imposed by any discrete unit. It cannot be adequately mapped by the spatial coordinates of a territorial jurisdiction, nor can it be mapped by the temporal coordinates of the nineteenth century. Its full contours become legible only on a much larger scale, operating not on the level of the individual, and not even on the level of the nation, but across the length and width of human life, the level on which long-term results can emerge.

This emphasis on long-term results suggests that the very definition of "woman" has to be changed. Rather than centering on the biological individual, it can now take in processes that go beyond biology.[2] In practice, what this means is that "woman" must now be tracked as a durational as well as extensional phenomenon. It has the same elongation, and the same morphology, as the human species itself. Its database is nothing less than the full recorded history of the planet.

GEOLOGY AND ASTRONOMY

I want to call attention to this large-scale model, so much at odds with our customary view of the nineteenth century, a century, we are repeatedly told, of rugged individualism. That, it now seems, is not the whole story. If Fuller's feminism is any indication, rugged individualism would seem to be only one side of a dialectic, with a structural counterpoint, a negative force pulling in the opposite direction. Self-reliance, because it is so heavily dramatized, so heavily leaned upon, can end up becoming

a stress point and a fault line. Its positive value can cross over into negative territory, taking us to the very limits of that concept, the point where
its claim collapses under its own weight.

This should not surprise us. The nineteenth century was nothing if not
a dialectical century, and a crucial part of that dialectics was fueled by
the new, antihumanist findings of the large-scale sciences. These sciences
revealed not only the dumbfounding largeness of the universe but also
the dumbfounding smallness of human beings. Astronomy and geology
were especially merciless in disabusing us of any illusion of grandeur.
The former, discovering in the cosmos distances measured by billions of
light-years, and the latter, discovering on our planet itself a long record
of prehistoric fossils, made it clear that the universe as a whole and even
our own planet is operating on a time frame grossly asymmetrical to the
human life span.

This asymmetry of scale makes human knowledge infinitely problem-
atic. There is no way of reconciling the gulf between the space and time
we have at our command and the space and time we need in order to understand the full range of cause and effect. There is no way of reconciling this gulf between the capacity of the human brain and the staggering
accumulation of data that needs to be processed. The French astronomer
and mathematician Pierre Simon Laplace, in his *Essai philosophique sur
les probabilités* (1795), underscored this point:

> We ought then to regard the present state of the universe as the effect
> of its anterior state and as the cause of the one which is to follow.
> Given for one instant an intelligence which could comprehend all the
> forces by which nature is animated and the respective situation of the
> beings who compose it—an intelligence sufficiently vast to submit
> these data to analysis—it would embrace in the same formula the
> movements of the greatest bodies of the universe and those of the light-
> est atom; for it, nothing would be uncertain and the future, as the
> past, would be present to its eyes. The human mind offers, in the per-
> fection which it has been able to give to astronomy, a feeble idea of
> this intelligence.[3]

The feebleness of the human mind was, in some sense, the central discovery of the nineteenth century. It serious implications were clear even
to the most determined advocate of self-reliance. Emerson (who had
been reading Laplace since at least 1823)[4] was no exception. In a lecture
entitled "The Relation of Man to the Globe," given in December 1833, he
observed, "There are many facts which from their nature cannot suddenly
be known and which can only be disclosed in long periods of time." The
planet is a cumulative archive that none of us can decipher on our own,
for it is "a monument on whose surface every age of perhaps numberless

centuries has somewhere inscribed its history in gigantic letters—too deep to be obliterated—but so far apart, and without visible connexion, that only the most diligent observer—say rather—an uninterrupted succession of patient observers—can read them."[5] In particular, Emerson singled out astronomy and geology as the two sciences challenging us the most. These two, he said, had not only downgraded our planet from "a first rate globe in heaven to a diminutive speck utterly invisible from the nearest star," they had also downgraded humanity itself to the status of a "deposed king from off whose back has been stripped the purple, and from whose head has been torn the crown."[6] All of this would seem quite discouraging, but Emerson, characteristically, was not discouraged. In a universe so vast, he said, all human differences vanish. As far as the cosmos is concerned, qualities that we call great and qualities that we call small are equally inconsequential: "In the eternity of nature centuries are lost as moments are. In the immensity of matter there is no great, no small."[7]

STATISTICS

This is what scale enlargement does: it changes the perceptual field, changes the threshold of differentiation, raising the bar so high that what once looked like huge differences now fall below the line. They disappear into the woodwork. There is an inverse correlation, in other words, between the magnitude of the scale and the robustness of distinctions. On a large enough canvas, distinctions can become very unrobust indeed; they can lose their claim to visibility altogether. Emerson was fascinated by this idea. He trotted it out on all occasions, as he did during one of the conversations Margaret Fuller held in Boston, on March 8, 1841.[8] Caroline Dall, who was in the audience, reported the event:

> Emerson pursued his own train of thought. He seemed to forget that we had come together to pursue Margaret's. He said it was impossible that men or events should *stand out* in a population of twenty millions as they could from a population of a single million, to which the whole population of the ancient world could hardly have amounted. As Hercules stood to Greece, no modern man could ever stand in relation to his own world.[9]

An analytic scale pitched at the level of populations does not give a special status to anyone, because the perceptual field here is organized to highlight what holds true for the system as a whole, what exhibits patterns of regularity. These patterns, emerging as a result of scale enlargement, make it possible to speak of *frequencies* of recurrence, frequencies that are scale-induced, mathematically determined, and therefore also mathematically calculable. A law of large numbers comes into play when the database is sufficiently large. This law turns each individual, however exceptional, into a systemic effect, a quantifiable instance.

This too is a legacy of the large-scale sciences. There is a logical connection between the mathematics of cosmological and geological time and the mathematics of aggregation and prediction.[10] Charles Lyell's geology looked forward to modern quantitative reasoning, paving the way for a "statistical paleontology," Martin Rudwick has argued.[11] In the case of astronomy, this overlap between large-scale science and statistical thinking was even more pronounced: Laplace was not only an astronomer but also the author of *Essai philosophique sur les probabilités*, an early advocate of the science of calculable frequency, calculable margin of error.

And indeed, no other mathematics better captured the ambition of the Enlightenment, its desire to give the plenitude of the world a rational form, the form of numerical order. Beginning with an unknowable vastness of data, probability makes a virtue of this fact, deriving from it the most thoroughgoing mathematical determinism. The large databases are unknowable in the individual instances that comprise them, but they are aggregately calculable. Given millions of people, we can count on the existence of at least one good basketball player. Given millions of people, we can count on the existence of someone with perfect pitch. The exceptional individual, in other words, is simply the mathematical consequence of a large enough populational pool. He or she is not so much an aberration as a rare but nonetheless systemic effect. The law of large numbers applies to this individual no less than to the rest of the population. What looks like an exception is, in fact, part of the rule.

This elimination of exceptions means that there is no circumference wider than the law of large numbers. This is a truly global postulate, generalizable in every phenomenon. In the hands of Adolphe Quetelet, it would become consolidated into a new science, statistics, the most foundational and most encompassing of the modern sciences, one that makes an aggregate population the determining ground for every individual occurrence. Emerson invokes it in his essay, "Fate" (1846), which mentions Quetelet by name and pays tribute to the law he expounds:

> It is a rule that the most casual and extraordinary events, if the basis of population is broad enough, become matter of fixed calculation. It would not be safe to say when a captain like Bonaparte, a singer like Jenny Lind, or a navigator like Bowditch would be born in Boston; but, on a population of twenty or two hundred millions, something like accuracy may be had.[12]

For Emerson, the law of large numbers is both infinitely deflating and infinitely reassuring. Deflating, because things that look exceptional turn out not to be. But also reassuring, because the fact that these things are not exceptional means that they will come around again in a rotational cycle: they have a guaranteed frequency, a periodic rate of return.

NONBIOLOGICAL REPRODUCTION

For Fuller, even more than for Emerson, this periodic rate of return makes all the difference in the world. It suggests that biological reproduction is not the only game in town, that there is a principle of likeness not reducible to its terms. As we can see from the example of De Staël and the New England schoolgirls, a large-scale paradigm makes for a different kind of kinship. Given enough space and time, given a big enough population, there will be other human beings similar to De Staël. These human beings are not her *biological* offspring; they are her *statistical* offspring. Their kinship with her is a populational effect. The tyranny of biology, in other words, has been upstaged by a mathematical law that performs the same reproductive function, doing so not through female anatomy but through the law of probability. And it is on the ground of probability that De Staël might be said to be a "benefactress" of these New England schoolgirls. Her very existence is statistically significant; it carries the prediction that there will be descendants.

This prediction, this enactment of a collective likelihood, has nothing to do with the goodwill of any single person. In fact, agency now resides in a much broader domain. The paradigm here is anti-intentionalist, and indeed antihumanist. And yet, the unfolding of such a paradigm not only has consequences for the human species as a whole but also affirms it as such: as a species distinguishable from others on the strength of its claim to more than just biology, more than bare life.[13] The "humanness" of all of us, in other words, emerges as the logical entailment of a large-scale model that, at first glance, would seem to have wiped us completely off the map.

This is an interesting paradox, a kind of antihumanist humanism. Scale enlargement here not only gives rise to a mathematical determinism that empties out the volition of the individual actor; it also gives rise to something else, something running counter to it, namely, a conception of the "human" that grants the species the power to perpetuate its handiwork: handiwork finite but not trivial, emanating from the physical body but not ending with its biological end. This nonending means that every member of the species can count on the species as a whole to serve as a buffer as well as a solvent: a vast, ever-expanding, and ever-receptive archive, compiling and collating all that we have done and all that we would ever want to do. Human beings are the only creatures on the planet who reproduce through archives. They are the only ones who can have "kin" above and beyond what biology permits. *Woman in the Nineteenth Century* honors this kinship and gives it the largest possible scope, not only by embracing the history of the entire species, but also by refusing to distinguish between those who now inhabit the earth and those who once did, those who have a kind of territorial sovereignty in the present moment and those who, in dying, have lost that sovereignty.

Posthumous Kinship

I would like to explore the implications of what it means to challenge territorial sovereignty in this way, to offer shelter to one particular class of aliens: those who have no citizenship in any territorial nation because they have no citizenship in the living world. The dead, Robert Pogue Harrison has recently argued, represent a category of humanity in most urgent need of theorization.[14] Margaret Fuller, I would like to suggest, has already begun to think along those lines. And, in recovering an archive that reaches back to this group of noncitizens, she gives us a feminism stretched almost beyond recognition. "Woman" is generalized rather than localized here, offered less as a subset than as a synecdoche for the species as a whole. Since the burden of biological reproduction has always fallen on this group, it is also the group with the most to gain from any lightening of that burden. Fuller's archive is feminist in just this sense. Making gender a non-issue in reproduction, it broadens the definition of kinship to include statistical likenesses emerging across the life of the species, applicable to both sexes, and embracing not only the living but also the dead.

Woman as a population thus falls on both sides of mortality, just as the planet as a habitat does. Its rank and file includes former tenants no less than current ones. Such demographics fly in the face of territorial sovereignty, for the time frame here extends from the oldest recorded history, an arc longer than the duration of any nation-state. To acknowledge this arc, to see the grave as the midpoint rather than the endpoint of human relations, is to call for a new ethics, a new politics, and a new aesthetics, all based on a broader definition of the species as partly actual and partly virtual, constituted by its unended as by its uncommenced life.[15] Such a time frame mocks our biological finitude but also affirms in it a relational continuum. In its large-scale coordinates, it reduces us to nothing; but, in reproducing us, perhaps against our will, it gives us a deep field of kinship, more robustly expressive of our humanity than our own life span.

OPENING OF THE MOUTH

What would ethics, politics, and aesthetics look like if kinship were defined in this way? The center of gravity, first of all, might not coincide with anything Western, certainly not anything modern. When it comes to kinship with the dead—providing for their needs and saving them from the terrible fate of nonexistence—the ancient civilizations remain unrivaled.[16] Even a cursory glance at Egyptian mortuary texts shows a well-developed practice based on the ongoing ties between those still walking this earth and those no longer able to do so. To care for these people, complex rituals were performed to make sure they would remain human after death. Remaining human, they journeyed beyond the grave and came back once again to the realm of light and air.

The vast corpus of the *Book of the Dead* was dedicated to just this purpose.[17] Its Egyptian title (*Reu nu pert em hru*) literally means "Chapters of Going Forth by Day." This alignment of death with *daybreak* might seem odd to a modern sensibility, but logical to the ancient Egyptians, for death was not just the end of a cycle but also the beginning of a new one. The dead were buried underground, beneath the face of the earth; but they were also solar beings; they streamed out, flooding and illuminating the world as does the sun.

The *Papyrus of Ani* (an especially well-preserved instance of the *Book of the Dead* from Thebes, ca. 1250 BCE) thus opens with an appeal to both these realms: a hymn to the Sun-god, Re, followed by a hymn to the god of the underworld, Osiris. The postmortem journey of Ani comes after these hymns, made up of "chapters of going out into the day, the praises and recitations for going to and fro in the God's domain."[18] First, the heart of the dead man is weighed (to make sure that he is guilty of no wrong); then follows an important ceremony, the Opening of the Mouth, to make sure he is restored to the power of speech: "May you give me my mouth with which I may speak, and may my heart guide me at its hour of destroying the night."[19]

This Opening of the Mouth was a well-developed ritual in Egypt, dating back to the Fourth Dynasty, around 2600 BCE.[20] During this ceremony, a set of flint tools were applied to the mummified body or to a surrogate statue, magically opening the deceased's mouth, eyes, and ears for renewed use. That was what was done to resurrect Osiris. And since

Figure 3-1. The Opening of the Mouth Ceremony from the Book of the Dead of Hunefer, ca. 1310 BCE. Courtesy of the British Museum.

this god was the prototype for all of us—since all dead human beings could aspire to come back from death, as he did—the same rituals must now be performed for Ani, so that he could indeed become Osiris, literally taking on his name, as "Osiris Ani" or "Osiris N." It was the obligation of the living to make sure this would happen.

The *Book of the Dead* dramatized this obligation. In the images accompanying the hieroglyph, the Opening of the Mouth was portrayed in a detailed scene (fig. 3.1). At the door of the tomb, the dog-headed god, Anubis, holds the mummy of the deceased, before whom kneels the weeping wife. In front of them is a table of funeral offerings, tended by three priests. One wears a panther's skin and holds in his hand a libation vase and censer. Another holds in his right hand a mouth-opening tool, *ur heka*, in the shape of a ram-headed serpent, and in his left hand another tool, the *Meskhet*, in the shape of an adze. With the former he will touch the mouth and eyes of the mummy; with the latter, he will touch the mouth once again to make sure it is indeed opened. Just to be safe, the papyrus puts in an extra set of tools, standing just behind the priests, comprising the *Meskhet*, the collection of adzelike devices, and the *Pesh-en-kef*, the libation vases.[21]

Without these tools, without the dedication and ingenuity of the living, Ani would be doomed to eternal silence. Luckily for him, dedication and ingenuity are not lacking, and he cries out in gratitude:

My mouth is opened by Ptah and what was on my mouth has been loosened by my local god. Thoth comes indeed, filled and equipped with magic, and the bonds of Seth which restricted my mouth have been loosened. Atum has warded them off and has cast away the restrictions of Seth.

My mouth is opened, my mouth is split open by Shu with that iron harpoon of his with which he split open the mouth of the gods.[22]

Thanks to these gods, and thanks to the human beings who so carefully perform these rituals, the gag order that comes with mortality has been lifted. Regaining his power of speech, Ani loses no time asking for a customary privilege granted the Egyptian dead—freedom of travel, freedom, in effect, to leave the underworld immediately and go back once again to his former home: "May I enter into and go forth from the God's Domain, without my *Ba* being hindered. May I see the sun and may I behold the moon every day."[23]

How is this possible? In what form can the dead come back to life? As we can see from Ani's phrasing, he does not expect to come back exactly as he was; only his *Ba* would make the track back. The *Ba* is one of three words (the other two are the *Akh* and the *Ka*) used by Egyptians to describe the soul of the dead.[24] It is usually depicted as a bird, a stork. In that form, it is sometimes shown perched on the mummiform coffin, but, given its avian nature, its chief function is to fly, to be swift and vigorous in its passage. It dramatizes the ability of the soul of the dead person to come and go as it pleases, "in the manner it did on earth." Motion, in other words, is one of the few attributes *not* subject to the dividing line imposed by mortality. It is a crossover attribute, claimable by the dead as by the living. On this score, dead human beings are actually not the same as Osiris. The god of the underworld is immobile; he is always shown in a mummified form; from his head down he is featureless, lifeless, his legs stuck together, clearly not ambulatory in any way. His kingdom is chthonic, and his iconography reflects that airtight jurisdiction. The human dead, on the other hand, have a much more flexible citizenship.[25] Their legs as well as their mouths aspire to move in a realm of light and air.

PLUTARCH'S ISIS

Margaret Fuller would not have known about these particular funerary rituals; the first English edition of the *Book of the Dead* appeared only in the late-nineteenth century. However, she did have a keen interest in ancient Egypt, sparked by an eyewitness account from a first-century

Greek author, Plutarch, who had traveled to Egypt twice and who devoted a long, celebrated essay in his *Moralia* to the "ancient religion and philosophy of Egypt," commonly referred to as *De Iside et Osiride*. The Renaissance Humanists rediscovered this text and republished it in 1509, with the help of Erasmus. It was translated into Latin and the vernacular languages from the sixteenth century onward. Philemon Holland's English translation appeared in 1603. This was followed by a late-seventeenth-century translation, "by several hands," the fifth edition (1718) of which Emerson owned and circulated among his friends.[26] On May 30, 1837, Fuller wrote to say that the volume was now in her hands.[27] But this was hardly her first encounter with Plutarch, for she already had prior knowledge of him from her education in Latin and Greek since age six. In 1834, in her first published work, a response to George Bancroft in the *Boston Daily Advertiser*, she had been able to clinch her argument by citing Plutarch.[28]

Plutarch wrote very much as a foreigner and latecomer. The worship of Osiris dated back to the Fourth Dynasty;[29] it was already "ancient"— an over-two-millennium-old phenomenon—by the time Plutarch wrote *De Iside et Osiride*, around AD 120.[30] The great antiquity of the god meant that he was a composite figure, sedimented through many chronological periods, taking in a multiplicity of features from Egypt's polytheism. It was not uncommon (as we can see from the *Papyrus of Ani*) for four different gods to be meshed together: benign gods like Ptah, Thoth, and Shu, and nonbenign ones like Seth. And there were many more, a bewildering pantheon, with abundant mixing, overlap, changes of name, deities morphing into one another, some fading and others rising to new prominence.

Isis is a case in point. In the Middle Kingdom (as evidenced by the *Book of the Dead*) she had an honored but marginal place, appearing almost always as an appendage to Osiris, and almost always in conjunction with Nephthys, her sister and co-attendant. In the succeeding centuries, however, she was increasingly singled out. A magnificent temple was built specially for her at Philae during the early Ptolemaic reigns (265 BCE).[31] As shown in the Hellenized late additions to this temple, Egypt was by then part of the Graeco-Roman world, and Isis reflected that sea change.[32] Her features became Graeco-Roman. Herodotus mentioned her in book 2 of his *Histories*, as the local name for a cosmic principle, "the Egyptian equivalent of Demeter."[33] Plutarch, likewise, took pains to construct a Greek etymology for her, tracing the word Isis to τò ὄν and ἴσειον.[34] In short, "the name of Isis is Greek, and so too is that of her adversary Typhon, who, being puffed up through ignorance and mistake, pulls in pieces and destroys that holy doctrine, which she on the contrary collects, compiles, and delivers."[35]

Isis, Osiris, Typhon

With this sleight of hand, Plutarch gave Isis an etymological home in the Greek language. And, by pairing her with another character with a Greek etymology—Typhon, her nemesis—he shifted the focus of the story away from the resurrection of Osiris to an earlier, less happy moment, when the god was killed. Typhon was the killer. It was he who trapped Osiris in an ark and floated it out to sea. When Isis found out, she wandered up and down, with her hair shorn, looking for the dead body. Finally finding it, she "threw herself down upon the chest, and her lamentations were so loud, that the younger of the king's two sons died for very fear."[36] Looking for her husband's dead body, Isis turned another human being into a dead body. And her murderous grief did not end. When she "laid her cheeks upon the cheeks of Osiris, and embraced him and wept bitterly, [a] little boy seeing her came silently behind her, and peeping saw what it was; which she perceiving cast a terrible look upon him in the height of her passion; the fright whereof the child could not endure, and immediately died."[37]

Mourning Osiris's death, Isis ravaged the lives of those who had the misfortune to be close by. Murderousness was not something external, a principle of evil locatable outside of herself. Rather, it was one of two alternate pathways, a right turn and a wrong turn each threaded through her, or as Plutarch put it in a striking passage, "by reason of two contrary origins and opposite powers—whereof the one leads to the right hand and in a direct line and the other turns to the contrary hand and goes athwart."[38] In her susceptibility to that "contrary hand," Isis was hardly distinguishable from Typhon. His "ignorance and mistake" were equally hers, fatal flaws that compromised what she did, opening her endlessly to blame. Having tracked down Osiris's body and buried it, she could not foresee that Typhon, while hunting, would come upon the body a second time. This time he tore Osiris's body into fourteen parts and scattered all the pieces. Plutarch dwelled on Isis's utter helplessness at this point: "Which when Isis had heard, she went to look for them again in a certain barge made of papyrus, in which she sailed over all the fens. . . . And this (they say) hath occasioned the report that there are many sepulchres of Osiris in Egypt, because she made a particular funeral for each member as she found them. . . . But of all Osiris's members, Isis could never find out his private part, for it had been presently flung into the river Nile, and the lepidotus, sea-bream, and pike eating of it, these were for that reason more scrupulously avoided by the Egyptians than any other fish."[39]

According to J. Gwyn Griffiths, the loss of Osiris's private parts is not corroborated by Egyptian sources, which emphasize instead the god's virility. This particular detail is probably not Egyptian at all. There is every indication here of an "intrusive Greek element": the fate of Uranus, it seems, had been superimposed upon Osiris.[40] Hybridizing Osiris in this way, Plutarch also turned the happy ending into a mixed ending, layered over and compounded by opposing forces. Typhon's act of mutilation could not be erased. Isis might try to undo it, but her action was overwritten by his, bearing his stamp and issuing in a joint signature, a vexed case of dual authorship. Plutarch would not allow anything more upbeat than this, for "it is impossible for the ill one to be quite extinguished, because much of it is interwoven with the body and much with the soul of the universe."[41] There could be no unsullied, unvacillating outcome. The best one could hope for was an ending energized by its negativity, every action followed by "an overturning, and again a leaping over."[42]

One is tempted to call this pattern a dialectic. Its volatility, in any case, became the rhythm of time when Plutarch made Typhon a key player. Margaret Fuller, drawing on Plutarch in her turn, paid special tribute to this vexed oscillation. "I have a great share of Typhon to the Osiris, wild rush and leap, blind force for the sake of force," Emerson remembered her to have said.[43] This being the case, neither Plutarch nor Fuller could see the Isis story as an edifying story. At no point did Isis have the last word; at no point could she impose closure where she would like to have seen closure. Osiris was lost to her, not once but twice: he was first murdered, then he had to suffer the indignity of being dismembered. Isis could not prevent these things from happening; she could not even recover all of the pieces of his body. Goddess that she was, she was brought to her knees again and again, powerless to right all the terrible wrongs, and doomed therefore always to mourn those wrongs.

FALLIBILITY ACROSS TIME

It might seem odd for Fuller to recall this fallible figure from several thousand years ago and include her in *Woman in the Nineteenth Century*, claiming her as an emblem of "divine wisdom never yet surpassed" (51). But fallibility, I would argue, is what generates kinship across such long distances. What Isis exemplifies is not power, mastery, efficiency in execution, but the absence of all these things. It is this absence that makes her durable and reproducible, bearer of an attribute that can be predicated of many human beings, an ever-growing population. For if this goddess had failed so abysmally in something that meant so much to her, chances are that most of us will as well. The law of large numbers is most ironically potent here: it suggests that our *errors* are equally probabilistic, and therefore equally predictable. Herodotus was right to see Isis as a cosmic force, called by different names but more or less universally recurring—the "Egyptian equivalent of Demeter"—because what these two goddesses exemplify is nothing less than a time-honored statistics: a rhythm of imperfection, of miscarried words and deeds.[44] On this point Fuller was one with Herodotus and Plutarch. In fact, she linked together the two goddesses for just this reason (though calling Demeter by her Roman name, Ceres). Both got less than what they wanted; both had "to seek in weary pain for what after all can be but half regained. Ceres regained her daughter, but only for half the year. Isis found her husband, but dismembered."[45]

Finding a dismembered husband was not the exclusive fate of goddesses. It was very much the fate of human beings, the fate, for instance, of another figure from antiquity, an Assyrian princess, Panthea, also dramatized in *Woman in the Nineteenth Century*, taken this time from Xenophon's *Cyropaedia*.[46] Panthea, in gratitude to Cyrus for his courteous conduct, persuaded her husband, Abradatus, to join the Persian king in his campaign against the Egyptians. Abradatus was promptly killed in battle. When Cyrus came to pay his final respects,

> he took [Abradatus] by the right hand, and the hand of the deceased came away, for it had been cut off with a sword by the Egyptians. He, at the sight of this, became yet much more concerned than before. The woman shrieked out in a lamentable manner, and, taking the hand from Cyrus, kissed it, fitted it to its proper place again, as well as she could, and said: "The rest, Cyrus, is the same condition, but what need you see it? And I know that I was not one of the least concerned in these his sufferings, and, perhaps, you were not less so; for I, fool that I was! frequently exhorted him to behave in such a manner as to appear a friend to you. . . . He is dead, therefore," said she, "without reproach, and I, who urged him on, sit here alive."[47]

The dismemberment of Abradatus rehearsed the fate of Osiris, except that in this case there would be no reassembly of the body parts, and no resurrection. The dead would always be dead. Being dead, Abradatus paradoxically turned into an undying form of reproach, interminable, impossible for Panthea to shake off. She had counseled war, but she had not foreseen its outcome; and now, outliving him, she had the lasting guilt of never being able to make amends. The different pieces of Abradatus's body would never be fitted back together; they would never become whole. Putting Panthea forever in the wrong, he also put her forever under an obligation, an obligation devolving upon her on the strength of a simple fact, namely, that while he was dead, she was still "sit[ting] here alive."

Being alive, as a state of being radically different from being dead, carries an ethical imperative for just that reason. This imperative might be seen as the propositional form of our existential condition. For what distinguishes us from the dead is surely our active presence on earth, and therefore the *privilege* of making mistakes. The dead, as Panthea says, are "without reproach," in the sense that they are no longer susceptible to that peril. The living, on the other hand, are not only susceptible but also constituted as ethical subjects by that fact. "Fool that I was!"—this lamentation, coming out of the mouth of Panthea, could have come out of the mouth of every one of us. To take this as the ground of kinship, to grant it predictive power over what we do, and to bind ourselves to the dead in its harsh light, is to embrace an ethics in which error is both an obligation and a form of clemency. Obligation: because as the living members of the species we must pick up where the dead leave off, though we are bound to fall short. And clemency: because falling short is no more than what we would expect, a predictable outcome, forgivable for that reason, and in turn compelling future humans to act on our behalf. Rather than a lapse, a sign of inadequacy, a deviation from the benchmark, failure is now itself the benchmark. It is the statistical norm that grounds our efforts, that seals our tie to the species, and the statistical norm to which, sooner or later, each of us will return.

Fuller's ethics, like Kant's, issues a categorical imperative. But the categorical imperative here has nothing to do with the moral law. Instead, it has everything to do with a postulate of fallibility: the postulate that we have always made mistakes and will always make mistakes, that these are the punctuation marks we bring to time. Since this is the case, a mistake is not reprehensible, not even remarkable. It is simply a periodic occurrence, one that translates into a collective injunction for the entire species. All of us are obligated, by these mistakes, to face up to the burden of time as the burden of things having always gone wrong, and therefore the burden of a cry for repair, for mending. Two other philosophers, Charles Sanders Peirce and Paul Ricoeur, would later develop philosophies parallel to this, based on "fallibilism" or the "fallible man."[48] Fuller has anticipated them, both in the severity of her judgment and in the amplitude of what she affirms. Fallibility is not the end here. Rather, it is the beginning of a measure of time humanized by our finite efforts, our failures to complete what we set out to do. Embracing these failures, we embrace the unfinished task of the dead even as we embrace their unlapsed membership in our species. This membership gives them the right to come back once in a while and to make noise in the ethics, politics, and aesthetics of the living.

Noisy Ghosts

Margaret Fuller likes noise. In appendix A to *Woman in the Nineteenth Century*, she has a long description of Isis, quoted from the *Metamorphosis of Apuleius* in Thomas Taylor's 1822 translation. This is how the goddess looks—and *sounds*:

> But that which most excessively dazzled my sight, was a very black robe, fulgid with a dark splendor. . . . Glittering stars were dispersed through the embroidered border of the robe, and through the whole of its surface, and the full moon, shining in the middle of the stars, breathed forth flaming fires. . . .
>
> What she carried in her hands also consisted of things of a very different nature. Her right hand bore a brazen rattle, through the narrow lamina of which, bent like a belt, certain rods passing, produced a sharp triple sound through the vibrating motion of her arm. (182)

Isis is in black, the color of mourning. But this blackness is not a uniform blackness; it is interspersed with points of light. In keeping with Fuller's cross-mapping of the temporal and spatial axes, the visual rhythm here echoes the sonic rhythm produced by a rather ungainly object in Isis's right hand, a "brazen rattle," which she keeps constantly in motion, making not sweet melody but a jarring note, a "sharp triple sound."

Taylor had a useful gloss at just this point. He included a picture of the rattle and supplied a cross-reference to three other texts: "The rattle (in the original *crepitaculum*) of Isis, is the same with the celebrated *sistrum* of that Goddess, as is evident from what is asserted of the latter by Martial, Propertius, and Plutarch."[49] Plutarch, as always, was in the picture. Taylor made a point of citing him on the meaning of the *sistrum*: "The sistrum likewise indicates that it is necessary that beings should be agitated, and never cease to rest from their local motion. . . . For they say that Typhon is deterred and repelled by the sistra; manifesting by this, that as corruption binds and stops [the course of things], so generation again resolves nature, and excites it through motion."[50]

Fuller copied this passage into her reading notes.[51] This image of the sistrum—ungainly, ungentle, and unquiet—spoke to her as nothing else did from ancient mythology.[52] "She chose the *Sistrum* for her emblem," Emerson later recalled, "and had it carefully drawn with a view to its being engraved on a gem." He added, "I know not how many verses and legends came recommended to her by this symbolism."[53] In 1844, Fuller wrote a poem specifically titled "Sistrum":

Triune, shaping, restless power,
Life-flow from life's natal hour,
No music chords are in thy sound;
By some thou'rt but a rattle found;
Yet, without thy ceaseless motion,
To ice would turn their dead devotion.
Life-flow of my natal hour,
I will not weary of thy power,
Till in the changes of thy sound
A chord's three parts distinct are found.
I will faithful move with thee,
God-ordered, self-fed energy,
Nature in eternity.[54]

It is the ragged energy of the sistrum that Fuller dwells on, the fact that it produces no harmonies, "no music chords," no unification of sound. Its "triune" tonalities, with "three parts distinct," seem a replay of the drama of Osiris, Isis, and Typhon, also "three part distinct"—a drama not only of resurrection, but also of death, of frequent and unavoidable error. These three will endure till the end of time. They are present to every newborn, at the "life-flow of [the] natal hour"; and they never leave us, for death and error, no less than life, are the ligaments of the species, what binds us in kinship across time. Without them, our seemingly oxymoronic "dead devotion" would have been truly dead. Here, then, is a form of afterlife born of the earth and reflecting its finiteness: not the quickening of the dead, but the death-induced quickening of the living, a quickening that allows noisy ghosts to be noisy always, garrulous beyond the grave. Fuller knew nothing about the Opening of the Mouth ceremony in ancient Egypt, but in the ceaseless rattling of the rattle, she had found a working parallel.

FULLER AND MARX

Fuller could have had an interesting conversation with Marx on this point.[55] Both wrote for the *New York Tribune*;[56] both were interested in human history on a large scale, but they had the opposite membership criterion for what counts as "human." Marx's criterion is as strict as could be. In *The Eighteenth Brumaire of Louis Bonaparte*, he famously complains about the intrusive presence of the dead, complains about the 1848 revolution as a ghost-filled event, where "the tradition of all the dead generations weighs like a nightmare on the brain of the living."[57] And he goes on:

From 1848 to 1851 only the ghost of the old revolution walked about, from Marrast . . . down to the adventurer, who hides his commonplace repulsive features under the iron death mask of Napoleon. An entire people, which had imagined that by means of a revolution it had imparted to itself an accelerated power of motion, suddenly finds itself set back into a defunct epoch and, in order that no doubt as to the relapse may be possible, the old dates arise again, the old chronology, the old names, the old edicts, which had long become a subject of antiquarian erudition, and the old minions of the law, who had seemed long decayed. The nation feels like that mad Englishman in Bedlam who fancies he lives in the times of the ancient Pharaohs.[58]

For Marx, the time of the Pharaohs is "defunct," and a forward-looking revolution must leave this corpse behind, spurn it, make sure its "ghost" will never again walk about.[59] Fuller has a different philosophy. For her, "old dates," "old chronology," "old names," and "old edicts" are indeed ghostly; they matter for just that reason. Always on the verge of oblivion, they cry out to be revived and, in that cry, make of us obligated hearers. We are the only creatures on this planet capable of hearing the dead; that auditory range makes us relational beyond the limits of biology. This is what it means to be "human": what it means to belong to a species constituted on both sides of mortality and conversing across that dividing line. For Fuller, and pace Marx, it is that conversing—and the ghosts it brings back—that sustains the idea of "revolution," saving the events of 1848 from utter futility, a stillborn hope.

EUROPE 1848

Fuller was there as an eyewitness. She was in Italy from March 1847 to January 6, 1850, and, in the dispatches that she sent to the *New York Tribune*, was able to chronicle in full the birth and death of Republican Rome.[60] On May 7, 1848, she wrote that this revolution seemed an experiment in "a nobler commonwealth than the world has yet known."[61] The commonwealth was "common" in many senses, not least because it sprang from a common past, as much Fuller's as anyone else's. On December 2, 1848 she wrote: "The great Past enfolds us, and the emotions of the moment cannot here importantly disturb that impression. From the wild shout and throng of the streets the setting sun recalls us as it rests on a hundred domes and temples—rests on the Campagna, whose grass is rooted in departed human greatness. Burial-place so full of spirit that Death itself seems no longer cold."[62] It was in just such a burial place, against a death warmed by human continuity, that Fuller could in turn assert her continuity with Europe, as a living experiment against the buried hope of America: "In Europe, amid the teachings of adversity a nobler spirit is struggling—a spirit which cheers and animates mine. . . . This is what makes *my* America. I do not deeply distrust my country. She is not dead, but in my time she sleepeth, and the spirit of our fathers flames no more, but lies hid beneath the ashes."[63]

And, because those ashes were so prevalent, because so much lay in ruins under them, the crushing death of the Roman Republic seemed almost unsurprising. In the same dispatch Fuller wrote: "Should my hopes be dashed to the ground, it will not change my faith."[64] These words were to prove more than prophetic, for in just a couple of months Rome would fall under the bombardment of the French army, which, by the cruelest irony, would enter the city on the Fourth of July. Fuller's hopes *were* dashed to the ground, but this did not in fact change her faith. In the last dispatch she sent, she had this astonishing thing to say: "God be praised! It was a dark period of that sceptical endeavor and work, only worthy as helping to educate the next generation, was watered with much blood and tears. God be praised! that time is ended, and the noble band of teachers who have passed this last ordeal of the furnace and den of lions, are ready now to enter their followers for the elementary class."[65]

The year 1848 represents only preschool in the temporal career of humankind. Having gone through that, we are ready now to move on, to grade school. The failed revolution is no more than that: it is not even the beginning, but what comes before the beginning. Its very primitiveness, the very fact that it has miscarried, that it has come to nought, gives it a predictive power in reverse. It has a claim on the emergent shape of the world precisely because it has failed to achieve a shape on its own. A failure like that generates a negative dialectics, as Adorno has taught us to understand that term.[66] It *is* a categorical imperative, perhaps even in the Kantian sense, because it puts all of us under the obligation to come up with a sequel, even though that sequel will, in its turn, lead to an outcome that will be less than adequate. It is that "less than" that will be carried over and carried forward, binding the species in kinship, and affirming the continual membership of the dead even as it redefines membership for the living.

Fuller gives us a haunting image of this species membership based on death and error. On July 4, 1849, one year after the fall of the Roman Republic, she wrote:

A contadini showed me where thirty-seven braves are buried beneath a heap of wall that fell upon them in the shock of one cannonade. . . . A pair of skeleton legs protruded from a bank of one barricade; lower a dog had scratched away its light covering of earth from the body of a man, and discovered it lying face upward all dressed; the dog stood gazing on it with an air of stupid amazement.[67]

The field of time is a field littered with corpses, too many to count. Rather than simply digging them up and looking at them in stupid amazement, as the dog does, humans must affirm the humanity of the dead as only our species can—by some act of recall, some Opening of the Mouth ceremony. Each must bring back her own dead, reciting their failures but reciting them in a different voice. Such a gesture is indeed both humanist and antihumanist. Humanist, because it does put forward a claim on behalf of the species as one distinct unto itself. And antihumanist, because this claim both presumes and requires this species to be fallible, to be shortsighted, incapable of processing all the data of the world, incapable of writing a complete script.

POETICS OF FAILURE

That presumption, not surprisingly, gives rise not only to a politics but also to a poetics, likewise humanist and antihumanist in this double sense. Fuller's account of Madame De Staël points to some of its salient features; her account of Goethe gives these features an even sharper definition.

The essay on Goethe—in fact, a supposed defense of him against the harsh judgment of Wolfgang Menzel—was published in *The Dial* in January 1841.[68] Once again, Fuller freely conceded that this author was not quite where he ought to have been: "Had he but seen a little farther, he would have given this covenant a higher expression"; but, as it was, "a too determined action of the intellect limited and blinded him for the rest of his life."[69] This might look like a devastating critique, but, once again, it is the limitations of Goethe that give him a life across time, a flawed and yet fecund entry into a future that will always pronounce him "incomplete."[70] He is a poor relation to all of us, a dependent, finding shelter in a script written not by him but by the populational dynamics of the entire species. "That he has failed of the highest fulfillment of his high vocation is certain," Fuller says, but it is just this failure that "gives him a claim to all our study."[71]

What would that "study" be? One thing is clear: it will not harmonize sweetly with what it studies. In her translator's note to Eckermann's *Conversations with Goethe*, Fuller faults Eckermann for being too much of an echo and too little of a counterpoint to his idealized author:

The simple reverence, and thorough subordination to the mind of Goethe, which make Eckermann so transparent a medium, prevent his being of any value as an interpreter. Never was satellite more completely in harmony with his ruling orb. He is merely the sounding-board to the various notes played by the master's hand; and what we find here is, to all intents and purposes, not conversation, but monologue.[72]

Given Fuller's praise of the "sharp triple sound" of the sistrum, its refusal of unity, her own relation to Goethe will be deliberately harsh. Indeed, the German author is for her largely a negative principle, an entity falling short and therefore in dire need of a rerun. "[H]e did not in one short life complete his circle."[73] That incomplete circle makes him species-dependent, and affirms the rest of us as his kin, his extension. For such a species, individual finitude is both a given and a goad, both the measure of bodily limit and the starting point of large-scale aggregation and transmission. A poetics operating on such a scale makes authorship too large to be borne by any one person. It is borne, instead, by the longitudes and latitudes of the planet and the full length of its recorded history. This is the deep field of time. Asymmetrical to our biological life span, it makes the predictable failure of each of us the condition for our ongoing life.

CHAPTER FOUR

Genre as World System:
Epic, Novel, Henry James

WHAT WOULD LITERARY HISTORY look like if the field were divided, not into discrete periods, and not into discrete bodies of national literatures? What other organizing principles might come into play? And how would they affect the mapping of "literature" as an analytic object: the length and width of the field; its lines of filiation, lines of differentiation; the database needed in order to show significant continuity or significant transformation; and the bounds of knowledge intimated, the arguments emerging as a result?

In this chapter—thinking about Henry James, and thinking about the novel and the epic—I propose one candidate to give us a new heuristic map: the concept of genre. Genre, of course, is not a new concept; in fact, it is as old as the recorded history of humankind. Even though the word itself is of relatively recent vintage (derived from French, in turn derived from the Latin *genus*),[1] the idea that there are different kinds of literature (or different kinds of poetry) goes back at least to ancient Greece. Traditionally it has been seen as a classifying principle, putting the many subsets of literature under the rule of normative sets.

Theorists like Benedetto Croce have objected to it on just these grounds. "[I]nstead of asking before a work of art if it be expressive and what it expresses," genre criticism only wants to label it, putting it into a pigeonhole, asking only "if it obey the *laws* of epic or of tragedy." Nothing can be more misguided, Croce says, for these *"laws of the kinds"* have never in fact been observed by practicing writers.[2] Derrida makes the same point. "As soon as genre announces itself, one must respect a norm, one must not cross a line of demarcation, one must not risk impurity, anomaly, or monstrosity." This sort of border policing is madness, he says, for the law of genre is an impossible law; it contains within itself a "principle of contamination," so much so that the law is honored only in its breach.[3]

FAMILY RESEMBLANCE

Keeping these objections in mind, I invoke genre less as a law, a rigid taxonomic landscape, and more as a self-obsoleting system, a provisional set that will always be bent and pulled and stretched by its many subsets. Such bending and pulling and stretching are unavoidable, for what genre is dealing with is a volatile body of material, still developing, still in transit, and always on the verge of taking flight, in some unknown and unpredictable direction. "Genre is much less of a pigeonhole than a pigeon," Alasdair Fowler has suggested. Movement is key, and if this movement is vested in the concept of *kinds*, it is not as "permanent classes," but as "families subject to change."[4]

This analogy to "families" is especially worth thinking about. It reminds us that genre is not just a theory of classification but, perhaps even more crucially, a theory of interconnection. *Kin* is every bit as important as *kind*. And by kin, what I have in mind is not necessarily a genealogical connection, but, just as often, a broad spectrum of affinities, interesting when seen in conjunction, but not themselves organically linked. Likeness here is probabilistic and distributional; it has less to do with common ancestry than with a convergence of attributes, issuing from environments roughly similar but widely dispersed. What matters here is not lineage, but a phenomenal field of contextually induced parallels. Born of the local circumstances that shape them and echoing other forms shaped by circumstances more or less alike, they make up a decentralized web, something like what Deleuze and Guattari call a "rhizome."[5]

This web can be further elucidated by a concept from Wittgenstein: "family resemblance."[6] Wittgenstein uses it to talk about a conceptual elasticity that classifies tennis, chess, and ring-a-ring-a-roses under the same heading—"games"—constituting this as a "family," with a largely undefined and infinitely expandable membership. Tennis, chess, and ring-a-ring-a-roses have no common ancestry; they do not go by the same operating principle; there might not even be a single attribute common to all three. Instead, what allows them to be grouped together is "a complicated network of similarities overlapping and criss-crossing: sometimes overall similarities, sometimes similarities of detail."[7]

Family resemblance is multilocation, multiplatform, and multidimension. Relatives might resemble one another in broad strokes, in shape and size; they might also resemble one another in some small detail, such as a stylistic tic. Kinship is not limited to one feature, one modality, or one scale. It can emerge even when the two things being compared are manifestly unlike. Tennis and chess, different in almost every way, are alike in one thing: each has a structured outcome, each divides its players into winners and losers. This outcome does not hold, however, for ring-a-ring-a-roses, whose similarity to the other two has much less to do with the terminal effect than with something much more general, something like fun. The "family" made up of these three games revolves not on a single plane, but on many axes, brought into being by "spinning a thread . . . fibre on fibre. And the strength of the thread does not reside in the fact that some one fibre runs through its whole length, but in the overlapping of many fibres."[8]

Fractal Geometry

The spinning of threads is an especially apt metaphor for the twists and turns that run from one genre to another, a family whose tensile strength lies in just this sinuousness. These interconnections have little to do with linear descent. What they exemplify instead is a loosely integrated circuit, with structural entanglement from various angles and at various distances, a complex geometry. This loosely integrated circuit is very close to what Lévi-Strauss understands by "kinship," which, for him, is more *mathematical* than biological. In *Structural Anthropology*, he emphatically says: "kinship does not consist in the objective ties of descent or consanguinity between individuals."[9] Rather, it is a permutative prism, effected by different degrees of rotating, combining, and scattering, and generating different clusters of relations, clumped together on different platforms. Kinship is "a network of different types of orders."[10] It is a geometry that spills over onto several scales at once.

For Lévi-Strauss, this spilling over creates a problem for the researcher, for it is not clear on what scale the analysis is to proceed, what mathematics should be summoned. On the one hand, kinship relations are "considerably more numerous than those dealt with in Newtonian mechanics"; on the other hand, they are "far less numerous than would be required to allow a satisfactory use of the laws of statistics and probability. Thus we find ourselves in an intermediate zone: too complicated for one treatment and not complicated enough for the other."[11]

Writing in 1963, Lévi-Strauss did not know about a new mathematics that was soon to appear, one that goes far beyond the Euclidean geometry of Newtonian mechanics even as it transforms statistical analysis, introducing scalar refinement previously unimaginable. This new mathematics pays special attention to the "intermediate zone," phenomena that spill over between dimensions. It goes by the name "fractal geometry." From the first, it is interdisciplinary (and interlingual) in its scope. Its inventor, Benoit Mandelbrot, is at home in at least four fields:

A graduate of École Polytechnique; Caltech M.S. and Ae.E. in Aeronautics; Docteur des Sciences Mathematiques U. Paris. Before joining the IBM Thomas J. Watson Research Center, where he is now an IBM Fellow, Dr. Mandelbrot was with the French Research Council

(CNRS). . . . he has been a Visiting Professor of Economics and later of Applied Mathematics at Harvard, of Engineering at Yale, of Physiology at the Albert Einstein College of Medicine, and of Mathematics at the University of Paris-Sud, and has been with M.I.T., first in the Electrical Engineering Department, and most recently as an Institute Lecturer.[12]

Aeronautics, economics, engineering, physiology—all these disciplines converge in this new mathematics. Its practical value is great enough, furthermore, to merit a paying job at IBM.[13] And, just as it underscores the kinship among fields, its very name is a testimony to the kinship among languages. *Fractal* has an interesting etymology, which Mandelbrot calls attention to: "*Fractal* comes from the Latin adjective *fractus*, which has the same root as *fraction* and *fragment* and means 'irregular or fragmented'; it is related to *frangere*, which means 'to break.' The stress should logically be on the first syllable, as in fraction."[14]

Fractal is a set of points that cannot be plotted as one, two, or three dimensions. It is a geometry of nonintegers, a geometry of what loops around, what breaks off, what is jagged, what comes only in percentages. Mandelbrot is moved to propose this new geometry because of his dissatisfaction with Euclid's. "Many important spatial patterns," he writes, "are either irregular or fragmented to such an extreme degree that *Euclid*—a term used in this Essay to denote all of classical geometry—is hardly of any help in describing their form."[15] Unlike the Euclidean objects—squares, circles, and triangles, with their clean resolution—the shapes that interest Mandelbrot are shapes with serried outlines: the wispy puffs of clouds, the lacy fronds of ferns, the pocked and porous surface of the sponge, the coiled dimensions inside a ball of twine.

The Problem of Scale

These whirling, percolating, clumping shapes make length indeterminate. In his celebrated chapter, "How Long Is the Coast of Britain?" Mandelbrot points out that there is no single answer to this question, since everything depends on the scale adopted and the degree of refinement it permits. If an observer were to measure the coastline from the air, from a distance of twenty thousand feet, that aerial vision would yield a clean line—and a shorter distance—since all the nooks and crannies would be passed over. If the observer were on the ground, measuring the coast at close range and on foot, in units of eight or nine inches, the coast of Britain would be much longer, thanks to the zigzags newly recorded. And, if the observer were not a human being at all, but a snail, using *its* feet as the unit of measurement, the zigzags would be even more pronounced, and the coast of Britain longer still. In short, as the scale "is made smaller and smaller, every one of the approximate lengths tends to become larger and larger without bound. Insofar as one can tell, each seems to tend toward infinity."[16]

Fractals is the geometry of the irregular and the microscopic, what gets lost in a big picture. It does what aggregating and averaging cannot. To aggregate and to average, Mandelbrot says, is like wrapping a tinfoil around a sponge: the former does "measure" the latter, but only by completely obliterating every detail of its texture. Refusing to do this, fractals would seem opposed to any large-scale paradigm. This turns out not to be the case. Mandelbrot's geometry of the minuscule is, in fact, matched by a geometry of what gets "larger and larger without bound." It is a geometry of infinity, of what keeps spinning out, in endless spirals. These two—finite parameters and infinite unfolding—go hand in hand. The latter is embedded in the former, coiled in the former, and can be released only when the former is broken down into fractional percentages. For it is only when the scale gets smaller and the details get finer that previously hidden dimensions can come swirling out. Scalar opposites here generate a dialectic that makes the global an effect of the grainy.

The fractal database thus comes as a spectrum, ranging from the microscopic to "phenomena on or above Man's scale."[17] Aeronautics, economics, engineering, and physiology all benefit from this duality of scale. Literary studies would as well, for this discipline, like the others, is energized by the feedback loops between the very large and the very small. Mandelbrot finds (this is strangest feature of his geometry) that whether one magnifies or reduces the unit of measurement, some deviation is bound to occur: some turbulence, some "noise," some irregular beat or bump on the linear frequency. Such irregularities are not limited to just one scale; they are much more deeply transitive, and much more robustly self-propagating. They carry over tenaciously from one metric to another, spewing out countless copies of themselves on countless dimensions.

Mandelbrot calls this "self-similarity." It is a reproductive system of sorts, but statistical rather than biological, taking the form of a scalar recursiveness. What is repeated here, over and over again, is a sporadic but also quite durable quirk, an off-scale excrescence that breaks up and messes up the straightforward causation of any linear system. Roughness is more elementary than we may think. It is certainly more reproducible. More so than cleanness or smoothness, it is the rough weave of the fabric, the bumpy surface of pits and pocks, that is threaded throughout the world, in infinite extension and infinite regress. Mandelbrot speaks of these pits and pocks as "fractal kin," a "family of shapes."[18] Such a family, going all the way up and all the way down, all the way out and all the way in, loops the gnarled contours of the globe through the gnarled contours of every single node.

Endless Kinship

Here then is the mathematics Lévi-Strauss was looking for: one that is robust across scales, keeping track of kinship at every level. Fractal geometry is the lost twin of anthropology. And—as must be clear—I would like also to propose it as the lost twin of literary studies, especially the study of genre. Here as well, what this geometry allows us to see is a tangle of relations, one that counts as a "system" precisely because its aberrations are systemwide, because pits and bumps come with many loops and layers of filiation. Even literary forms that look quite different at first sight turn out to have some quirks in common. That family resemblance runs through them even as their trajectories diverge. And, depending on context, this family resemblance can be extended, modified, and recombined in any number of ways. The process is ongoing, and will never be complete, since there is no end to such irregularities, no end to the second and third and fourth cousins coiled within each ball of deviance.

Literary history becomes a different kind of history when it follows the careers of these second and third and fourth cousins, in turn having cousins of their own. Periodization becomes much more complicated then, for a population of kin is bound to scatter and reconnect at odd intervals. Their oddities, echoing one another from far off, force us to go back and periodize all over again. It is an unfinished business, messing up any paradigm that assumes its data to be complete. We don't know where any particular genre might spiral out, what offshoots might spin off from it. We don't know how much time it will take, or how much space it will string together. Literary genres are, after all, as old, as widely dispersed, and as unpredictable as human beings themselves. The epic has thousands of years behind it, and so too does the novel. Both stretch from antiquity to modernity, both show up in every human habitat. Their longevity and ubiquity make them the durable threads that bind together the world.

Comparative Morphology

Franco Moretti, drawing on the work of Immanuel Wallerstein and Fredric Jameson, puts genre at the center of a "world-system" for just this reason.[19] He calls for a "comparative morphology," one that takes as its starting point a distributive map, reflecting the circulation and evolution of literary forms, and operating on the same scale as the planet. Only such a map can capture the full range of environmental input, the difference that each locale makes. What Moretti wants, in short, is a developmental database, assembled along both the axis of space and the axis of time, and tracking not only existing forms but also emerging ones. This developmental database is generalizable as a law, what he calls a "law of literary evolution."[20] For him, such a law would account for both continuity and change. Its history is in effect the history of recorded life, a history of the interaction between the local and the global.

Moretti's paradigm is crucial to any "world" approach to genre. I would like, at the same time, to caution against what strikes me as his overcommitment to general laws, to global postulates operating at some remove from the phenomenal world of particular texts. As Moretti forthrightly admits, what he advocates is a paradigm called "distant reading," so named because of its clear opposition to the better-known, "close" variety. Unlike close reading, distant reading is meant to track large-scale developments; it is not meant to capture the fine print. Moretti does not worry too much about this. According to him, "if the text itself disappears, well, it is one of those cases when one can justifiably say, less is more."[21]

Is this really true? Is the loss of the text a price worth paying in order to project literature onto a large canvas? If fractal geometry has anything to tell us, it is that the loss of detail is almost always unwarranted. There are any number of reasons I can name (such as the pleasure of reading), but probably the most pertinent one here is the fact that the literary field is still incomplete, its kinship network only partly actualized, with many new members still to be added. Such a field needs to maintain an archive that is as broad-based as possible, as fine-grained as possible, an archive that errs on the side of randomness rather than on the side of undue coherence, if only to allow new permutations to come into being. Rather than seeing comparative morphology as a thinning process, one that leads to a formalizable law, I would like to see it as a thickening process, one that keeps a full, cumulative, and not necessarily unified record, the better to meet emerging forms halfway.

BACKWARD EXTENSION

This sense of emergence can be extended, not only forward (which is the usual direction it takes), but also backward, to material that, for one reason or another, has been left out of standard literary histories. I am thinking especially of the phenomenal field of premodern and non-Western literature, and its undertheorized relation to two genres: the epic and the novel. It is a commonplace, of course, to speak of the "rise" of the novel in the eighteenth century, a rise supposedly coextensive with realism, with print culture, and with the rise of the middle class.[22] This is true to a large extent in the English case, but a broader frame—less narrowly periodized and less narrowly nationalized—yields a very different picture. Classicists such as Arthur Heiserman and J. J. Winkler have long called attention to the existence of the novel in ancient Greece.[23] Margaret Doody, while attentive to the eighteenth century, has also insisted that the archive is in fact much larger, that it ought to include premodern and non-Western material. In her wide-ranging book, *The True Story of the Novel*, Doody takes the genre much farther back and much farther east.[24] This backward extension seems to me crucial if we are to redraw the literary map, bringing below-the-threshold data back into the field of vision.

Rather than concentrating on the novel and tracing it back to antiquity, however, I would like to explore a broader paradigm, namely, the tangled pathways and fractional reproduction of literary forms. I begin not with the novel but with the epic: as a form possibly antecedent to it, and always bearing a nontrivial relation to it. Tracing the relation between these two across a range of environments, I put far-flung kinship at the center of any discussion of genre. This far-flung kinship, in turn, reminds us that irregularities need to be traced as far back as possible in order for each new instance to be seen anew. The quirks of genre, being venerable, have been discussed for quite some time. There is a critical literature going back to antiquity on just this point.

In what follows, I revisit this critical literature, beginning with Plato and Aristotle, and using these two as a springboard to a still more ancient past, a non-Western birthplace of genres, located not in Greece but in Mesopotamia. I discuss *Gilgamesh* as a salient instance of the epic surface, a surface that would reappear in its medieval European kin, *The Divine Comedy*. Then, as a counterpoint to this backward loop, I go forward, moving to Henry James but obliquely, circuitously, allowing for twists and turns. Through these coils of relations, I try to remap the tangled borders between the ancient and the modern, between the United States and the world, even as I retrace the fractal dimensions of the epic in the novel.

PLATO AND ARISTOTLE

In the *Republic*, Plato divides poetry into two modes: poetry that is imitative and poetry that is narrative. Since these are *modes*, they designate not particular works but their general orientations. And, as orientations, both might be present in the same work, though to different degrees. Rather than being a catalog of discrete types, Plato's landscape is a gradational landscape—a spectrum—with one mode presiding on one end and the other mode presiding on the other. In the middle, these two meet. This is a unique feature of the spectrum: its midpoint is a point of maximum contact, maximum interaction, aligned with both poles, with input from both. Multiplicity is a structural provision here, while each pole is singular. According to Plato, drama such as tragedy and comedy are singular in just this way: they are instances of the "wholly imitative." The dithyramb is also singular, being located at the other end, an instance of the "opposite style." Only one kind of poetry is perched in the middle, the point of maximum contact, with access to both ends, and encompassing the fullness of the spectrum: "the combination of both is found in epic."[25]

For Plato, the epic is the most full-throated of genres, most technically diverse. Not unified or monolithic, it is structured instead by the extensional force of a spectrum. This extensional force is given even more play by Aristotle, in turn pointing to a larger set of circumstances surrounding the genesis of the epic. For me, this is one the most interesting observations in the *Poetics*, though one that has been the least remarked upon. As we know, tragedy is what interests Aristotle the most, but the epic, being an adjacent genre, also comes in for a good bit of attention. According to him, these two have much in common, but they diverge on one point, namely, that "the epic has a very strongly marked special tendency towards extra extension of its bulk."[26] This tendency suggests two things. First, the bulky epic is heavier; it moves at a different pace, a different rhythm, with a different kind of propulsion, and, not infrequently. a different kind of inertia. Secondly, because it is moving so slowly, it also gathers together the world in a different way. Its kinship network is broader, with tributaries coming from afar, significant input from many foreign tongues.

FOREIGN WORDS

Central to Aristotle's argument about epic is a linguistic map, with a long-standing and ongoing loop of interaction between the center and the peripheries. Unfamiliar words spring up on the horizon and slowly filter in, changing the shape of the common tongue and recombining it on a different terrain. Aristotle discusses this phenomenon in section 22 of the *Poetics*, a section devoted to the use of foreign words in poetry. He writes:

> Impressiveness and avoidance of familiar language is achieved by the use of alien terms; and by "alien" I mean dialectical words, metaphor, lengthening of words, in short anything other than the standard terminology. But if the whole composition is of that sort, it will be either a riddle or a piece of barbarism: riddle if made up of metaphors, barbarism if made up of foreign words.[27]

Aristotle sees two dangers facing the poet. On the one hand, there is the dullness of "standard terminology"; on the other hand, there is the "barbarism" of unfamiliar words. Since the former is just as bad as the latter, a good writer needs to play one against the other in order to be fortified against both, using the alien as a check on the clichéd. Foreign words are, for that reason, not just barbarisms but *necessary* barbarisms. Aristotle takes them for granted; his very taxonomy presupposes their presence. According to him, "Of the various kinds of words, compounds are best suited to the dithyramb, foreign words to epic verse, and metaphors to iambic verse."[28] Different kinds of nonstandard diction are correlated, in short, with different kinds of poetic practice. Foreign words, it turns out, are the special province of epic.

Why? Aristotle offers this oblique explanation: "For the hexameter is the slowest moving and weightiest of all verses—that is why it is the most receptive to foreign words and metaphors."[29] The epic, in short, is a kind of linguistic sponge. Springing up at contact zones, it is also superresponsive to its environment, picking up all those non-Greek words that come its way, but not necessarily dissolving them, perhaps keeping them simply as alien deposits, grains or lumps that stick.

What might these words be, and how did they get into the picture in the first place? Aristotle offers no further explanation, but, with the help of recent scholarship, we can bring a more specific context to frame his conjectures, bringing a larger circumference to bear on Greek antiquity. If the *Poetics* is to be trusted, foreign input would seem always to have been an important part of the epic tradition. This tradition was prior to Aristotle, prior even to Homer, with antecedents going much further back, and going back to non-Western languages.

GILGAMESH

None of this would come as a surprise to students of Mesopotamia, who have been making just this argument for quite some time. Walter Burkert, for instance, argues in *The Orientalizing Revolution* that ancient Greece was on the receiving end of a civilization still more ancient, centered in Mesopotamia, with Akkadian, Ugaritic, Phoenician,

Aramaic, and Egyptian offshoots. A form of epic had flourished in this ancient civilization—notably the Sumerian epic and the Akkadian epic, such as the *Epic of Gilgamesh*. Many of the formal attributes of these Mesopotamian epics would also be found in the Greek epic. Burkert has a list of these. Above all, he points to one particular narrative convention, the use of direct speech and the repetitive, piled-on formula that introduces it:

> The lavish use of direct speech, the representation of whole scenes in the form of dialogue is, indeed, a peculiarity of the genre. In Akkadian, the introductory formula is, in literal translation: "He set his mouth and spoke, to [so and so] he said [the word]." The simple meaning of *speak* is expressed in three synonyms—just as with the well-known Homeric formula, "he raised his voice and spoke the winged words."[30]

The act of speaking is triply underscored in both the Mesopotamian epic and the Greek epic. This elaborate (and seemingly gratuitous) speech convention punctuates the epic, giving it its peculiar rhythm. The use of three synonyms obviously slows down the action. Taking note of this detail, along with Aristotle's observation about the presence of foreign words, we can make some guesses about the epic, using its form as an index to its history, both past and future.

First, the epic seems always to have been a genre spurred by cultural contact. Since this is the case, since the proximity of the alien is its genetic condition, it stands to reason that this genre should have some sort of formal vehicle to register that fact, to mark the foreignness of foreign words, their nontrivial departures from native speech. Its elaborate speech convention might have been one such vehicle, for while this convention is applied to everyone who speaks, it can also be used, if necessary, to highlight the nonstandard diction of one particular tongue. This is indeed the case in the *Epic of Gilgamesh*. Benjamin R. Foster points out that this Mesopotamian epic

> contains clear differentiations in the speech of individual characters, including style, diction, grammar, and even pronunciation. Utanapishtim, for example, expresses himself in the elevated, obscure style suitable for an antediluvian sage but has a curious mannerism of rolling or doubling consonants (*sharru* for *sharu*, *shaqqa* for *shaqa*, *ushaznannu* for *ushaznanu*, *niqqu* for *niqu*) . . . and Ishullanu, the gardener, uses a nonstandard form in Tablet VI, line 72 (this could be translated either as archaic and proverbial, "Hath my mother not baked?" or as a colloquialism: "Hain't my mother baked?").[31]

Nonstandard speech is a lexical marker that gives the epic its peculiar morphology. This lexical marker has implications for its structure of time. For what these archaisms point to is a prehistory, a deep time antecedent to and bearing a diacritical relation to the present. The *lexical* axis of the epic, in short, serves also as a *temporal* axis. Its deviations from the linguistic norm are testimonies to a receding but still active, still shadowing past. It pays tribute to that past by citing a mode of speech associated with it, a mode of speech that is cast either in a foreign tongue or in a tongue that has a foreign sound to it. The linguistic fabric of the epic is, for that reason, not in the least smooth. It is a rough cut, with dents and bumps, each representing a coil of time, a cystlike protuberance, in which an antecedent moment is embedded, bearing the weight of the past and burrowing into the present as a warp, a deformation. In this way, the lexical map of the epic is a map not only of space, but also of time. The cumulative life of humankind is captured here as a looping, bulging, swirling net, featuring both the linguistic norm and its nonstandard variants. It is this that gives the epic its scope. It also makes this genre a prime candidate for fractal geometry.

Dante's *Commedia*

Fractal geometry, in fact, describes not only the Mesopotamian epic, but, even more aptly, its medieval European counterpart. In a remarkable recent book, *Heaven's Fractal Net*, written by a religious historian, William J. Jackson, the *Divine Comedy* is cited as the most stunning instance of a recursive structure, repeated on several scales. Jackson points to the *terza rima* itself, a three-line unit, with each rhyme making "a small circle in its rhythm of returning sounds—interlinkings within larger interlinkings."[32] Likewise, the punitive logic of *contrapasso*, with the crime repeated in the punishment, makes hell a place of "infinite reiteration."[33] These are large-scale fractal structures. In the context of this chapter, I would like to focus especially on its small quirks, the dents and bumps in its lexical surface. Like *Gilgamesh*, the *Commedia* is spurred by cultural contact, pivoted at the point of maximum interaction. Its linguistic fabric reflects this. Non-Italian words show up almost as soon as the *Inferno* begins. *"Miserere di me"*—these are the first words spoken by Dante to Virgil. It is surely no accident that Latin should be used on this occasion, when the two poets are brought face to face for the first time, when Dante is asking Virgil to have pity on him. That older poet has to be addressed in the language he had originally used, a language older than any of the Italian vernaculars, and still a common tongue for the educated when Dante wrote.[34]

Like *Gilgameth*, then, the *Commedia* also has a bumpy fabric, riddled with words that do not synchronize. Aristotle has been proven right in both Akkadian and Italian: the lexical surface of the epic is indeed sponge-like, full of holes, porous to nonstandard diction. Latin is, for that reason, not the only foreign words on exhibit in the *Commedia*. If it marks a point of lexical elevation, elevated from the vernacular of the poem, there are plenty of other usages to give foreignness a low definition. These include, most obviously, the crude profanities of the demons, including what seems to be nonwords made up by them, for instance, "Pape Satan, pape Satan aleppe," spoken by Plutus in *Inferno* 7 or "Raphel may amech zabi almi," spoken by Nimrod in *Inferno* 31. As Zygmunt Baranski points out, the *Commedia* is a kind of nonstop carnival when it comes to languages. Dante uses "every register of his native language, and further embellishes this with Latinisms, Gallicisms, a wide range of neologisms, regionalisms, words associated with particular literary genres, other kinds of technical vocabulary—drawn, for instance, from optics, astronomy, scholastic theology, mysticism, and language of merchants—and, finally, foreign words."[35] For Baranski, this virtuoso performance is meant for one express purpose, namely, to show off the impressive range of one particular vernacular, the Florentine tongue, to prove that it can harness all the linguistic resources of the world, that it can do everything that Latin can and do it better.

This is very much the case, within the context of authorial psychology, the psychology of Dante as a vernacular poet. Within the context of comparative morphology, however, it would also seem to be the case that this is part of a reproducible structure, a general effect of cultural contact. *Gilgamesh* is there to prove it. The Italian epic and the Akkadian epic are cousins for just this reason. Their kinship is a kinship in lexical bumps, produced by the nontrivial presence of foreign words, used to mark a prior layer of time. This prior layer comes into play not only when Dante uses Latin to address Virgil, it also comes into play when, in *Purgatorio* 26, he allows Arnaut to come forth to speak. Rendered in direct speech, and rendered in Provençal, this dramatized use of a foreign tongue once again brings into relief a roughed-up chronology, a roughness built into the epic and marking it as a genre.[36]

Updating Bakhtin

What is also built into the epic, then, is a differential axis of time. This is what Mikhail Bakhtin singles out as its generic signature in his classic essay "Epic and Novel." Bakhtin writes: "The world of epic is the national heroic past. . . . The important point here is not that the past constitutes the content of the epic. The formally constitutive feature of the epic as a genre is rather the transferral of a represented world into the past."[37]

A layer of prehistory is a given. Temporal distance is what gets the epic going; this is its structural prerequisite.

Of course, for Bakhtin, this structural prerequisite also means that the epic is an archaic genre, firmly locked into the past. Its horizon is a backward horizon, already behind it, with no point of contact with the contemporary world. Bakhtin writes:

> In its style, tone and manner of expression, epic discourse is infinitely far removed from discourse of a contemporary about a contemporary addressed to contemporaries. . . . We come upon it when it is already completely finished, a congealed and half-moribund genre. . . . it is impossible to change, to re-think, to re-evaluate anything in it. . . . it is impossible to really touch it, for it is beyond the realm of human activity.[38]

Bakhtin, of course, has his own reasons for defining the epic in this way, as a genre that has already run its course, that can have no further meaning, no further development in the modern world. The point of the exercise is to show that there is only one genre that is truly alive right now—the novel—an autonomous genre, not indebted to the epic and indeed completely replacing it, taking over the literary field at just that point where the epic is consigned to oblivion. According to him, only the novel is adequate to the competing languages of the modern world; only the novel can give voice to the heteroglossia that reflects human diversity.

And yet, as must be clear from our preceding discussion, this cannot be true. What Bakhtin takes as a generic attribute of the novel is in fact not unique to it. Nonstandard diction had a much longer history and a different genetic locale, finding its earliest home not in Europe but in Asia. Bakhtin is handicapped, not only by a too-restrictive database, but also by overlooking some less cited passages in what ought to be canonical texts. Still, his theory need not be jettisoned.[39] It only has to be amended, I think, by replacing his linear model of supersession with a fractal model of looping: a model of recursive kinship. In other words, rather than seeing the epic as an archaic genre, completely behind us and pronounceable as dead, I would like to see it as an archaic genre that has been threaded into the present: still evolving, still energized by foreign tongues, and reproducing itself across many scales, bearing witness to the input of many environments.

All we have to do is to look at Derek Walcott and his experimentations in *Omeros* to see just how *un*moribund the epic is, how vital it can be in a creolized medium. But I would like to make a related claim as well, a riskier claim, having to do not with the survival of the epic as epic, a poetic genre, but with its survival as a spilled-over phenomenon, spilling over into other dimensions of literature, and becoming a *fraction* of prose. This is one of the most interesting implications of fractal geometry. It theorizes the novel as a linguistic sponge in its turn, picking up the poetic genre, steeping it in a different medium, and preserving it only in percentages, as grains and lumps. It is this sponge that I would like to explore in Henry James. His novels—pulpy, knotted, and sometimes indeterminately concave—highlight not only the permeable borders between antiquity and modernity, and not only the permeable borders between poetry and prose, but also the tangled dimensions of the very large and the very small.

LARGE AND SMALL

Largeness and smallness preoccupy James, and understandably, given his frequent gyrations between different orders of magnitude and different lengths of time. In his preface to the New York edition of *The Wings of the Dove*, he excuses himself for "disguising the reduced scale of the exhibition, for foreshortening at any cost, for imparting to patches the value of presences, for dressing objects in an air as of the dimensions they can't possibly have." Such tricks are forgivable, he says, for it gives the author a "free hand for pointing out what a tangled web we weave when—well, when, through our mislaying or otherwise trifling with our blest pair of compasses, we have to produce the illusion of mass without the illusion of extent."[40]

Nor is this a late concern only. Largeness and smallness are crucial to early James. Here is a salient moment from *The Portrait of a Lady*:

> She had long before this taken old Rome into her confidence, for in a world of ruins the ruin of her happiness seemed a less unnatural catastrophe. She rested her weariness upon things that had crumbled for centuries and yet still were upright; she dropped her secret sadness into the silence of lonely places, where its very modern quality detached itself and grew objective, so that as she sat in a sun-warmed angle on a winter's day, or stood in a mouldy church to which no one came, she could almost smile at it and think of its smallness. Small it was, in the large Roman record, and her haunting sense of the continuity of the human lot easily carried her from the less to the greater.[41]

The passage shuttles back and forth: between two scales, two lengths of temporal measurement. Isabel Archer's suffering is trivial in one sense. It is inflicted upon her not by a nation or a public institution, but by a private individual, an expatriate, no less. No major event on the national calendar is inscribed in this puny ruin of one woman's happiness. James says as much: the suffering is small. And yet, this despicable size is just what makes it *not* despicable within the spongelike texture of the novel. Because the novel is, in fact, of uncertain dimensions. It can be bumped up to a much larger scale. That scale—the scale of "old Rome," of the "large Roman record"—keeps tally of two thousand years of suffering. Isabel's own is rendered "objective" by it. From the standpoint of that prenational time, there is nothing special about this suffering; it is utterly commonplace and unremarkable. And yet, being that, it is at least something. It is a small entry, but an entry nonetheless, to a large fact. Scale enlargement here undoes human singularity and preserves it through that undoing.

This is what novelistic subjectivity amounts to. Its frame is indeed global, but the global here, bearing the compass of time, enfolds rather than erases its scalar opposite. Isabel's suffering, trivially unremarkable, is vividly before us because it is both smaller and larger than the jurisdictional plane of the nation. The prenational and the subnational come together here to create an irregular beat, a fractal loop both above and below the nation's linear cross-section. Benedict Anderson cannot be more wrong about the temporality of the novel: there is no standard timetable here, no "clock and calendar" to dictate a flat, synchronized surface.[42] On the contrary, it is because novelistic time is not synchronized, not flat, because it is spongelike, with dimensions sunken and curled up, that it has a geometry different from Euclid's, and different from the plane geometry of the nation.

POUND AND AUDEN ON JAMES

What kind of an entity is the novel, then? This is not an indifferent question to James. "Everything," he says, "becomes interesting from the moment it has closely to consider, for full effect positively to bestride, the law of its kind. 'Kinds' are the very life of literature, and truth and strength come from the complete recognition of them, from abounding to the utmost in their respective senses and sinking deep into their consistency."[43]

And, on the question of kind, Ezra Pound—who edited a special issue of the *Little Review* on James and himself contributed an essay[44]—had one answer, an emphatic one. Enough has been written, he says, on the "minor James. Yet I have heard no word of the major James, of the hater of tyranny; book after early book against oppression."[45] This judgment might puzzle some of us, but Pound is adamant. "There was emotional greatness in Henry James' hatred of tyranny," he insists again. This goes hand in hand with "the momentum of his art, the sheer bulk of his processes, the (*si licet*) size of his fly-wheel." In short, "we may rest our claim for his greatness in the magnitude of his protagonists, in the magnitude of the forces he analysed and portrayed."[46] His canvas is, to be sure, not the traditional large canvas, "not a re-doing of school histories."[47] Instead, its largeness stems from the duration and extension of its generic form, planetary in scope, because James, for all his professions of smallness, "does, nevertheless, treat of major forces, even of epic forces."[48]

Henry James an "epic" poet? And a hater of tyranny to boot? This is not the way he is usually classified. It is worth thinking what American literary history would look like if we were indeed to accept the kinship proposed here, linking a nineteenth-century prose genre to a poetic genre as old as any on record. Pound is not the only one to claim James as kin. W. H. Auden, in his "Address on Henry James," delivered to the Grolier Club on October 24, 1946, does much the same, naming the novelist as one of the few "forerunners" to aspiring poets, a forerunner all the more necessary in the atomized and globalized world:

> As everyone knows, we live today in one world, but not everyone realizes that to live in one world is to live in a lonely world. . . . Like the Wandering Jew, each must go his way alone, every step of it. . . .
>
> Of teachers he will find few and even of them he should be wary. But of examples of those who in their day have dared, like the Prince Tamino, the trials by fire and water and survived them to enter the Temple of Wisdom, he will, thank God, find a number, and among these great forerunners there are few, if he writes in English, of whom he will think more often and more gratefully than of our noble, our prodigious, our—yes, let us risk an annihilating ṣnub to our presumption from his most formidable shade—our dear H.J.[49]

Once again, it is not altogether easy to see the resemblance between the garrulous Henry James and the taciturn Prince Tamino, the Italian hero of a Viennese opera, *The Magic Flute*, who stands his trials by successfully maintaining a vow of silence. Still, Auden's point is clear enough. There is something "prodigious" about the novelist in his scope of endeavor and width of filiation. The fact that he "writes in English" does not make him exclusively Anglo-American. And the fact that he writes in prose does not make him any less "epic."

That is very argument put forth by Ezra Pound. In canto 7 of the *Cantos*, Pound offers his version of literary history—a history of the epic—multilingual in its kinships, and multilingual in its spirals of poetry and prose. Pound begins with the Greek of Homer,[50] moves through the Latin of Ovid,[51] the Provençal of Bertrans de Born,[52] the Italian of Dante,[53] the French of Flaubert,[54] and winds up with Henry James:

The house too thick, the paintings
a shade too oiled.
And the great domed head, *con gli occhi onesti e tardi*
Moves before me, phantom with weighted motion,
Grave incessu, drinking the tone of things,
And the old voice lifts itself
    weaving an endless sentence.[55]

Quite aside from the reference to the endless sentence, James is immediately identified here by two clusters of foreign words, one Italian and the other Latin: *con gli occhi onesti e tardi* and *grave incessu*. This is not the first time James is bumped up to a different linguistic register. In the *Little Review* essay, Pound has also used one of these foreign clusters to describe the aged novelist: "The massive head, the slow uplift of the hand, *gli occhi onesti e tardi*, the long sentences piling themselves up in elaborate phrase after phrase."[56] The Italian phrase, *Con gli occhi onesti e tardi* (with eyes honest and slow), comes from Dante, from the *Purgatorio* (6.63). It is used there to describe the poet Sordello, and is itself a spin-off from an earlier phrase, *con occhi tardi e gravi*, used in the *Inferno* (4.112) to describe the pagan poets: Homer, Horace, Ovid, and Lucan. Pound takes these words from Dante, but also mixes in a Latin phrase from Virgil, *grave incessu*[57]—all of these for the benefit of Henry James, sticking his "old voice" into an even older babel of tongues. This author might be called an American novelist; he is something else in the company he keeps.

That company fractures the label "American," just as it fractures the label "epic." An American author who has to be looped through Dante and Virgil, who has to be described using Italian and Latin, consorts ill with the United States as a linguistic and jurisdictional unit. And an epic tradition that includes Flaubert and James consorts ill with any definition of the genre that presupposes a clean break between the ancient and the modern, between poetry and prose. Pound scholars have, to some extent, always been skeptical of such a rigid separation: Hugh Kenner begins *The Pound Era* with a chapter on Henry James.[58] It is worth following that example, but in reverse, writing *The James Era* but beginning and ending with Pound: as a fractal offspring, theorist, and practitioner of an epic spiral, prenational in its genesis and subnational in its babel of tongues.[59]

LUKACS ON EPIC AND NOVEL

That epic spiral is the implicit subject of Georg Lukacs's *The Theory of the Novel* (a deceptively narrow title). Guided by Hegel, rather than

Marx, at this stage of his thinking,[60] Lukacs sees different genres—epic, novel, tragedy, and lyric—as a transverse process, historical variants of the same dialectic. For him, the epic and the novel are phenomenally distinct but structurally kin. Each rotates on an axis of totality and subjectivity. In the epic, totality and subjectivity are fused in the image of a journey, suspenseful, but ultimately completable. In the novel, totality and subjectivity are split apart, the former reduced to an idea, a higher-order abstraction not manifest in and not graspable from everyday life. The two genres are polar opposites, but with the same spin, the same differential axis rotating in each. Novel and epic must be studied together for this reason, for one becomes salient only against the weight of the other:

> The novel is the epic of an age in which the extensive totality of life is no longer directly given, in which the immanence of meaning in life has become a problem, yet which still thinks in terms of totality. It would be superficial—a matter of a mere artistic technicality—to look for the only and decisive genre-defining criterion in the question of whether a work is written in verse or prose.[61]

For Lukacs (as for Rosalie Colie, Vladimir Propp, Tzvetan Todorov, Hans Robert Jauss, not to say Alasdair Fowler and Franco Moretti),[62] the interest of genres comes from their widening circumference, their cross-stitched and gyrating paths. To label them strictly on the basis of whether they are written in poetry or prose is much too rigid a criterion. For there is an animating hybridity built into the classifying process itself: the taxonomic force has always been bent by spillovers. Genres are thus weakly designative and weakly determinative. The structural properties of each and the infrastructural relations among them are subject to local variation and to large-scale transformation over time. That is why literature has a *history* to begin with. This history is not the story of a single genre, and can never be told using only one. Nor can it can be told as the story of a single language, a single chronology, a single territorial jurisdiction, for it is the scattering and mixing of genres that make literary history an exemplary instance of human history, which is to say, multipath, multiloci, multilingual.

A Theory of the Novel is a crucial corrective to any single-nation or single-genre approach. Among its many challenges, one bears directly on Henry James. If literary history need not be segregated according to "whether a work is written in verse or prose," the kinship between epic and novel might turn out to be one of the most fruitful areas of inquiry. Meshing Lukacs's insights with the insights of fractal geometry, I study that kinship as a kinship in lexical bumps, bumps that dot the surfaces of both epic and novel, that spin out into indeterminate lengths. These are coils of words, including foreign words. They are also coils of time. Dilating and contracting, they generate a vital nonsynchrony, with horizons rising and falling, a landscape both ancient and not ancient.

COILS OF TIME

The Golden Bowl opens with just this landscape:

> The Prince had always liked his London, when it had come to him; he was one of the modern Romans who find by the Thames a more convincing image of the truth of the ancient state than any they have left by the Tiber. Brought up on the legend of the City to which the world paid tribute, he recognized in the present London much more than in contemporary Rome the real dimensions of such a case. If it was a question of an *Imperium*, he said to himself, and if one wished, as a Roman, to discover a little the sense of that, the place to do so was on London Bridge, or even, on a fine afternoon in May, at Hyde Park Corner.[63]

The course of empire has long run westward, away from the Rome of two thousand years ago, to the London of the early-twentieth century. But the shades of the "ancient state" remain, coiled in the Latin that bears its stamp. It is fitting that the word *Imperium* should appear at this juncture, deliberately foreign and deliberately ancient, but also easily recognizable to the English speaker, requiring no translation. For empire is indeed easily recognizable in London, an offshoot of Rome that has reproduced the very "dimensions" of its forebear, signaled by "objects massive and lumpish, in silver and gold . . . tumbled together as if, in the insolence of the Empire, they had been the loot of far-off victories" (3). This is the terrain of the *Aeneid*, the sumptuous objects serving as narrative emblems of both epic and conquest.[64] But this is an updated epic, after all, with input from a different environment. So its hero, the Roman prince, is updated as well: to those with "a shallow felicity," he looks as if he might be "a refined Irishman" (4). Looking Irish, he is matched by two figures still more modern—Americans, father and daughter—whose solicitude, extended even to his lawyer, Calderoni, makes him think of the latter's "bestowal of his company for a view of the lions" (4).

The twists and turns on the coils of time are dizzying. In the space of a paragraph, we go from imperial Rome to an imperial England with its ethnic snobberies, to an imperial America newly arrived but already outstripping both, an America whose "easy way with [its] millions" (5) is rewriting the annals of the Colosseum, but in a different ink. For this is the twentieth century, and no blood will be shed in "American City," or other cities bearing its imprint. There is no danger that either Calderoni or the Prince himself will be fed to the lions. There is no danger that anyone will be torn apart, converted to bits and pieces of flesh. The Prince might fantasize about it: "I'm like a chicken, at best, chopped up and smothered in sauce; cooked down as a *crème de volaille*, with half the parts left out" (8). But such quartering would never take place, not in the manner of the Colosseum, and not in the manner of French haute cuisine. American greenbacks have a different mode of execution: they hold on to the object purchased. The Prince will be kept exactly as he is, intact, a precious relic from long ago, never to be fractionalized, never to be converted into modern currency and broken up into small change: "It was as if he had been some old embossed coin, of a purity of gold no longer used, stamped with glorious arms, medieval, wonderful, of which the 'worth' in mere modern change, sovereigns and half-crowns, would be great enough, but as to which, since there were finer ways of using it, such taking to pieces was superfluous" (23).

The Ververs are the most magnanimous and most astute of buyers. If there is a risk that the Prince might devalue on their hands, might bring in fewer "sovereigns and half-crowns" than they have expected, the thing to do is never to cash him in, never to have his value ascertained. His is to be a sealed case, never to be reopened. It is no longer an active term in bookkeeping: "He felt therefore just at present as if his papers were in order, as if his accounts so balanced as they had never done in his life before and he might close the portfolio with a snap. It would open again doubtless of itself with the arrival of the Romans; it would even perhaps open with his dining to-night in Portland Place, where Mr. Verver had pitched a tent suggesting that of Alexander furnished with the spoils of Darius" (19).

Spoils of Alexander

Unfortunately for the Ververs, the portfolio does indeed open of itself, with more complicated mathematics spinning out, making the bookkeeping messy and continually worrisome. For the "old embossed coin" that is the Prince turns out to be more than a relic. Still active, still in play, it is a form of "currency" the Ververs have not bargained for. Even though their desire is never to update it, never to convert it to "modern change," it has already done so of its own accord, liquifying itself, spilling over into many replicas. Among these, none is more striking than the golden bowl. It is this reproductive spiral from the past to the present that poses the greatest threat to the Ververs, to "the American way" (7). For this spiral not only enmeshes the Prince in a much longer coil of time than his own life span; it also brings the same coil of time to bear on the Ververs themselves, putting their cherished self-image through an acid bath. Maggie thinks of Americans as the most innocent people alive, babes in the woods, which is "just what makes everything so nice for us" (11). Her father's relation to the things he owns, she explains to the Prince, is "beautiful—is absolutely romantic. So is his whole life over here—it's the most romantic thing in the world" (12). The Prince, being Roman, sees things differently. Ancient history is on his mind, and the open-palmed beneficence of the Americans is somehow mixed up with the names of Darius and Alexander.

These are resonant names for James, mentioned more than once in his writings. In his essay "Venice" (1882), subsequently published in *Italian Hours* (1909), James has an even more extended reference to these two figures, in turn casting up more names, more artistic genres beyond the medium of print, and a host of institutions housing them. Darius and Alexander turn out to have a tangled life in a number of paintings, on display in Venice and beyond Venice. James notes that there are "painters who have but a single home," but

> Veronese may be seen and measured in other places. . . . You may walk out of the noon-day dusk of Trafalgar Square in November, and in one of the chambers of the National Gallery see the family of Darius rustling and pleading and weeping at the feet of Alexander. Alexander is a beautiful young Venetian in crimson pantaloons, and the picture sends a glow into the cold London twilight.[65]

What James is referring to is a painting by Veronese, *Family of Darius before Alexander*, purchased by the National Gallery in 1857. It features Alexander as a victor after the Battle of Issus, fought in 333 BCE, the first of two epic defeats for Darius III, the last of the Persian kings. Darius managed to escape, but his entire family had fallen into the enemy's hands: his wife, Statira, his mother, Sisgambis, his two daughters, Statira and Drypetis. These are the "spoils" won by Alexander. But he is nothing if not magnanimous. Plutach writes:

> [H]e gave them leave to bury whom they pleased of the Persians, and to make use for this purpose of what garments and furniture they thought fit out of the booty. He diminished nothing of their equipage, or of the attentions and respect formerly paid them, and allowed larger pensions for their maintenance than they had before. But the noblest and most royal part of their usage was, that he treated these illustrious prisoners according to their virtue and character. . . . Nevertheless Darius's wife was accounted the most beautiful princess then living, as her husband the tallest and handsomest man of his time, and the

Figure 4-1. Paolo Veronese, *The Family of Darius before Alexander.* Courtesty of the National Gallery, London.

daughters were not unworthy of their parents. But Alexander, esteeming it more kingly to govern himself than to conquer his enemies, sought no intimacy with any of them.[66]

Here then is magnanimity on a par with Adam Verver's. Plutarch, writing in Greek, is no doubt partial to his compatriot. But Veronese, working in the medium of paint, actually has more resources to turn that magnanimity into an art. Since there is some worry, evident even in Plutarch, that Darius's wife, Statira, "the most beautiful princess then living," might be a problem (and the pregnancy that resulted in her death in childbirth in 331 BCE certainly raised suspicions),[67] Veronese shifts the focus to a different woman altogether. It is not Statira, but Sisgambis, mother of Darius, who is put at the center of the canvas (fig. 4.1). Middle aged and plain faced, with her jaw slightly dropped open, she is covered from head to toe in the "ermine-topped velvet robe of a Dogaressa of Venice," as Cecil Gould points out in a pamphlet on the painting put out by the National Gallery.[68] Never are low suspicions more firmly put to rest. Furthermore, not only is Sisgambis put at the center; the focus is specifically on an embarrassing mistake she has made. This is a detail not mentioned in Plutarch, but recounted by several late Classical writers: Arrian, Quintus Curtius Rufus, Diodorus Siculus, and Valerius Maximus. As summarized by Cecil Gould, the incident is this: "after the battle of Issus, Alexander the Great chivalrously set out to comfort the womenfolk of his defeated enemy, Darius. He went to their tent, accompanied by his close friend, Hephaestion. Since the latter was taller than Alexander, the mother of Darius mistook him for the king and made obeisance to him. When her mistake was pointed out, Alexander magnanimously relieved her confusion by saying of Hephaestion that he too was Alexander."[69]

Veronese's painting catches the story at just that moment—the gracious hand gesture of Alexander extended frontally to Sisgambis and sideways to Hephaestion, magnanimous toward both. This is a magnanimity that comes on top of the prior granting of "larger pensions" to the women, a gesture now fully sanitized. *Family of Darius* is a portrait of what a conqueror ought to look like, as idealized as can be. Indeed, the conqueror does not look like one at all. As James says, Alexander is a "beautiful Venetian youth in crimson pantaloons." Conquest, so charmingly personified, ensures that there is only mild unease on the part of the conquered, but no pain, no devastation. This is not a military camp, with no hint of bloodshed, but a splendid palace, complete with marble columns, arches, and pilasters, with sculptures in high relief in the spandrels and even a graceful fountain between Sisgambis and Alexander. The geometry is serene, harmonious, Euclidean.

It is perhaps not surprising that this should be the picture of choice for the National Gallery, acquired at a time when the British Empire would like to see itself in just that idealized light. Sir Charles Eastlake, director of the National Gallery, examined the picture in person at the Palazzo Pisani in Venice, on October 14, 1856.[70] The museum ended up paying £13,650 for it. This was considered an exorbitant price. It sparked a debate in the House of Commons in July 1857.

James and Ruskin

Ruskin, troubled by the uproar, wrote to the *Times* on July 7, 1857, to defend the purchase. "Permit me to add further," he said, "that during long residence in Venice I have carefully examined the Paul Veronese lately purchased by the Government. When I last saw it, it was simply the best Veronese in Italy, if not in Europe (the "Marriage in Cana" of the Louvre is larger and more magnificent, but not so perfect in finish); and, for my own part, I should think no price too large for it; but putting my own deep reverence for the painter wholly out of the question, and considering the matter as it will appear to most persons at all acquainted with the real character and range of Venetian work, I believe the market value of the picture ought to be estimated at perhaps one-third more than the Government have paid for it."[71]

It did not trouble Ruskin too much that the "best Veronese in Italy, if not in Europe" should end up in the National Gallery in London. That was none of his business. His focus was much more concentrated, fastened on one detail. On this occasion, it happened to be the excellent bargain the British government was making, the excellent value it was getting for £13,650. This concentrated focus, redirected in volume 5 of *Modern Painters*, would produce an equally concentrated account of the painting, read at such close range that the entire canvas becomes a single detail:

> There is a pretty little instance of such economical work in the painting of the pearls on the breast of the elder princess, in our best Paul Veronese (Family of Darius). The lowest is about the size of a small hazel nut, and falls on her rose-red dress. Any other but a Venetian would have put a complete piece of white paint over the dress, for the whole pearl, and painted into that the colors of the stone. But Veronese knows beforehand that all the dark side of the pearl will reflect the red of the dress. He will not put white over the red, only to put red over the white again. He leaves the actual dress for the dark side of the pearl, and with two small separate touches, one white, another brown, places its high light and shadow. This he does with perfect care and calm; but in two decisive seconds. There is no dash, nor display, nor hurry, nor error. The exactly right thing is done in the exactly right place, and not one atom of color, nor moment of time spent vainly.[72]

Like the letter to the *Times*, this account of *Family of Darius* is obsessed with economy. It insists that expenditure should be cost-efficient, that there should be no waste, "not one atom of color, nor moment of time spent vainly." This focus produces a reading as exquisite as it is selective. The fact that these women are kneeling hardly matters; the fact that this is the aftermath of a bitter military defeat also vanishes in the "two small separate touches" that are the pearl. This is small-scale reading at its most dedicated and demented. Henry James, infinitely more crude in his comment on the women "rustling and pleading and weeping at the feet of Alexander," at least has kept those two facts in the picture.

How does James feel about Ruskin? *Italian Hours* is full of snide jabs at the older writer. In "Italy Revisited," James writes: "I had really been enjoying the good old city of Florence, but I now learned from Mr. Ruskin that this was a scandalous waste of charity." Whereupon "I am almost ashamed to say what I did with Mr. Ruskin's little books. I put them in my pocket and betook myself to Santa Maria Novella."[73] This is not simply jest. Ruskin's "little books" are things James fancies he can put in his pocket, for the former does miniaturize where the latter does not. That difference also leads to a different understanding of what constitutes "economy" and "waste" when art changes hands, when a powerful nation takes it upon itself to acquire beautiful objects from abroad.

OLD, OLD HISTORY

In "Two Old Houses and Three Young Women"—another essay in *Italian Hours*—James speaks of the steps "almost soft enough for a death-chamber," leading to the "beautiful blighted rooms" in a "despoiled *decadula* house" in Venice. The inhabitants of that house are three sisters, living blighted lives, haunted by "the shrunken relics of nine Doges" and "their great name and fallen fortunes."[74] And James goes on:

> One of the sisters had been to London, whence she had brought back the impression of having seen at the British Museum a room exclusively filled with books and documents devoted to the commemoration of her family. She must also then have encountered at the National Gallery the exquisite specimen of an early Venetian master in which one of her ancestors, then head of the State, kneels with so sweet a dignity before the Virgin and Child. She was perhaps old enough, none the less, to have seen this precious work taken down from the wall of the room in which we sat and—on terms far too easy—carried away for ever; and not too young, at all events, to have been present, now and then, when her candid elders, enlightened too late as to what their sacrifice might really have done for them, looked at each other with the pale hush of the irreparable. We let ourselves note that these were matters to put a great deal of old, old history into sweet young Venetian faces.[75]

What James is referring to here is another Veronese painting, *The Adoration of Kings*, bought by the National Gallery in 1855.[76] Economy on the part of British government lays waste other parts of the world. Such transactions do put "old, old history" into the young. The Venetians in "Two Old Houses" are not the only ones to have grown ancient in that way, nor the only ones to carry with them a "pale hush of the irreparable" as they visit the museums of the imperial capitals. The Prince in *The Golden Bowl*—son-in-law to a collector who is planning to build a magnificent museum in American City—is afflicted with an "antenatal history" (16) for the same reason. Its "presence in him was like the consciousness of some inexpugnable scent," clinging to "his clothes, his whole person, his hands and the hair of his head" (16). This scent is so overpowering that it is almost as if he and his kind were not quite washed, not quite Westernized, as if their long and smelly history were a lapse in sanitation, making them racial renegades, dubiously Caucasian. The Prince, his marital contract notwithstanding, remains a part of this unsanitized past: "His race, on the other hand, had had [vices] handsomely enough, and he was somehow full of his race" (16). To that "race," coming from "backward old Rome" (31), London "will be more or less another planet. It has always been, as with so many of *us*, quite their Mecca, but this is their first real caravan" (25).

Ancient Rome is part of the Near East in its backwardness. This eastward alignment gives *The Golden Bowl* a historical canvas stretching across thousands of years. Its horizon is not unlike the one composed by Veronese, a genre in paint that haunts its cousin in print. Citing the painting, the novel becomes momentarily and fractionally epic as it knots itself into a coil of time, winding its way through the monumental art of Venetian patronage as well as the monumental chambers of the National Gallery, coming to rest, finally, in the Battle of Issus of 333 BCE. This is the "third infusion or dimension" James alludes to elsewhere,[77] making the novel no more purely American than it is purely English or purely Italian. Any literary history would be remiss without taking into account this citational geometry and the lively input of visual genres into the print medium.

VERONESE AND TIEPOLO

And there is a further wrinkle, a further bump. James speaks of Adam Verver as having "pitched a tent suggesting that of Alexander furnished with the spoils of Darius." This citation makes no sense if we limit ourselves to Veronese, for there is in fact no tent in that sumptuous painting. In his desire to highlight the trappings of civil life, an extension of the nobility and civility of the conqueror, Veronese has banished from his canvas any sign of violence, any sign that this is a military venture, with military casualties. The tent has no place in such a setting. James's not particularly elegant phrasing seems to be inelegant as well in getting things mixed up. His citation cannot simply be to Veronese; something else must have given him the idea that a tent is involved. His source could have been Plutarch's passing reference—although, as his schoolmate Thomas Sergeant Perry pointed out, what James read in school was "a fair amount of Latin literature. Like Shakespeare, he had less Greek."[78] Plutarch was not his favored text.[79] This particular detail, then, most probably came to him through a visual rather than textual tradition, for the tent of Alexander was nothing if not a kinship network in its own right: a topoi painted over and over again for three hundred years. Cecil Gould notes that though "Veronese himself dispensed with the tent altogether," in "the versions by Sodoma and Taddeo Zuccari before Veronese, and Le Brun, Mignard, Ricci and Tiepolo after him, the setting included a tent."[80]

Tiepolo's version is especially interesting. Painted in 1743 for a villa in nearby Vicenza (the Villa Cordellina in Montechhio Maggiore), this

Figure 4-2. Giambattista Tiepolo, *The Family of Darius before Alexander.*

fresco was well known as a pastiche on Veronese.[81] There is one major departure—Tiepolo has put in a gigantic tent, taking up almost one-third of the compositional space (fig. 4.2). And there are other, subtler departures as well. Michael Levey calls attention to Tiepolo's curious "tendency to fail in presenting heroic men . . . as if he felt they were too absurdly heroic for him. . . . Alexander especially, with his rigid bearing and distinctly unimpressive physique, might be the castrato of this *opera seria* : assertive, even arrogant, but slightly ludicrous amid the firmly characterised, robust, bearded baritones and the impressive range of so-pranos who yet all depend on him."[82] This is a very different conqueror

Figure 4-3. Giambattista Tiepolo, *The Family of Darius before Alexander,* detail of Alexander's face.

from Veronese's (fig. 4.3). Maria Elisa Avagnina, Fernando Rigon, and Remo Schiavo point to other disturbing details, randomly scattered and sinuously echoing, ranging from the "tragic mask of the queen mother, old, bleary-eyed and toothless" to many grimacing faces, half disclosed in the ornamental backdrop of the fresco: "In sharp contrast to the solemnity that surrounds the great historical figures, a 'malign' note is struck in the grotesque heads of monsters that decorate the armour, sandals, jars and even the phalera of the horses."[83] These are fractional glimpses, dotting the canvas like a filigree of malice. They emerge only at close range; once seen, they are impossible to forget (figs. 4.4 and 4.5).

Tiepolo's *Alexander and the Family of Darius* belongs to a "family" that is worrisome indeed. Cousin to Veronese, its vexed kinship is such as to turn the other painting into a much longer story, with unfolding dimensions hitherto unsuspected. These dimensions are the very air its victims breathe. Conquest of this sort menaces even when it is idle, even when it is embodied by persons less than impressive. This is the mystery of power. The gigantic tent dramatizes this. With splendid embroidery

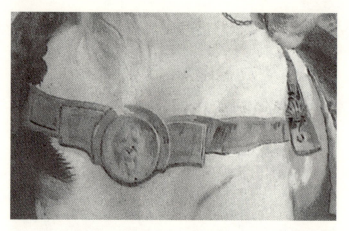

Figure 4-4. Giambattista Tiepolo, *Family of Darius*, detail of phalera.

on top, signaling the royalty of the person occupying it, the rest of it is simply a looming shape, like a curtain, dwarfing the human figures, but impenetrable, its intentions veiled, matching the blank look on Alexander's face.

FAMILY OF DARIUS

The Prince in *The Golden Bowl* is struck by just such a curtain. On the eve of his marriage, he senses that there is "that element of the impenetrable which alone slightly qualified his sense of good fortune" (22). He is reminded of "a wonderful tale by Allan Poe, his prospective wife's countryman," in which

> the shipwrecked Gordon Pym, who, drifting in a small boat further toward the North Pole—or was it the South?—than any one had ever done, found at a given moment before him a thickness of white air that was like a dazzling curtain of light, concealing as darkness conceals, yet of the colour of milk or of snow. There were moments when he felt his own boat move upon some such mystery. The state of mind of his new friends, including Mrs. Assingham herself, had resemblances to a great white curtain. (22)

The Narrative of Arthur Gordon Pym, of course, ends abruptly at this point. After the encounter with the great white curtain, there is nothing more to say. *The Golden Bowl* is more intrepid, for as the Prince gets "a little nearer the shroud, he promised himself virtually to give the latter a twitch" (24). That twitch is not unlike Tiepolo's. Pulling and tugging at

Figure 4-5. Giambattista Tiepolo, *Family of Darius*, detail of jar.

an angle, it makes everything that seems straight go awry. And, since this going awry explodes into a novel that goes on for hundred of pages, it will reveal, among other things, a twisted Adam Verver, whose magnanimity does not prevent him from "holding in one of his pocketed hands the end of a long silken halter looped round [Charlotte's] beautiful neck." James writes: "He didn't twitch it, yet it was there; he didn't drag her, but she came."[84] And all the while, his "two or three mute facial intimations . . . amounted perhaps only to a wordless, wordless smile, but the smile was the soft shake of the twisted silken rope" (288). It says to Maggie: "Yes, you see—I lead her now by the neck, I lead her to her doom, and she doesn't so much as know what it is, though she has a fear in her heart which, if you had the chance to apply your ear there that I, as a husband, have, you would hear thump and thump and thump" (288).

The Golden Bowl belongs to a "family" of indeterminate depth. There is nothing pretty about this kinship: it is fractional, coming in bits and pieces, darkly concave and endlessly grating, with a backward loop as far as Mesopotamia, and many cousins along the way, too many to count. James and Tiepolo probably did not know about a Roman mural from Pompeii depicting the marriage of Alexander to Statira, daughter of Darius. Partly to consolidate his dominion over Persia, Alexander decided in 324 BCE to make Statira his second wife. This mural, painted around 200 BCE, seems less a celebration of that event than a mean stab at Alexander's puniness. The artist here shows him as a stick of a man, not handsome, shorter than Statira, and inexplicably much darker than she is (fig. 4.6). As Maggie might say, speaking of her "Father's form": "It strikes me he hasn't got any" (7). Statira, meanwhile, glaring into space, with arms akimbo, is graphic in her loathing. This is not a happy family. The force of recoil here is infinitely greater than the bond of filiation. There is such a thing as negative kinship.

James, for instance, never loses a chance to have a jab at Ruskin. In *Italian Hours* he takes delight in the fact that "Mr. Ruskin [seems] to be put out of humour by Titian and Tiepolo."[85] This is true. In "The Shrine of the Slaves" (appended to volume 3 of *The Stones of Venice*), Ruskin has some unkind things to say. Tiepolo, he says, "is virtually the beginner of Modernism; these two pictures of his are exactly like what a first-rate Parisian Academy student would do, setting himself to conceive the sentiment of Christ's flagellation, after having read unlimited quantities of George Sand and Dumas. It is well that they chance to be here; look thoroughly at them and their dramatic chiaroscuros for a little time, observing that no face is without some expression of crime or pain, and that everything is always put dark against light or light against dark."[86] Tiepolo is faulted for many things: his failure to be purely Italian; his dalliance with the French novel; his "Modernist" way of injecting into everyone "some expression of crime and pain." Ruskin is speaking of Tiepolo's frescoes at St. Alvise rather than at Montecchio Maggiore, but the same objections apply. And those objections could have been leveled at James as well, for what he depicts is also something less and something more than magnanimity, putting many black holes into that curtain of light.

The "family of Darius," in this sense, is not only fractional, but downright fractious. This is what keeps it going. In his autobiography, *The Middle Years*, James offers his own gloss on this edgy kinship. He finds himself, he says, once again in the "old National Gallery, where memory mixes for me together so many elements of the sense of an antique world."[87] And he is struck again by an epic canvas, oblivious to the shake-ups it has endured, thriving indeed on the "rearrangements and reversals," on the "blighting new lights and invidious shattering comparisons":

Figure 4-6. Marriage of Alexander and Statira, Roman mural, Pompeii.

I look at it to-day as concomitantly warm and closed-in and, as who should say, cosy that the ancient order and contracted state and thick-coloured dimness, all unconscious of rearrangements and reversals, blighting new lights and invidious shattering comparisons, still pre-vailed and kept contemplation comfortably confused and serenely sur-reptitious, when not indeed at its sharpest moments quite fevered with incoherences. The place looks to me across the half century richly dim, yet at the same time both perversely plain and heavily violent—violent through indifference to the separations and selections that have become a tribute to modern nerves; but I cherish exactly those facts of benightedness, seeming as they do to have positively and blessedly conditioned the particular sweetness of wonder with which I haunted the Family of Darius.[88]

CHAPTER FIVE

Transnational Beauty:
Aesthetics and Treason, Kant and Pound

DOES BEAUTY come under the jurisdiction of the nation-state? Is it a controlled phenomenon, the handiwork (and perhaps the handmaiden) of a territorial regime? Or is it more primitive, more unruly, having a deeper relation to humans as a species? If so, can it be invoked as a common ground of sorts, a platform for our shared humanness, over and against what would divide us?

The recent surge of interest in aesthetics[1] makes these questions all the more urgent. In this chapter I test the extent to which beauty can be aligned with a human commonality, rather than with one particular nation-state. I take my cue from Terry Eagleton, not exactly a fond champion of the concept. Eagleton pointed out some years ago that while the aesthetic is an idea steeped in bourgeois ideology, it nonetheless "provides an unusually powerful challenge and alternative to these dominant ideological forms," for its "contradictory" energies are such as to keep alive a "residually common world."[2] This residually common world suggests that there might be principles of human association older and more elementary than those dictated by territorial jurisdictions. The aesthetic, in this way, gestures toward a *species-wide* domain, as wide as the planet in its duration and extension.

I am not the first to see the aesthetic in this light. Immanuel Kant, in *Critique of Judgment* and, relatedly, in his political writings, most especially in *Perpetual Peace*, has already done much to lay the groundwork for such a claim. Kant sees the aesthetic as a species-wide category of experience, one emanating from the human perceiver rather than the perceived object. What interests him is not the ontological status of the thing we judge to be beautiful, but rather the mental operation that enables us to make that judgment.[3] This mental operation is the pivot of humanity. According to Kant, it is the clearest evidence we have of a *noncontradictory* relation between the subjective and the universal. Beauty is a quality each of us evaluates; it affirms our freedom each as a separate judge. This freedom, however, is held in check by one constraint, the constraint of universal assent: it must be acceptable to everyone else. This marks the projected scope as well as the limiting condition of our subjective judgment. The aesthetic is both local and global in this sense, both particular in its instantiation and generalizable in its ground. Through this duality, the species is able to individuate each of its members even as it affirms its collective integrity. A basis for agreement both connects us and makes each of us singular. That is why we count as a species, a taxonomic order accommodating each and every human being.

Of course, for Kant, this claim on behalf of the aesthetic is argued on strictly a priori (which is to say, logically necessary) grounds. Empirical data, according to him, prove nothing definite; no binding maxim can rest upon them. I reverse his strategy. Relying heavily on empirical data—in this case, the much publicized attack against one set of poems, the *Pisan Cantos*, the work of an alleged "aesthete" and "traitor"—I explore the aesthetic as a term activated on both ends of the political spectrum: speaking to state sovereignty on the one hand, global humanity on the other. Kant's theory, tested by this empirical archive, will be fully vindicated, and ironized beyond recognition. The spectacle of an American poet recklessly embracing the aesthetic heritage of the world, and recklessly giving himself over to an anti-American cause, fulfils just what Kant predicts, but only by giving it a bad name. The "aesthetic" here is indeed a challenge to the "national," although few would find it reassuring. Even so, and perhaps because it is *not* reassuring, this vexed term continues to name a deviant zone, namable at the taxonomic limits of the nation. An alternate conception of the species emerges here, possibly (and in this case demonstrably) monstrous, but, in its vision of a deep common denominator, going all the way with Kant.

WORLD FEDERATION

And Kant goes far. In *Perpetual Peace*, he offers this blueprint:

> The condition which must be fulfilled before any kind of international right is possible is that a lawful state must already be in existence. . . . Now we have already seen above that a federative association of states whose sole intention is to eliminate war is the only *lawful* arrangement which can be reconciled with their *freedom*. Thus politics and morality can only be in agreement within a federal union, which is therefore necessary and even *a priori* through the principles of right. And the rightful basis of all political prudence is the founding of such a union in the most comprehensive form possible.[4]

Writing in 1795, in a Prussia under the thumb of Frederick William II, Kant had every reason to dream about a "federative association of states," a world polity not under that thumb.[5] This world polity, however, is meant not to supersede the state but to protect it.[6] For the sole charge of this entity is to eliminate war, which, for Kant, is the most vicious destroyer of nations: both in the literal sense of bringing down particular regimes and in the subtler sense of killing off civil liberties in a militarized state. Only a world polity can put an end to this dual destructiveness. Only a world polity can speak to the human species as a whole, protecting individual freedom by safeguarding international peace.

And yet, living as he did in a Europe ravaged by war, Kant knew better than to see this international peacekeeper as anything other than a utopian dream. *Perpetual Peace*, while not ironic in the substance of what it proposes, is overflowing with irony when it comes to the likelihood of its ever being adopted. The treatise begins with the caption "The Perpetual Peace" followed by this line: "A Dutch innkeeper once put this satirical inscription on his signboard, along with the picture of a graveyard."[7] Only among the dead is peace a viable option. Among the living it will always be a stillborn hope, dead on arrival.

ARENDT ON KANT

Hannah Arendt, struck by this uncharacteristic irony on Kant's part, has argued that *Perpetual Peace* is just a self-mocking indulgence, "reveries" that "Kant himself did not take . . . too seriously."[8] This overtly political essay and several others like it do not amount to much, Arendt insists. They do not represent the full extent of Kant's thinking, for "there exists a political philosophy in Kant but that, in contrast to other philosophers, he never wrote it" (31). Where then is this "nonwritten political philosophy" (19) to be found? Arendt devotes the whole of her *Lectures on Kant's Political Philosophy* to this question.[9] Her answer is as perverse as can be. The "nonwritten" can only be inferred, she says, and inferred from the most unlikely source, namely, a treatise that on the face of it has nothing whatever to do with politics. "Since Kant did not write his political philosophy, the best way to find out what he thought about this matter is to turn to his 'Critique of Aesthetic Judgment,' where, in discussing the production of art works in their relation to taste, which judges and decides about them, he confronts an analogous problem" (61).

A theory of aesthetics doubling as a theory of politics? The judging of beauty "analogous" to the keeping of peace? This counterintuitive approach has not persuaded everybody.[10] Still, the paradigm Arendt sets forth cannot be more suggestive. Any hope for a species-wide ordering of the humanities—and any hope for a species-wide ordering of the world—will have to come to terms with her argument.[11] In what follows I test her hypothesis in just that light. Reading *Critique of Judgment* as she advises, as a meditation on two fronts, I explore it as a deeply architectured, and therefore a robustly non-ironic version of *Perpetual Peace*. The aesthetic theory here affirms the unity of the species by way of the faculty of judgment, offered by Kant as evidence of the deep agreement among human beings, extendable to the political realm and grounding his hoped-for elimination of war.

Of course, whether war can ever be eliminated is a sad question at the moment. Do we, as a species, have a basis for agreement and, if so, can that basis be strengthened to the point of guaranteeing peace? This is a supremely uncomfortable subject for all of us, not just Kant and Arendt. And nothing adds more to the discomfort than the example of Ezra Pound. To be a party of humanity, in his case, meant not only to be anti-war but also to be a fan of Mussolini, a propagandist for the fascist state, a traitor against his native country in his Rome Radio broadcasts. Very few of us see a hopeful future in his dubious example. If such empirical data mean anything at all, they point to a deep fault line in Kant's theory (and Arendt's reading of it), a fault line running all the way through the projected hope of species unification. That hope is probably too fragile to bear all the weight put upon it. In fact, it is probably the ugly twin, *dis*unity, that would end up bearing that weight: as an unhappy but not altogether unhopeful condition, giving rise to its own negative dialectic. But this is getting ahead of the story.

COMMON TASTE

It is useful to begin with the *Critique of Judgment* and its aspirations for the species. The key vehicle of these aspirations is something called "common sense," defined in §20 of the "Critique of the Aesthetical Judgment" as that "subjective principle which determines what pleases or displeases only by feeling and not by concepts, but yet with universal validity."[12] Here then is the crucial Kantian pivot, the overlap between the subjective and the universal, between the species-individuating and species-integrating poles of the aesthetic. This dynamics he further elucidates in §40, where the commonness of aesthetic judgment is given a sharper definition through its Latin name:

> But under the *sensus communis* we must include the idea of a sense *common to all*, i.e. of a faculty of judgment which, in its reflection, takes account (*a priori*) of the mode of representation of all other men in thought, in order, as it were, to compare its judgment with the collective reason of humanity. . . . I say that taste can be called *sensus*

communis with more justice than sound understanding can, and that the aesthetical judgment rather than the intellectual may bear the name of a sense common to all, if we are willing to use the word "sense" of an effect of mere reflection upon the mind, for then we understand by sense the feeling of pleasure. We could even define taste as the faculty of judging of that which makes *universally communicable*, without the mediation of a concept, our feeling in a given representation. (136, 138)

"Taste," the most private of our senses, is singled out by Kant as the most public, its contents most universally communicable, its field of action of the largest scope. It is an odd choice. Taste is not usually given this kind of global mandate. Unlike sight, a faculty deemed "objective" because of its representation of external objects, taste is not objectively representational. It registers only a feeling on our part, our like or dislike of something presented to the palate, but it yields no descriptive image. Sight tells us about the measurable shape, size, and color of an apple; taste tells us no such thing. It says only that this apple is delicious or passable, a judgment entirely internal to us, with no outward extension in the world. Taste is bounded by the bounds of our subjectivity. It is the most primitive of our senses.

It is this primitive sensory faculty that occupies the central place in Kant's aspirations for the species. Not only is taste identified with aesthetic judgment; in that capacity it is given a further task, the all-important task of species unification. It is the "aesthetic"—rather than the "intellectual"—that is the unifying force for Kant, and the distinction between these two says much about his conception of humankind. The intellectual is a specialized category, a high-end, high-order phenomenon; it rests on a cognitive apparatus, it requires the "mediation of a concept." Intellectual activities take place on an upper stratum of our mental life. This high-end phenomenon is not "universally communicable": mathematics, for instance, is not something that can be explained to everyone; it is the privilege of a few. The "aesthetic," on the other hand, is the province of everybody; it is the lowest of the low. It requires no mediation at all, no high-flying concept, nothing special, since it is just a gut "feeling," the liking or disliking occasioned by what comes our way. That feeling expresses itself as the judgment that the encountered object is good or bad, beautiful or ugly, delicious or passable. And it does not take much to arrive at such a judgment. Aesthetic feeling (according to Kant) is instinctive and instantaneous; it is preconceptual at the very least, and, in some cases, perhaps even precognitive. It is the most basic feature of human life, the only part of our mental existence that is truly across-the-board, available to every member of the species.[13] And it is because it is so basic, because it occupies the lowest rung of the mind, that "the aesthetical judgment rather than the intellectual may bear the name of a sense common to all."

Aesthetic judgment is the name that Kant gives to the baseline of humanity. The word *beautiful*, most common of words, is that baseline. There is no phenomenon that cannot be positively or negatively described by this term, and no human being who will not at some point resort to its usage. Kant is not usually regarded as a patron saint of cultural studies, but he should be. Aesthetics and cultural studies do not have to be segregated, as if the latter were solely the province of the mindlessly low and the former solely the province of the snobbishly high.[14] Kant, on the contrary, sees the "beautiful" as a low-end phenomenon, experienced across the board, encompassing the full range of objects in the world and the full range of judges. "It is by beauty," Ernst Cassirer says of Kant, that humankind "passes beyond the sphere of empirical individuality . . . to a common basis—to that basis which in the *Critique of Judgment* is called *das übersinnliche Substrat der Menscheit*, the intelligible substratum of humanity."[15] That is why the word *beautiful* is such a common word, why its usage says something basic about us. Hannah Arendt, enlarging on this point, sees the *Critique of Judgment* as a theory about species being, about what can be collectively predicated of the "human." It is a theory of "an original compact of mankind as a whole, and derived from this idea is the notion of humanity, of what actually constitutes the humanness of human beings, living and dying in this world, on this earth that is a globe, which they inhabit in common, share in common, in the succession of generations" (76).

What are the chances of this idealized sense of the "human" actually materializing among human beings? Can the aesthetic, the *sensus communis*, the substratum of humanity, overcome the appetite of nation-states for war? Much depends on the ontological status of this term, the depth of that substratum. Is the *sensus communis* something *constitutive*, a unity antecedently given and binding its members at every level, unifying any individual judgment with the judgement of everyone else as a precondition? Or is the *sensus communis* merely *regulative*, not really a substratum at all, but much more tenuous, secured only through a negotiated give-and-take, with each judge appealing to a kind of species tribunal for validation? Paul Guyer, in his careful analysis of the these two definitions of the *sensus communis*, one strong and one weak, argues that they represent an unresolved tension in Kant.[16] That tension will have large consequences for the claim of the aesthetic and its ability to unite humankind against the nation and against war.

In §19, Kant seems to be coming down firmly on the side of the strong claim. "The judgment of taste," he says, "requires the agreement of everyone, and he who describes anything as beautiful claims that everyone *ought* to give his approval to the object in question and also describe it as beautiful. . . . We ask for the agreement of everyone else, because we have for it a ground that is common to all; and we could count on this agreement" (74). This is clear indeed. The ground for agreement is antecedently given, truly a substratum, we can count on it. Kant is not, of course, so misguided as to think that this ground has in any way been actualized in the world. Even a fool can see that there is no consensus about beauty just yet. But a consensual ground potentially exists. In fact, it logically *has to exist*, for otherwise our feeling of beauty would have been entirely arbitrary. And it is because this feeling is not arbitrary, because it is justified by some preexisting and nonidiosyncratic norm, that it can count as a "judgment" in the first place. A judgment, to be such, carries the binding force of an *ought*. It points to a generalizable rule as its genetic condition. We call something "beautiful" with the understanding that we are passing a normative verdict, that other human beings might concur with this norm, and that, under ideal conditions, they ought to.

Aesthetic judgment affirms the unity of the species as a *logical necessity*. As Terry Eagleton says, "It is as though, prior to any determinate dialogue or debate, we are always already in agreement, *fashioned* to concur; and the aesthetic is this experience of pure contentless consensus where we find ourselves spontaneously at one without necessarily even knowing what, referentially speaking, we are agreeing over."[17] Such logical agreement seems not to mesh with the known facts of human life. Even in Kant, complications set in almost right away. The normative "ought," for instance, sometimes has a petulant air to it, as it does in §22:

> In all judgments by which we describe anything as beautiful, we allow no one to be of another opinion, without, however, grounding our judgment on concepts, but only on our feeling, which we therefore place at its basis, not as a private, but as a common feeling. Now this common sense cannot be grounded on experience, for it aims at justifying judgments which contain an *ought*. It does not say that everyone *will* agree with my judgment, but that he *ought*. (76)

Here the *ought*, rather than being the bearer of a logical necessity—a preexisting common ground—becomes instead an order, a fiat. It is a counterfactual assertion that imperiously wipes out what disagrees with it. That disagreement can only be an aberration as far as it is concerned. Judgment here is "regulative" in the worst sense of the word. Extended from an individual opinion and generalized into a universal norm, it takes any nonconcurrence as a mistake, an ipso facto error, to be duly corrected. The premise of unity, in other words, carries in reserve a punitive clause. It carries in reserve the right to name as deviant those who stray from its normative common sense.

AESTHETES AS TRAITORS

Kant is so wedded to the idea of aesthetic judgment being one and the same with the *sensus communis* that he cannot fully acknowledge this punitive scenario. Nor can he acknowledge another scenario, also punitive, in which the *sensus communis*, far from being one with the aesthetic, instead cordons it off, draws a sharp line around it, as a marked target, a negative definitional pole. The "aesthetic" then becomes a name for what this imagined community jointly castigates, jointly exorcizes, as an agreed-upon object of condemnation. The twentieth century has witnessed many enemies of the people branded with that label. The United States has had its share of these, and none more vexing than Ezra Pound.

The condemnation of Pound reached a climax when the *Pisan Cantos* was awarded the first Bollingen Prize in 1949. To Robert Hillyer (then president of the Poetry Society of America and a winner of the Pulitzer Prize), this was the last straw, the ultimate affront of a "new estheticism, the literary cult to whom T. S. Eliot and Ezra Pound are gods."[18] He was not alone in being thus affronted. The formidable *Saturday Review of Literature*, which published his articles, fully shared his outrage. In an accompanying editorial, Norman Cousins and Harrison Smith, editor and president of the *Saturday Review*, made their own case against Pound and named his offense in no uncertain terms:

> Like Mr. Hillyer, we were profoundly shocked to see the name of the United States Library of Congress, and therefore that of the United States Government, associated with the Bollingen $1,000 award to Ezra Pound. It is not enough to say that Ezra Pound is a traitor. It is not enough because it is important to know exactly what kind of traitor he is, and what he is a traitor to. Ezra Pound is not merely the traitor who deserts his country in order to impart secrets which are useful to the enemy. . . . [but] the world's No. 1 sneerer at America and its traditions and its people.[19]

Pound might have been called a fascist, an anti-Semite, but these names did not in fact figure largely in the *Saturday Review* editorial. Instead, the name of choice, the name that trumped all other names, was "traitor." This was the proper designation for Ezra Pound, and one the *Saturday Review* used advisedly. Technically speaking, of course, Pound's "treason" against the United States was somewhat nebulous, not at all cut-and-dried.[20] He had not, after all, acted as a spy; he had not passed on valuable secrets to the enemy. He had been guilty only of "sneering" at America in his radio broadcasts.

Still, "traitor" was the right name, and the *Saturday Review* was on good authority in using it. This word—or at least its more technical, punishable sibling, "treason"—had originated from the legal proceedings initiated by the U.S. Attorney General. On July 26, 1943, Pound was indicted by a grand jury in the District of Columbia for violation of the Treason Statute (section 1, title 18, U.S. Code, 1940 edition):

> That Ezra Pound, the defendant herein . . . being a citizen of the United States, and a person owing allegiance to the United States, in violation of his said duty of allegiance, knowingly, intentionally, wilfully, unlawfully, feloniously, traitorously, and treasonably did adhere to the enemies of the United States, to wit, the Kingdom of Italy, its counsellors, armies, navies, secret agents, representatives, and subjects, and the military allies of the said Kingdom of Italy, including the Government of the German Reich and the Imperial Government of Japan, with which the United States at all times since December 11, 1941, have been at war, giving to the said enemies of the United States aid and comfort within the United States and elsewhere.[21]

The words "United States" appeared obsessively, like some sort of mantra. The grand jury needed to invoke it over and over again, for it was this sanctified name that in turn gave a name to Pound's offense. "Treason" is an offense against the state; more than that, it is an offense defined *by* the state, named as a prosecutable relation to its "enemies," and, in that naming, affirming the sovereignty of the state at the very point of its alleged breach. This is a nation-based taxonomy in its full glory; "treason" is its star player.

That starring role is not limited to courtroom verdicts. As evidenced by the popularity of Ann Coulter's recent book, *Treason: Liberal Treachery from the Cold War to the War on Terrorism* (2003), the word is versatile, it can do double and triple duty.[22] That was very much the case with the *Saturday Review*: the word condemned Pound both on the ground of political allegiance and on the ground of literary merit. And there is no reason why it should not be versatile in this way, interchangeably literary and political, for "traitor" is indeed a judgment operating on both registers if we see literature strictly in national terms, if we judge Ezra Pound solely and exclusively as *American*. Pound has not been a good American, not in his political loyalties, and not in his literary affiliations. With nationality as the sole yardstick, his "poetical and propaganda activities" can rightly be condemned using one and the same term.

Robert Hillyer was merely executing that logic when he entitled his first article "Treason's Strange Fruit":

> Ezra Pound is quite simply under indictment for treason because during the last war he served the enemy in direct poetical and propaganda activities against the United States. . . . In view of Pound's hatred for the democracy of his native country, it is ironic that among the conditions of the award is the stipulation that the recipient must be an American citizen. By some tenuous legality Pound may be a citizen, but he knows nothing and cares less about civic obligations. . . . He has seldom set foot in America since he was twenty-three. His country's elections, wars, aspirations, and exploits have left him untouched if not hostile.[23]

As an American, Ezra Pound was deficient indeed. Anyone judging him by that criterion would have reason to spurn him, to resent his legal citizenship, an empty name, without substance. Against that taxonomic imposture, Robert Hillyer, the *Saturday Review*, and the grand jury of the District of Columbia were united in their outrage and united in their determination to set things right. The false name, "American citizen," had to be stripped away, and the real name, "traitor," pronounced with the combined authority of the court and a mass-circulating magazine.

Since it was a question of calling things by the right name, it was not just Pound who had to be called out. He was the easy target in "Treason's Strange Fruit," but Hillyer actually had in mind a larger prey. The problem with the Bollingen Prize, he said, was not only that the wrong man got the award, but that the *judges* decided to give it to him in the first place. Who were these judges? They were a group known as the Fellows of the Library of Congress in American Letters, and included, among others, Conrad Aiken, Robert Lowell, Katherine Anne Porter, Karl Shapiro, Allen Tate, Robert Penn Warren, as well as two names listed with a parenthetical aside: "Wystan Hugh Auden (a native of Great Britain who is now an American citizen)," and "T. S. Eliot (a native of the United States who has become a British citizen)." Hillyer did not mind Auden, but Eliot incensed him. And so the article that began with the treason of Pound ended up with the treason of Eliot, heavily underlined:

> Eliot's whole life has been a flight from his native St. Louis, Missouri. He has gone far, and doubtless, if he survives Masefield, he will be the next English laureate. In America he is so enhedged with nebulous divinity that people are shocked, as by blasphemy, at anything said against him. This is occasioned not so much by his writings as by the awe for a man who managed to get contemporary America out of his

system, an aspiration of many new poets and critics. . . . What is to be done? The 1949 Bollingen Award is a permanent disgrace and cannot be expunged. But preventive measures against a similar choice can be taken. The first step would seem to be for the expatriate T. S. Eliot to be dropped from the jury.[24]

Once again, those magic words—"American" and its opposite, "expatriate"—are made to do double and triple duty, naming in one and the same convenient gesture the crime of treason, the crime of being a bad poet, and the crime of being a bad judge. Since everything boils down to nationality, since nothing escapes its naming, its sovereignty is thereby absolute. It will not tolerate any competing lexicon, any word that offers a different description of a poet or of a judge on a prize-selection committee.

Un-American

The "aesthetic" was unforgivable for just that reason. The idea that poetry might be written (or read) with an evaluative criterion other than its American-ness was treasonable in itself. Hillyer's dislike of the offending word began with its spelling. His object of condemnation was the "new estheticism"—and no good American would spell it any other way. Under this spelling, he obviously included those "Americans and one expatriate on the Bollingen jury," those "esthetes [who] crowned Pound as their laureate."[25] But, as he made clear in the title of his second article, he also meant to include a much larger group, named by him as "Poetry's New Priesthood." This comprised a group of readers, those "self-styled 'new critics,'" who had the nerve to look to beauty as an evaluative criterion. Hillyer found it ominous that these "new esthetes" had gone so far as to compile a taxonomy of their own, with this title, "A Glossary of the New Criticism."[26] Not finding words such as "traitor" and "treason" in that glossary, Hillyer hurled at these delinquent judges a charge they were to receive again and again: "To a world eager for the clearest vision of poets they offer only the analysis of disillusioned irony, word by word."[27] Close reading was downright unpatriotic. What made it even worse was that the practice seemed to be quite common; college professors and even high-school teachers were addicted to it:

> Their power is enormous, especially in the colleges and even the preparatory schools. A large proportion of funds for cultural purposes from the great charitable foundations is earmarked for their use. *Poetry: A Magazine of Verse*, seems to be falling into the hands of the new esthetes. In their April number the editors comment on what a

hard time poor Ezra Pound must have had from lack of appreciation and add that "nothing is more understandable than that he should have adopted a rather cross attitude towards America." Some day someone is going to adopt a rather cross attitude towards the editors of *Poetry*. Maybe America.[28]

Hillyer was right. Just two months after the publication of his *Saturday Review* articles, a Joint House and Senate Committee directed the Library of Congress to stop sponsoring the Bollingen Prize.[29] "America" did indeed decide to have nothing to do with poetry. And for good reason. Twentieth-century poets and their readers were not exactly flag-waving patriots: Louise Bogan, Robert Lowell, Wallace Stevens, Robert Penn Warren, and Allen Tate were all opposed to World War II.[30] The fact that *Poetry* magazine had actually come out with a mild apology for Pound gave Hillyer just the ammunition he needed. The war is not over yet, he insisted, for treason is in our midst: "the clouds of an intellectual neo-Fascism and the new estheticism have perceptibly met and on a horizon too near for comfort."[31]

Here then is the charge that trumps all else: aestheticism and fascism are one. Uncannily, Hillyer is echoing a celebrated dictum of Walter Benjamin's: "The logical result of Fascism is the introduction of aesthetics into political life."[32] What Benjamin means, and what he goes on to say, is that to "render politics aesthetic" in this way is "culminate in one thing: war." Fascism makes war both inevitable and pleasurable, since "[w]ar is beautiful because it combines the gunfire, the cannonades, the cease-fire, the scents, and the stench of putrefaction into a symphony."[33] Read out of context, Benjamin's complex account of war can sound like a simple equation of aesthetics with a reprehensible politics. It is this that Russell Berman objects to, pointing out that this equation flattens a much more complicated process, flattens, in particular, the mediating role played by the nation.[34] In the United States, that mediating role was such as to turn Benjamin's indictment on its head. Here the aesthetic, far from being staged as official spectacle, as in Germany and Italy,[35] was deployed instead as a commonsense term of condemnation, a shorthand for all that gave offense. It was lined up with the word "treason" and the word "Fascism" to name any deviance from the patriotic norm.

That naming must be seen in the context of another word then current, "un-American," one of the most remarkable words in the twentieth century. The designative power of the House Committee on Un-American Activities was fully behind it. This committee, appointed by Congress in 1938, and exclusively targeting communists and fellow travelers in the decades to follow, initially had a different mission, with a different group of subversives on its agenda. The name of the committee was coined by Representative Sam Dickstein of New York, who proposed that "[t]here should be a standing committee of this House known as the Committee on Un-American Activities, which should watch every subversive group in this country." He was thinking especially of the Nazis. According to him, there were 25,000 men and women in Nassau County alone, "going crazy, dressed in uniforms and goose-stepping their way for miles at all hours of the night." And, outside Nassau County, "there are 200,000 people in this country who should have their citizenship papers canceled," for they are "men of the Bund ready to put on uniforms and to use a gun."[36]

From that beginning, the word "un-American" would go on to enjoy a rather different career.[37] At every point of its flourishing, it was an index to U.S. nationalism, an index to a taxonomy that named its positive term through a marked and denounced negation. "American-ness" needs a subversive foil, called by different names, but each affirming in reverse the ideal it is said to have subverted. The *Saturday Review*'s attack on the "new estheticism" must be seen in this light. The "introduction of aesthetics into political life" was very much an exercise in name-calling, branding the culprit through its guilt by association with an enemy abroad. Those who launched the attack and those being attacked were both aware of the stakes involved. As the Fellows of the Library of Congress in American Letters said in a formal response to the *Saturday Review*: "This charge of irresponsible aestheticism . . . linked sometimes with charges of Fascist-mindedness" in effect imposed a "standard-brand positive Americanism as a test for literary worth."[38]

In the case of Pound, though, the links between aestheticism and fascism were not only real but proudly advertised. The *Pisan Cantos* wore their politics on their sleeves. Canto 74 begins by mourning the death of Mussolini:

> The enormous tragedy of the dream in the peasant's
> > bent shoulders
> Manes! Manes was tanned and stuffed,
> Thus Ben and la Clara a Milano
> > by the heels at Milano[39]

Benito Mussolini and his mistress, Clara Petacci, were overtaken by the Italian Partisans on April 27, 1945 and shot, their bodies brought back to Milan and hanged by the heels. To Pound, the hope for humankind in general and for the Italian peasants in particular died that day. Mussolini, after all, had embarked on ambitious agricultural reforms, including reclaiming 150,000 acres of the Pontine Marshes in 1931 and distributing them to 75,000 peasants;[40] he had made the promise that each of those peasants would have a house of his own in eighty years.[41]

Pound, obsessed with economic reform ever since his ten-year stint at the British Socialist magazine, the *New Age*, was particularly drawn to this aspect of fascism, its promised redistribution of wealth.[42] He thought Mussolini's estimate too modest: "I don't the least think he expects to take 80 years at it, but he is not given to overstatement. . . . It is possible the Capo del Governo wants to go slow enough so as not to see, in his old age, an Italy full of fat peasants gone rotten. . . . All this is poesy and has no place in a critical epistle."[43]

Politics was indeed aesthetics for Pound, called by its name: "poesy." And it was in tribute to that "poesy" that he would write, with poetic license in turn, his most controversial piece: *Jefferson and/or Mussolini*. As its title indicates, this treatise is dedicated to the proposition that the American president and the Duce have much in common. In Pound's own words: "The heritage of Jefferson, Quincy Adams, old John Adams, Jackson, Van Buren is HERE, NOW in the Italian peninsula at the beginning of the fascist second decennio, not in Massachusetts or Delaware."[44] It is an outrageous claim, a theory of American (and Italian) history hardly anyone would agree with.[45] As Pound himself said, this manuscript had the distinction of being refused by "40 publishers."[46] What sort of judgment inspired him to write something so out of step with everyone else's? As evidenced by the reference to Mussolini's "poesy," that judgment seemed to have been largely aesthetic in nature. "His god is beauty," D. H. Lawrence once said of Pound.[47] That god gave him a historiography as well as a poetics. It is much more beautiful, much more striking, to think of the shape of human history as an arc rather than a straight line, the legacy from Jefferson and Adams swerving to the side, curving to Europe, winding up in the hands of an Italian. In canto 74 Pound himself has made "poesy" out of a similar claim, chronicling an arc of cultural transmission also swerving to the side:

> But a snotty barbarian ignorant of T'ang history need not deceive
>   one,
> nor Charlie Sung's money on loan from anonimo[48]

The Chinese (like the Greeks) are fond of calling foreigners "barbarians." Pound adopts that word, the prejudiced word of an ancient civilization. And it is he, Ezra Pound, who can afford to be prejudiced in that Chinese way, for it is he, the non-native, who has T'ang history in his safekeeping, while the supposed native, Charlie Sung, clearly has in *his* safekeeping something very different.

Jefferson and Mussolini, Mussolini and Pound: there is a symmetry between these two sets of relationships.[49] The arc of cultural transmission that makes the Italian the recipient of an American legacy also makes the American the recipient of a Chinese legacy. It is a beautiful symmetry. But

"beauty" of this sort, intoxicating to Pound, is nonsensical to most people. Aesthetic judgment is most often, and most powerfully, a lone judgment. Its force is never generalizable, for that force is measured by its
peculiar grip on one person, a grip that bears the imprint of one subjectivity, as it does no one else's. It is at this point, where an across-the-
board "taste" turns into something much more luminous (and much
more obsessive) for one particular person that aesthetic judgment can be
said to be a vital mental event, an event that marks that person. That
mark cannot serve as a blueprint for human unity, for its very intensity
inflects it, rigs it as subjective, the terrain on which disagreement thrives.
The aesthetic thus points to a deep divisiveness among human beings; it
is a foreshadowing of war rather than a deterrent to it. "Art cannot con-
cretize Utopia, not even negatively," Adorno has argued. "Without a
perspective on peace art would be untrue, just as untrue as it is when it
anticipates a state of reconciliation. The beautiful in art is the illusion of
peace in empirical reality."[50]

That "illusion of peace" would hit Ezra Pound with full force. Writing
his *Cantos* as a grand epic of humankind, a rejection of war, he ended up
by himself, in a cage, a traitor and a prisoner in the American Disciplinary Training Center at Pisa. He concedes as much:

> sunt lumina
> that the drama is wholly subjective
> stone knowing the form which the carver imparts it
> the stone knows the form[51]

The poesy of fascism is subjective drama. The "form" of symmetry between Jefferson and Mussolini, and between Mussolini and Pound, is
known only to Pound himself. It is emphatically not shared by the grand
jury of the District of Columbia and the readers of the *Saturday Review*.
But, if it is true that the aesthetic is no more than subjective, no more than
the individualized ground for disagreement, that "no more" nonetheless
carries a nontrivial force, especially when it happens to be pitted against
a patriotic norm so naturalized as to become common sense. Disagreement with that norm is suicidal then; it is terrifying to witness.

In his sixth radio broadcast, the first recorded after the Japanese attack on Pearl Harbor, Pound opened with this offhand remark: "On Arbour Day, Pearl Arbour Day, at 12 o'clock I retired from the capital of
the Old Roman Empire to Rapallo to seek wisdom from the ancients."[52]
The ancients in question were Confucius and Mencius, whose Chinese
ideograms, "of extreme beauty," he was trying to translate.[53] The national catastrophe of Pearl Harbor meant nothing to Pound. He did not
mourn the casualties, he did not pour his patriotic furor on Japan, he did
not call the Japanese barbarians. On the contrary he noted only this:

> Anybody who has read the plays entitled Kumasaka and Kagekiyo, would have AVOIDED the sort of bilge printed in Time and the American press, and the sort of fetid imbecility I heard a few nights ago from the British Broadcasting Company . . . the Awoi no Uye, Kumasaka, Nishikigi, or Funa-Benkei. These are Japanese classical plays, and would convince any man with more sense than a pea hen, of the degree of Japanese civilization.[54]

Pearl Harbor or not, Japan would always remain for Pound a luminous name. His admiration for that country, like his admiration for Mussolini, was aesthetic: he had translated those Japanese classical plays himself, from Ernest Fenollosa's notes, and the task had seemed not a task, but simply "the pleasure of arranging beauty into words."[55] That beauty must have meant nothing to his compatriots. In any case, beauty is beside the point in the wake of Pearl Harbor.

Is beauty beside the point or not? And what does it mean to speak of the beauty of ancient plays when torn bodies are crying out for vengeance? Then as now, Pound's will always be a minority voice, laughable in its naive and stubborn attachment, blind to the patriotic fury of a wounded nation. Kant is right about this at least: the aesthetic is not intellectual, it is the most primitive of our faculties. It is not astute, not savvy, not expedient—which is why, in spite of Pearl Harbor, Pound would still insist on making this radio broadcast:

> The United States had been for months ILLEGALLY at war, through what I considered to be the criminal acts of a President whose mental condition was NOT, as far as I could see, all that could be or should be desired of a man in so responsible a position.[56]

Statements like this explain why the word "aesthetic" can so easily be made into a synonym for the word "un-American."

CHAPTER 6

Nonstandard Time:
Robert Lowell, Latin Translations, Vietnam War

DEEP TIME is "un-American" in conforming neither to a national chronology nor to a national map. It nourishes a politics as well as an aesthetics: a devotion to ancient beauty that can lend itself to the charge of treason. Ezra Pound is an extreme case. Robert Lowell, in his attachment to Latin and his opposition to the Vietnam War, would seem to be rehearsing much the same dynamics. Rather than pitting him against the *Saturday Review*, I return now to a more theoretical argument of this book, having to do with the depth of literary culture and the sinuous threads spun of it. In chapter 4, I invoked fractal geometry to talk about those threads, coiling and uncoiling, generating indeterminate lengths within the lexical surface. In this chapter I speculate some more on these indeterminate lengths, citing them in counterpoint to the numerical measurement of distance. Literary culture is a solvent that breaks down this numerical regime, that allows nonstandard space and time to emerge. Lowell is the central exhibit here, but Aristotle, Newton, and Einstein will all come into the picture.

NUMERICAL TIME

I begin with the concept of "numerical time." What is it? No ready answer comes to mind. The phrase is not idiomatic or even vaguely recognizable, because *time* is rarely qualified by this adjective, or qualified at all. It seems to come all in one piece, in one flavor. It is an ontological given, a cosmic metric that dictates a fixed sequence of events against a fixed sequence of intervals. It is present everywhere, the same everywhere, independent of anything we do. It carries no descriptive label and has no need to advertise or to repudiate that label.

When it is seen in this way, as a given, time is also seen as quantifiable, measurable as uniform units. It is made up of segments that are exactly the same length, one segment coming after another in a single direction. This unidirectionality means that there is only one way to line up any two events, one way to measure the distance between them. Time is imagined here as if it were a kind of measuring tape. There is of course no physical evidence of such a tape. Still, we assume it is there. And we need to assume this, for it is only when time is vested in this concrete form that we can impute to it a fixity of distance. One year, one month, one minute—these unit lengths have to be "real" unit lengths. They have to be objectively measurable. And, as proof of this, they have to come already stamped, already serialized. We speak of one particular minute as, say, 5:10, followed by the next minute, 5:11, just as we speak of one particular year as, say, 1965, followed by the next year, 1966. This serial designation puts time under the jurisdiction of number.

This is not exactly an innocent step. But—I think it is fair to say—it is a step taken quite uncritically by most of us. We don't think twice when we refer to one particular year as 1965, because a numerical bias is by now so deeply ingrained in us that it works as a kind of mental reflex. That is why dates have a kind of summary authority, why we ascribe to them such descriptive and explanatory power. We don't doubt that a number, 1965, can be assigned to one particular slice of time. We don't doubt that this numerical designation is meaningful, that it exercises a binding power over all events thus designated. Number, in this way, works as a kind of automatic unifier. It imposes a temporal identity across the board, because numerical chronology is of course the chief means by which time can be standardized, can be represented as a sequence of units, each homogenous, each calculable. The location of any event is fixed by this sequence, and so too is its proximity or distance to any other event. 1965 is separated by only twenty years from 1945, so it has to be closer to this year than to the year 65, from which it is separated by 1900 years.

This numerical bias is the unspoken norm for humanists no less than for scientists. Under New Historicism, this unspoken norm has sometimes turned into a methodological claim, producing a spate of scholarship whose very ground of analysis is numerical time. It is quite routine for us to seize upon one particular number—the date of a text's composition—and use it to set the limits of an analytic domain, mapping the scrutinized object onto a time frame more or less standardized. One year, five years, ten years: these are the unit lengths we use, as a matter of course, when we proceed to "contextualize." To contextualize, defined in this way, is simply to synchronize. Events are deemed pertinent to one another only if they fall within the same slice of time, only if they are bound by two serial numbers so close to being consecutive that the distance between them can be measured by single digits. This short duration is assumed to be adequate, to capture both cause and consequence: both the web of relations leading to the making of the text and the web of relations flowing from its presence in the world.

PLATO AND ARISTOTLE ON NUMBER

In this chapter, I take issue with this reign of the synchronic by way of the numerical. What does it mean to construct an analytic domain bound by two serial numbers with a minimum degree of separation? As a time frame, how adequate is this brief duration and serial lineup? What sort of phenomena fall within its purview, what falls outside? What effect does this conception of time have on the institutional shape of literary studies? And what effect does it have elsewhere, in other disciplines? How far should we go, how interdisciplinary should we get, to put our synchronic model in perspective?

It is worth taking a risk here, looking beyond our usual intellectual allies, since the question of time—its ontology and numerical measurement—turns out to be a central issue in one field ordinarily seen as quite remote from the study of literature, namely, physics. Interdisciplinarity between these two fields stretches the limits of each, for literary studies and physics, currently located on two ends of our intellectual spectrum, can come into contact only through a backward loop, a reengagement with some long-standing and as yet unsettled disputes. The detour is helpful, not only to anchor a specific argument about time but also to propose a more extended analytic horizon: not coinciding with our usual disciplinary borders, and not coinciding with the geography and chronology of the United States.

I begin with a debate between Plato and Aristotle, featuring two different conceptions of time, two ways of mapping time against number. Plato, with his belief in the transcendent reality of mathematics, argues, not surprisingly, for the priority of number over time. Time for him is an effect, an epiphenomenon, something deduced or derived from number. Past and present, Plato says in the *Timeaus*, are no more than shadows cast by an everlasting and ever-unchanging mathematical structure. They are a "moving image of eternity," "moving according to number."[1] Number, in short, is a preexisting order of reality; it is a structural antecedent that grounds all events, that gives the world an eternal order.

Aristotle is not so sure. Book 4 of his *Physics* is devoted to complicating and qualifying Plato's formulation. "Time is a number," Aristotle concedes, but then quickly adds a caveat that sharply limits the operative parallel between the two. "But 'number' may mean either that which is numbered, or that by which we number it; time is number in the former sense."[2] This might seem hair-splitting, but Aristotle does not think so. The distinction between what does the numbering and what is being numbered is crucial. He adds, "Time is not the number we count with but the number counted."[3] In other words, time can perhaps be enumerated, but it is not the vehicle with which we do the enumerating. A measuring rod can perhaps be put to it, but it itself does not generate that measuring rod.

Having made this operative distinction, Aristotle then goes one step farther, insisting now on an ontological distinction between time and number. Number is sharp-edged and clean-shaven; time is not. "Time is a number not as a self-identical point has a number in respect of its being both beginning and end."[4] Every number is a discrete entity: it is self-contained, self-identical, ending exactly where it begins. It is a modular unit, pointlike in its ontology. Time is anything but that. The relation between any individual instant and time in its totality is not in the least cut-and-dried. Rather, it is a sinuous overlap, a fold within a voluminous fabric, registering the continual emergence of relations. This interactive process goes backward as well as forward, producing adjacencies between what was and what will be. "Being the number of what is continuous, it is itself continuous."[5] Clean resolution, in other words, is not at all possible given the ontology of time. Years, decades, and centuries are endlessly connected even when they are discretely numbered. There can be no stable partitions here, and no clean breaks.

Rather than segmenting evenly, along lines fixed by serial numbers, time for Aristotle is a continuum: a continuum that, at any given moment, can be cut in any way. These "cuts"—their lengths, their angles of incision, the folds being gathered together as a result—are generated on a strictly ad hoc basis, which is to say, under the shaping hand of particular events. As these events resonate with the past, drawing it into the orbit of the present, distance can become sharply foreshortened. Events otherwise far apart can find themselves suddenly side-by-side, rendered simultaneous for the moment. This "simultaneity" is not the effect of a fixed coordinate. It does not come stamped with a serial number. It is simply a chance meeting, brought into being when the distance between two events happens to collapse. It owes its existence to something like a gravitational pull, a force that can have a drastic effect on the numerical length of temporal separations. Aristotle does not mince words on this point: "if to be simultaneous in time is to be in the same now, then if both what is earlier and what is later are in one particular now, the events of 10,000 years ago will be simultaneous with those of today, and no event will be earlier than any other."[6]

NEWTON

This is of course a scandalous thing to say. Espousing it, in the teeth of Plato's numerical determinism, Aristotle challenges anyone who wants to think seriously about time. Unfortunately, that challenge has gone largely unheeded. In the centuries that followed, it was not Aristotle's conception of time, but a new version of Plato—Newton's version—that would reign triumphant, dominating the field of physics and a broad swath of Western culture outside physics, as Peter Gay, Margaret Jacob, Garry Wills, and I. Bernard Cohen have shown.[7] Newton's descent from Plato (and our descent from both) can be gleamed from the opening pages of the *Principia*:

> Absolute, true, and mathematical time, of itself, and from its own nature, flows equably without relation to anything external, and by another name is called duration. . . . Absolute space, in its own nature, without relation to anything external, remains always similar and immovable. . . . As the order of the parts of time is immutable, so also is the order of the parts of space. . . . All things are placed in time as to order of succession; and in space as to order of situation. It is from their essence or nature that they are places, and that the primary places of things should be movable, is absurd. These are therefore the absolute places.[8]

Time is "mathematical" for Newton, which is to say, quantifiable, expressible as a numerical constant. It flows everywhere at the same pace, in the same direction, and everywhere yields the same measure. It is an immutable sequence, calibrated by an immutable metric. But to say this is to realize, with a shock, that Newton's time is simply "time" for most of us, generalized and naturalized, not called Newton's because no attribution need be made to the individual who invented it. Instead, its numerical nature is taken for granted, as a fact of nature, the stuff of common sense. We are Newtonians precisely because we never carry that label.

Given this silent hegemony, this dominance of one conception of time and the erasure of all competing versions, it is especially important to take a new look at Newton, bringing into the open his unstated premises, the freighted corollaries locked into place by his numerical model.[9] It turns out that, for Newton, "absolute, true, and mathematical Time" does not come alone. It is part and parcel of a larger conceptual edifice: inseparable from and, it would seem, all but interchangeable with "absolute space." Time and space are mentioned in the same breath; one dovetails into the other. To quote Newton again: "All things are placed in time as to order of succession; and in space as to order of situation. . . . These are therefore the absolute places." Not only is space adduced here as a parallel to time, it is actually the antecedent, the originating idea from which time derives its shape, as a longitudinal "order of succession," much like a latitudinal "order of situation." It is space that provides the mental image for time, space that dictates the ontology of both.[10] Conceived in this light, time functions in exactly the same way as a spatial coordinate. It is a place, a location, a fixed term on a numerical sequence—and, for all those reasons, a container to which any event can be assigned.

Newtonian physics stands or falls on this image of time as a container. Since this is the case, time is perhaps less a measuring rod than a filing cabinet. Any event can be automatically put into one of a nested sequence of slots—into a century, a year, a month. Placement is crucial: everything must be filed away, locked into a receptacle bearing a uniform number. Newton spatializes time and, in the same gesture, standardizes it. The temporal axis now becomes a series of synchronic planes, a series of numbered cross-sections. Events are assumed to be unified if they happen to fall on the same plane; their common identity is guaranteed by their common serial address. Newtonian physics thus assigns a tremendous regulative power to simultaneity, the condition of being at an identically numbered cross-section.[11] And for Newton, this simultaneity is not a contingent fact, true within one particular frame of reference. It is absolute, a mathematical truth, unified at any given point, and binding in every instance. What this means is that every event is permanently tied to two sets of serial neighbors: to one set of events that comes before it and one set that comes after it, a sequence as immutable as the march of numbers.

This numerical chronology—probably the least examined dogma of modern thought—governs our sense of duration and the historical relations it permits. Under its dispensation, there is just one way to measure the distance between two events: they are either simultaneous or not, either far or near. That distance never varies, for it stands as a numerical constant. And such constants are morphologically ironclad. There is a dividing line—a clean break—between them, even when consecutive. They never fold into each other or spill over into each other. This ironclad ontology is indeed the ground on which most of us envision history as well as our own life spans, as we assign historical events to absolutely numbered slots and ourselves to durations the numerical length of our lives. This is what it means to be Newtonians. Historians—Newtonians in this sense—thus divide history into numbered periods and speak of them as if they were objective units. And literary critics, Newtonians as well, lock a text into a brief duration, a numbered slice of time, as if that slice were a container.

Beyond Serial Numbers

How to loosen up this stern regime? The consequences for the humanities are far-reaching, especially for literary studies. In an important essay, "DissemiNation: Time, Narrative, and the Margins of the Modern Nation," Homi Bhabha suggests one approach.[12] Bhabha argues that time has no phenomenal unity, that it is a vital analytic axis precisely because it is fractured. Lived memories and lived subjectivities do not always yield the same measure, sequenced by the same directional metric. Experienced through individual filters, time can take on any length and width, beginning and ending in odd places, with strange effulgences and conjunctions. No numerical chronology can homogenize them into a synchronic platform. And, in escaping homogenization, experiential time works against the putative unity of *any* construct, not least the construct called the nation.

For Bhabha, then, the breakdown of a single, enforceable chronology stands as one of the most powerful challenges to the sovereignty of the state. It directly contradicts the regime of "simultaneity" adduced by Benedict Anderson as the hallmark of the nation. Against that regime— against Anderson's account of national time as "homogeneous empty time . . . measured by clock and calendar"[13]—Bhabha calls attention to many alternate temporalities: "disjunctive" narratives, written at the margins of the nation and challenging its ability to standardize, to impose an official ordering of events.[14] "Postcolonial time," Bhabha says, "questions the teleological traditions of past and present, and the polarized historicist sensibility of the archaic and the modern."[15]

Bhabha does not mention Newton in his essay; and yet, the postcolonial time he describes marks a break not only from the synchronic plane of the nation-state, but also from the numerical jurisdiction of Newtonian physics. It is helpful to bring the latter squarely into the foreground as we explore an alternate conception of time: at odds with number, and working most immediately against the chronology of the nation, and more deeply against the dictates of seriality.

Here, I invoke an earlier essay by J. M. Coetzee, published in 1982, entitled "Newton and the Ideal of a Transparent Scientific Language."[16] Coetzee singles Newton out partly because of his mathematical absolutism, but also partly because he is a user of words like the rest of us, facing a problem we all face. Specifically, Coetzee asks what it means for Newton to aspire to a purely mathematical language, a notational system untouched by the embedding, localizing, and contaminating effects of metaphor. The *Principia*, in this light, becomes nothing less than a language experiment. It is an attempt to do away with the messiness of ordinary speech and to replace it with the precision of number: completely clear, completely unambiguous, universally true. It is a noble experiment, but doomed to fail, Coetzee says. Because every time Newton tries to take a mathematical truth into an experiential realm—every time he tries to translate a numerical relation into a language spoken by the rest of us—an extra layer of meaning sets in: unintended, unwelcome, and unstoppable. Ordinary language, it seems, is metaphoric by nature, in the sense that it is always stuck in some particular analogy, muddled by the semantic surcharge of what is meant merely to be an illustrative instance. The way we talk is quite different from the way mathematics talks. There can be no one-to-one mapping between these two languages, between the freighted particularity of words and the burdenless universality of numbers.

For Coetzee, then, Newton dramatizes a problem all of us should recognize, namely, the problem of translation, the impossible task of trying to unify two languages with very different referential claims on the world.[17] Taking his point, but putting a slightly different spin on it, we can think of Newton's problem not only as one of translation, but, more pragmatically, also of jurisdiction. How much of the world is under the rule of number? Not all, if Coetzee is right. A mathematical description has its limits: it does not cover everything, and its serial logic is not everywhere honored. What then is the *other* realm not fully collapsible into number? Can we give it a name, can we embrace it as an alternate habitat? What are the circumstances for its emergence? And what shape of time unfolds in its midst? If numerical jurisdiction relies on the clock and the calendar, how is time kept in this other, non-Newtonian realm?

Einstein

Here the history of physics can come to our aid. For in a remarkable turn, Newton's conception of time has actually been undermined on his home turf—and by none other than Einstein. In a dramatic moment in his "Autobiographical Notes," Einstein writes:

> Enough of this. Newton, forgive me; you found the only way which, in your age, was just about possible for a man of highest thought and creative power. The concepts, which you created, are even today still guiding our thinking in physics, although we now know that they will have to be replaced. . . .
>
> "Is this supposed to be an obituary?" the astonished reader will likely ask. I would like to reply: essentially yes.[18]

Newton's obituary has to be written, for all his assumptions about time—as uniform and numerical, as predicated on fixed simultaneity—have now been challenged. Indeed, the turning point in modern physics, for Einstein, rests on his "difficulty with all physical statements in which the concept 'simultaneous' plays a part."[19]

Rather than accepting simultaneity as an article of faith, Einstein asks whether it is generalizable at all. Is there such a thing as a synchronized "now," unified across the board, expressible as a numerical constant? Is synchrony itself an absolute fact that eternally stands between two temporal neighbors? Does the motion of an object make any difference to its space and time coordinates? And if so, what difference does *that* make to the concept of simultaneity? To answer these questions, Einstein considers the phenomenal world as seen from two reference frames in two different states of motion. Using a moving train as one frame of reference and the railroad embankment as the other one, he asks whether the timing for two flashes of lightning can be synchronized for these two reference frames. Can they be seen as simultaneous in both places?

With palpable satisfaction Einstein writes: "the answer must be in the negative."[20] The two flashes of lightning A and B might be simultaneous for the observer standing still on the embankment. But, if this is the case, they will not be simultaneous for an observer on the train moving away from A toward B. Since this observer is shortening his distance to B and lengthening his distance to A, he "will see the beam of light emitted from B earlier than he will see the one emitted from A."[21] In other words,

> Events which are simultaneous with reference to the embankment are not simultaneous with respect to the train, and vice versa (relativity of simultaneity). Every reference-body (coordinate system) has its own particular time; unless we are told the reference-body to which the statement of time refers, there is no meaning in a statement of the time of an event.[22]

Simultaneity turns out not to be generalizable. Two events might be simultaneous in one frame of reference, but in a different frame they would not be. The "now" experienced in one location, then, cannot be the same as the "now" experienced in a differently moving location. These two nows cannot be unified: for the simultaneity that defines one turns out to be nonexistent in the other. Einstein, in this way, turns Newton's absolute truth into a contingent truth, specific to one set of coordinates, not generalizable beyond them. This is what he calls relativity. Of course, for Einstein, relativity is itself a mathematical concept. It is derived from non-Euclidean geometry, the peculiar geometry exhibited by space-time under the requirement that the speed of light be invariant.[23] And, in making the invariance of light the foundation of physics, Einstein is as committed as Newton to a formalizable mathematical language.[24] We are seriously mistaken if we imagine that there can be an easy translation from that language to ordinary speech.

OFFBEAT READING

Still, it is not impossible, even for laypersons, to have some experience of Einstein's basic idea: namely, that time is frame-dependent, that there can be no numerically unified now. At least one phenomenon from everyday life allows that idea to make nonmathematical sense. I have in mind the phenomenon of literature, routine enough, whose temporal ontology nonetheless upsets the coordinates of the routine, delivering not only a rebuff to Newton but also a tribute to Aristotle, giving his *Physics* an unexpected field of operation. Drawing on both Aristotle and Einstein, then, and translating their arguments into an argument about the temporal trajectory of words, I propose an intersection between literature and science, intersecting on a terrain I would like to call "nonstandard time." Here, measurement of distance is not absolute; experience is not bound by seriality. Inhabiting this domain, literature yields a temporal axis startling to contemplate: longer than we think, messier, not strictly chronological, and not chronological in a single direction. Literature is valuable "scientific" data in this sense: it is the clearest sign of a temporal order outside the jurisdiction of number.

I am thinking, in particular, of the experience of reading. What this activates is something like a "relativity effect": a telescoping of two time frames, yoked together, each putting pressure on the other, but remaining stubbornly apart, not unified by a number. This relativity effect comes about when we are drawn to words that came into being long before we did, not occasioned by us, and not referring to us. In one sense, they are entirely outside our life spans. But, in another sense, they are not outside, because thanks to the temporal foreshortening created by reading, they are actually, literally, in our hands. They have been pulled into our gravitational field, folded into our immediate environments. Perhaps this is a case of temporal colonization, an alien segment of time being domesticated. But—and this is important to recognize—any domestication we undertake is bound to be limited, limited by the paradox of these texts being ours and not ours, both in and not in our hands.[25]

In that paradox, two things happen. First, because domestication works only up to a certain point, these strange words retain a good part of their strangeness. They are here but they are not completely of the moment. This unyielding, unstoppable strangeness will always be a temporal thorn to the nation-state. The insecurity of its territorial borders is compounded by an even more fundamental insecurity: that of chronology. A year, a decade, a century—these time slots are not ironclad. They are not made like file cabinets. They cannot lock events into a sealed box; they cannot make the world walk in a single file.

Reading, I want to suggest, is a common activity that can have an extraordinary effect on the mapping of time, and on any kind of territorial sovereignty predicated on that mapping. It can generate bonds that deviate from the official timetable, since it is certainly not numerical chronology, not the clock and the calendar, that brings a reader into the orbit of a text, but something much more chancy, which is to say, much less regulated. Literary relations are idiosyncratic relations; they make time idiosyncratic. They bring distant words close to home, give them a meaningfulness that seems local and immediate even though they could not have been so initially, objectively. The distance between readers and the words they read is anything but a number. In this domain, at least, time is made up not of fixed lengths but of lengths variably generated— generated by each reader in the grip of a readerly passion, or, as Roger Chartier says, in "the dialectic between imposition and appropriation, between constraints transgressed and freedoms bridled."[26] There can be no such thing as a numerical now, a synchronic plane enforceable across an entire population.

It is helpful, then, to make a claim on behalf of a mode of time other than the standardized. *Deviation* from the national timetable surely matters as much as synchronization under the sign of the nation. Such deviation challenges not only the sequence of events dictated by a territorial regime, it also challenges the sequence of events dictated by a literary canon. Neither of these official narratives can line everyone up, for the effect of offbeat reading is to generate a temporal bond at odds with the chronological progression of the nation, and at odds with the chronological succession of sanctified texts. What results is a kind of serial unpredictability, the unexpected contact between points of time numerically far apart. Nowhere is this more salient than in the reading and translating of ancient texts: texts written in "dead" languages centuries ago.

LATIN TRANSLATIONS

In the rest of the chapter I explore one such instance of offbeat reading: Lowell's translations from Latin in the 1960s, in the midst of the escalating war in Vietnam and his own antiwar protests. Time is out of joint here, pulled in different directions, torn between different centuries, different locales. It is not one with the nation because it is not one with any synchronic map. Perhaps it is not even one with itself. Rather than being unified by a chronological date, it is energized instead by the tension between two time frames uneasily juxtaposed, at home neither in the American twentieth century nor in the Latin first century.

Lowell's interest in translation is longstanding, and he has many theories about it.[27] In his introduction to *Imitations*—his translation of Homer, Sappho, as well as Villon, Baudelaire, Rilke, and others—Lowell begins with a critique of those translators who aim only for fidelity to the original, who want only to head back to the century in which the text was written. Such people, he says, "seem to live in a pure world untouched by contemporary poetry. Their difficulties are bold and honest, but they are taxidermists, not poets, and their poems are likely to be stuffed birds."[28] Lowell has no desire to be a taxidermist. His principle of translation is very different: "I have been reckless with literal meaning, and labored hard to get the tone. . . . I have tried to write alive English and to do what my authors might have done if they were writing their poems now and in America."[29]

For Lowell, translation means not a rendition of the past in its pastness but the recasting of past words into "alive English," words that are kicking and screaming right at this moment. Bringing the original texts "up to date" and shooting for a contemporary sound, translation is above all a temporal exercise. It plays fast and loose with duration, twisting the numerical chronology into a new script. Two steps, at least, are involved here, something like a double alienation. First, there is a deliberate yoking together of a moment from the present and a moment from the past. On the heels of this, there is also a deliberate wrenching apart, a mutual tearing and mutual dislodging effected by the very act of conjoining. This double alienation produces a "relativity effect." It brings together two segments of time, each plied from its synchronic neighbors, brought within hailing distance of each other, but not allowed to coalesce into a unified now. The temporal structure that results is not expressible as a numerical constant, for not only are there two dates, two chronological numbers uneasily adjacent, they are adjacent in such a way as to yield the maximum friction, a repulsive force equal to the conjunctive one.

Translation in this sense is the art of "learning from those we walk on," as Lowell ambiguously puts it in "Half a Century Gone," a poem about the "mortal coil" behind him, the coil of his own life and that of others. These other people, "Dead now," nonetheless seem undeceased, unsubsided: they keep "rushing out / blackbordered letters like stamps from Turkestan."[30] We learn from these blackbordered letters, but we also "walk on" them, ride roughshod over them, as Lowell elaborates more fully later in the poem:

> We will remember then our tougher roots:
> forerunners hooped to the broiling soil,
> until their backs are branded with the coin
> of Alexander, small hexagonal sores—
> as if they were stretched on burning chicken wire,

skin cooked red and hard as a rusted tin can . . .
held twelve dynasties to a burning-glass
laid by the sanddrifts of Cleopatra—
what were once identities simplified
to a single, indignant, collusive grin.[31]

The act of remembering is analogous to the acts of hooping, broiling, branding, and stretching, endured by those ancestors in their own days, and now inflicted upon them again, by those who recall them in memory. This rough recall is the alternative to taxidermy, the dead preservation of dead forms. It produces not stuffed birds but the "coin of Alexander," currency still good, though it takes the form of "small hexagonal sores," a pain to have on one's back, and further irritated by random forces such as the "sanddrifts of Cleopatra." The violence they bear is the violence that wrings "alive English" out of dead words.

Lowell's Latin translations are especially interesting in this light, for no language is more dead, and yet no language is more vitally "hoopable" and stretchable in its coils. Unlike English, a language whose meaning is determined by its word order, Latin, a language based on inflection, is much freer, deriving its meaning not from word placement but from word endings. Words can go anywhere in a Latin sentence: the word order is infinitely more flexible and variable. Lowell's own poetic lines reflect his debt to that language (he had majored in Classics in college). And, of the Latin poets, it is probably Horace who is the greatest inspiration: Horace, who shares with Lowell the same precipitate movement from the public to the private, expecting the reader to know both and to put up with the jumps back and forth, from an encyclopedic history to a small packed detail.[32]

And yet, as Stephen Yenser points out, Lowell's translations of Horace in *Near the Ocean* (1967) are surprisingly inexact, often altering the sense of the original in a deliberate act of rewriting.[33] In "Cleopatra," for instance, Horace had written: "*dum Capitolio / regina dementis ruinas, / funus et imperio parabat.*"[34] The queen is plotting mad ruin for the Capitol and death to the Empire. Lowell changes this straightforward statement into something more reflexive and sinister, revising the relation between *ruinas* and *Capitolio*, so that ruin becomes not something inflicted upon the Capitol, but something growing from within. In his rendition, Cleopatra "plotted / to enthrone her ruin in the Capitol." Self-destruction is the organic form of the Empire. What reigns in the Capitol is ruin itself.

Lowell is probably thinking not just of the Roman Capitol, for ruin seems also to be enthroned in another Capitol, a modern one. The link between these two does indeed turn Horace's ode into a poem written "now and in America": the United States has more than a hand "translating" it. And yet the poem is not completely American either. The meeting of Latin verse and contemporary politics produces a twisted thread, uncoiling sometimes in one direction and sometimes in the other. It is not assignable to neither pole. It cannot be designated by a serial number.

CALIGULA

This breakdown of seriality animates not only Lowell's Latin translations, but also his poems invoking Roman history. I focus on one, "Caligula."[35] Caligula is Lowell's namesake. Ever since his schooldays at St. Mark's he had called himself "Cal," after the notorious Roman tyrant, translating that name into his own person, so to speak.[36] The poem "Caligula" was probably written around 1962 or 1963. The first version of it was published in the fall of 1964 in *For the Union Dead*:

> My namesake, Little Boots, Caligula,
> you disappoint me. Tell me what I saw
> to make me like you when we met at school?
> I took your name—poor odd-ball, poor spoiled fool. . . .
> Your true face sneers at me, mean, thin, agonized. . . .
> I live your last night. Sleepless fugitive,
> your purple bedclothes and imperial eagle
> grow so familiar they are home. Your regal
> hand accepts my hand. You bend my wrist,
> and tear the tendons with your strangler's twist.[37]

For Lowell, the Roman Empire is very much a contemporary phenomenon. Caligula is his classmate, they "met at school," the Roman Emperor's palace is "home" to the American poet. The two are wedded to each other at this moment. But, before we get too sentimental about this, Lowell is careful to remind us who Caligula is. The Roman face is a sneering face. The Roman hand extended to meet his is a hand that mangles and lacerates: "You bend my wrist,/and tear the tendons with your strangler's twist." Caligula is here, he is on the run, a "fugitive" in the twentieth century, but this hardly tames his malice, his fury, his unexplained but also unrelenting desire to harm his American offspring.

The possibility of being harmed—of having one's tendons torn and twisted—suggests that something odd has happened to the 1900 years supposedly separating the first-century emperor and the twentieth-century poet. That numerical distance has shrunk to nothing. Helen Vendler, struck by Lowell's habit of "keep[ing] ancient and contemporary history before him in one steroptical view," argues that it stems from a "contemptuous indifference," a "mortmain equalizing of any event to any other event."[38] This may be. I want to call attention, however, to the tremendous repulsive force generated by this contact, a force that both couples and decouples the emperor and the poet. The hands of these two are not exactly fused in unison. Far from being domesticated, Caligula remains a Roman tyrant, angry, evil-minded, mutilating the very hand that has brought him back to life. This tyrant is ungrateful, unassimilable. The fit between Roman history and Lowell's personal history is less than perfect—and that is probably the point. Caligula might be in the United States, but he remains a nonresident alien. That nonresidency dooms any attempt to translate him, though this does not, of course, stop Lowell from trying. For it is only by this attempted translation that the poet can give himself a name, even though, as he himself knows too well, it is a name that keeps lashing out at him, keeps trying to cut him up.

The two drafts of "Caligula" are instructive. In the first version of the poem, published in 1964 in *For the Union Dead*, Lowell ends with the line: "my namesake, and the last Caligula."[39] Five years later, in the much abbreviated version in *Notebook* (1970), this last line has been changed to its exact opposite: "my namesake, *not* the last Caligula" (my emphasis).[40] The name, then, has no terminal point. It is the name of a Roman emperor, it is the name of an American poet, and no doubt it is the name of someone else just around the corner. It is these endlessly enacted and endlessly incomplete translations that make Rome both far and near, both ancient history and not ancient history.

And indeed, Rome is both far and near for others beside Lowell. In the 1960s, the United States as a nation, flaunting its might as champion of the Free World, would seem to be ventriloquizing Rome, a "ghost" of the ancient empire, repeating its excesses as well as its horrors. No one was more aware of this than Lowell—deeply opposed to the war in Vietnam and deeply convinced, as well, that this destructive course was not national but planetary in scope:

> Pity the planet, all joy gone
> from this sweet volcanic cone;
> peace to our children when they fall
> in small war on the heels of small
> war—until the end of time
> to police the earth, a ghost
> orbiting forever lost
> in our monotonous sublime.[41]

This is Lowell's "Waking Early Sunday Morning," one of the best known political poems of the 1960s: "political," in the sense that it is haunted by the nation as by a "ghost," but not so haunted that it cannot see beyond—to the wreckage brought upon the whole world. *Peace*, an American word now, also has a peculiarly American meaning. It is what one succumbs to when one becomes another statistic in the endless cycles of violence, so endless as to be sublime.

The poem was written during the summer of 1965,[42] though it was hardly Lowell's sole preoccupation that summer. Indeed, those were feverish months for him, a political maelstrom clearly gathering on the horizon. Earlier that year, in February, American planes had extended their bombing from South Vietnam to North Vietnam. In March, the first U.S. combat troops—two battalions of marines—arrived in Danang. By April, antiwar demonstrations had spread across the nation, from Washington to many college campuses.[43] It was in this explosive climate that Johnson announced a White House of the Arts, to be held on June 14. Lowell was invited, initially accepted, but almost immediately changed his mind. His letter to Johnson was published in the front page of the *New York Times*, immediately stirring others to action. A telegram supporting Lowell was sent to the president, carrying the signatures of the nation's most prominent artists and intellectuals. The *New York Times* headlined this as well: "Twenty writers and artists Endorse Poet's Rebuff of President." The signatories were Hannah Arendt, John Berryman, Alan Dugan, Jules Feiffer, Philip Guston, Lillian Hellman, Alfred Kazin, Stanley Kunitz, Dwight Macdonald, Bernard Malamud, Mary McCarthy, Larry Rivers, Philip Roth, Mark Rothko, Louis Simpson, W. D. Snodgrass, William Styron, Peter Taylor, Edgar Varere, and Robert Penn Warren.[44] It was one of the most memorable public embarrassments for Johnson, a minor incident that spun completely out of control. Here is Lowell's letter:[45]

> Although I am very enthusiastic about most of your domestic legislation and intentions, I nevertheless can only follow our present foreign policy with the greatest dismay and distrust. What we will do and what we ought to do as a sovereign nation facing other sovereign nations seem now to hang in the balance between the better and the worse possibilities. . . . At this anguished, delicate and perhaps determining moment, I feel I am serving you and our country by not taking part in the White House Festival of the Arts.[46]

Lowell had no quarrel with Johnson's domestic policy, his "Great Society" program. He did have a quarrel with Johnson's foreign policy: the escalating use of force in Vietnam, the shotgun time frame of military action. The United States, as a nation at war, would like to have all its citizens marching in the same direction, to the rhythm of national chronology. But some citizens were obviously, dangerously, out of step.

Turning Back the Clock

Lowell dramatizes this rupture by creating a poetic form also deliberately contrarian, not always on the same emotional (or chronological) page even with itself. "Waking Early Sunday Morning" moves toward a vision of the world that has grown all too current, all too familiar: "Wars / flicker, earth licks its open sores, / fresh breakage, fresh promotions, chance / assassinations, no advance."[47] Its beginning, however, seems to be on a different plane altogether, luxuriating in a sense of freedom, oddly resistant to its predestined end:

> O to break loose, like the chinook
> salmon jumping and falling back,
> nosing up to the impossible
> stone and bone-crushing waterfall—
> raw-jawed, weak-fleshed there, stopped by ten
> steps of the roaring ladder, and then
> to clear the top on the last try,
> alive enough to spawn and die.[48]

The salmon does die, and encounters the bone-crushing waterfall in the fullness of that knowledge. And yet this foreordained end in no way detracts from the exhilaration of the journey upstream. It is as if the knowledge of death did not matter, as if the emotional uncertainty of whether one would be able "to clear the top on the last try" could actually outweigh the biological certainty that this achievement would in time be obliterated. This contrapuntal rhythm is captured in the metrical form of the poem itself. The off rhymes, the spondees, the enjambments—between "chinook" and "salmon," between "impossible" and "stone," between "ten" and "steps"—generate a sense of suspense, a length of time stretching indefinitely between the beginning and the end, an "aural analogue" to the still rushing, still unfolding life of the salmon.[49] That indeterminate length of time turns back the clock, so to speak, as if each and every salmon were trying for the first time, as if each individual instance were an entirely new instance. This newness will not vanish even when the end comes, for if that end is part of an eternal process, so too is the newness that precedes it. At the end of "The Ruins of Time," the last poem in Near the Ocean, Lowell seems to echo "Waking Early Sunday Morning," the opening poem of the volume:

> Animal
> despoiled of reason, each ascending sun
> dives like a cooling meteorite to its fall.

Do Rome and Carthage know what we deny?
Death only throws fixed dice, and yet we raise
the ante, and stake our lives on every toss.
The hours will hardly pardon us their loss,
those brilliant hours that wore away our days,
our days that ate into eternity.[50]

The arc running between the ascending sun and the cooling meteorite
gives the salmon its brief run upstream. It also gives us our brief run to
do what we will. In the end, we don't exactly know what that run
amounts to, how long our hours will be when we last, and how long
they will be when we are gone. For these hours do fold into eternity, and
are variously stretched, variously lengthened or shortened, by that folding. Even though our days are numbered, what *that* means is not entirely
clear either. It is certainly more complicated than mere seriality. And
nothing better dramatizes this nonserial time than the fact that Rome
and Carthage are still in our midst. "Do Rome and Carthage know what
we deny?"

It appears that they do. What Rome and Carthage know, and what we
are bent on denying, is the course of empire and the ruin organic to it,
enthroned in the Capitol. It is a fixed run, and yet it is no more fixed than
the run that yearly awaits the salmon. To resurrect Rome and Carthage,
and to put them in the midst of this yearly voyage, is to grant to these
empires—and to human beings who live under them—the freedom both
of a fixed script and of an endlessly extended reproductive cycle. It *is* a
relief to say that Lowell is a second Caligula, just as it is a relief to say
that America is a second Rome. "You search in Rome for Rome? O
Traveller! / in Rome itself, there is no room for Rome."[51] There is no
Rome in Rome because Rome is now in America, a far grander setting.
To see things in this light is no doubt to turn back the clock, to project
the American twentieth century into an un-American deep time. It is
Lowell's style of politics.

"I have never been New Left, Old Left, or liberal," he says in his acid
exchange with Diana Trilling. "I wish to turn the clock back with every
breath I draw, but I hope I have the courage to occasionally cry out
against those who wrongly rule us."[52] Turning back the clock is one
form of antiwar protest, perhaps the only one Lowell can bear. "The
theme that connects my translations is Rome, the greatness and horror
of her Empire," he says in his note to *Near the Ocean*. And he disingen-
uously adds, "How one jumps from Rome to the America of my own
poems is something of a mystery to me."[53] *Near the Ocean* came out in
1967, the same year that Lowell took part in the march on the Pentagon.
Jumping from Rome to America, it produces bits of Roman history writ-

ten over by Vietnam. Lowell needs these—needs the relativity effect they generate—in order to keep his clock turned back. He needs the tenth satire of Juvenal, "The Vanity of Human Wishes," in order to put himself, however briefly, outside the national timetable:

> And yet the boy will never be a man.
> Some prodigal seducer will seduce
> the parents—money never fails its giver.
> No overweight tyrant castrates the deformed.
> Trust Nero, Nero had an eye for beauty:
> he never picked a spastic or a lout.[54]

Lowell is translating Roman history, talking about the fate of young boys under the reign of Nero, who never reach manhood. But of course he is talking about something else as well: the fate of young boys who live under the draft, who never reach manhood either, since the draft, too, has a peculiar way of cutting short the lives of the handpicked. Nero, in this sense, is not the last Nero either.[55] Like Caligula, he too has a long afterlife, a ghostly hand extended murderously into the twentieth century.

But to recall Nero, his roving eye, his "overweight" body, in turn exposed to our eye, is to be struck by the difference between what this namable Roman tyrant can do and what can be done by his modern counterpart, without a name, without a body, and not called a tyrant at all. The yoking together of ancient and modern history once again generates a repulsive force, a double alienation, a sundering of these historical moments each from the other, and each from its own synchronic plane. To experience the Vietnam War inflected through the history of the Roman Empire is to be jolted out of any secure temporal mooring. It is to see the Latin first century in our midst: summoned, brought forward, but not domesticated, not unified by a serial number. What then, does the year 1965 mean for Lowell? This was the year in which he refused to take part in the White House Festival of the Arts. It was the year in which he wrote "Waking Early Sunday Morning." And it was also a year that was both near and far from the year 65, when Nero was concluding his run as Roman emperor and getting ready to move on, or so it seems, winding up in the United States, becoming a nonresident alien in the midst of the Vietnam War. 65, 1965—what exactly is the distance between these two dates? No one can say for sure. All we know is that it is nonstandard time. Not quantified by chronology, not quantified by serial numbers, it gives literature an analytic domain the full significance of which we have yet to explore.

CHAPTER SEVEN

African, Caribbean, American:
Black English as Creole Tongue

IS AFRICAN-AMERICAN LITERATURE national or is it diasporic? Just how important is the first half of that hyphenated word? Does "African" reside solely in the pigment of the skin, or is it more active than that, more complexly present, working its way into ritual and music, into the very words one uses and the grammar that strings those words together? Is there a research program embedded in the word "African," and if so, how does it square with the geography and chronology of the United States?

The "practice of diaspora" is emerging as a pivotal question in African-American literature.[1] In this chapter I explore it as a linguistic force—articulated in the vernacular rather in formal speech—and bearing witness to the global migration of tongues, the mixing of syntax and phonemes across continents. It is this global migration that makes African-American literature an exemplary paradigm not only for the broad contours of literature, but also for the outlines of a new human science, a creole anthropology, with intercontinental pathways threaded into nonstandard speech.

NATIONAL ANTHROPOLOGY

Since the diasporic has not been always accepted, it is worth recalling an earlier form of human science, more rigidly bounded, based on the analytic adequacy of the nation. According to this model, the "African-American" is no more than a *subset* of the "American." A bilateral entity turns out to be unilateral after all: two continents add up to one. "African," on this view, is dead on arrival; only a visual marker remains. Had it not been for their physical appearance, African-Americans would have vanished without a trace into the melting pot. They have no backward extension that might complicate that process, nothing prior to the Middle Passage carried over as a lasting tie. Their hyphenated state is skin deep: it makes no intellectual demands upon us, it never changes the temporal and spatial coordinates of the United States.

This was the premise of many sociologists and anthropologists writing in the early-twentieth century. R. E. Park spoke for a consensus when he wrote: "My own impression is that the amount of African tradition which the Negro brought to the United States was very small. In fact, there is every reason to believe, it seems to me, that the Negro, when he landed in the United States, left behind him almost everything but his dark complexion and his tropical temperament."[2] E. Franklin Fraizer turned this impression into a programmatic statement: "Probably never before in history has a people been so nearly completely stripped of its social heritage as the Negroes who were brought to America. . . . [O]f the habits and customs as well as the hopes and fears that characterized the life of their forebears in Africa, nothing remains."[3]

ABIDING TRACES

Linguists were the first to cast doubt on this presumed "nothingness" of the African past. Traces *do* remain, they argue, to be found (not surprisingly) in language, a medium intertwined with human history and bearing witness to its long life through the evolution and migration of words. In a paper presented at the annual Modern Language Association meeting in 1938, entitled "Western African Survivals in the Vocabulary of Gullah," Lorenzo Dow Turner from Fisk University offered an extensive catalog of such words, making survival rather than erasure the key term in the movement of languages from Africa to America. Subsequently expanded into his groundbreaking book, *Africanisms in the Gullah Dialect* (1949), this emphasis on survival opens up a new way to think about input from the past, the routes it travels, the housing it receives on the way, and the scale on which all of these are to be investigated. The planet emerges here as a single unit of analysis, for these exogenous words suggest that the world is "rhizomatic" (to take a word from Gilles Deleuze and Felix Guattari),[4] with many levels of grafting and mixing, generating linguistic kinships across vast distances and across the Western/non-Western divide. For the first time, it is possible to think of the black vernacular as a *creole* form, of tangled parentage and laterally reproduced, a significant departure from standard English.

Lorenzo Turner focuses on Gullah, a dialect spoken by the predominantly black populations on the Sea Islands off the coasts of Georgia and South Carolina. He argues that the ties between these regions and Africa were vital and dynamic well into the second half of the nineteenth century, a contention borne out by subsequent studies.[5] Slaves were brought to the Sea Islands throughout the eighteenth century; a conservative estimate gives the number at 100,000. This direct importation was officially banned by the Slave Trade Act of 1808, but an illegal traffic persisted. As

late as 1858, the slave ship *Wanderer* brought approximately 420 slaves
to the Georgia coast.[6]

This continued traffic meant that the influx of African languages continued well into the mid-nineteenth century. And, even after it came to
an end, residual (and increasingly creolized) forms of these languages
continued to flourish in areas with predominantly black populations, as
on the Sea Islands. According to Turner, "Africanisms" can be detected
in all aspects of the spoken tongue. In its phonology and, above all, in its
vocabulary—in its personal names, its forms of abbreviation and forms
of colloquialism—Gullah bears witness to a genesis not strictly Indo-
European. Languages from the West Coast of Africa—Wolof, Malinke,
Mandinka, Bambara, Fula, Mende, Vai, Twi, Fante, Ga, Ewe, Fon,
Yoruba, Bini, Hausa, Ibo, Ibibio, Efik, Kongo, Umbundu, Kimbundu—
all left documentable traces.[7] Two thirds of *Africanisms in the Gullah
Dialect* (188 pages) comprise a list of words derived from these West
African tongues.

Lorenzo Turner, writing as a linguist, understandably focuses on language as primary evidence. The anthropologist Melville J. Herskovits,
writing around the same time, proposes a larger domain of analysis.
The survival of Africanisms becomes a general paradigm for studying
every aspect of culture: not just the spoken tongue but also material objects, secular and religious practices, and the mental universes that underwrite their operations. All of these, according to Herskovits—in
effect the sum total of African-American life—can be adequately studied only when the adjective "African" is given as much as weight as the
adjective "American." What is called for, in short, is not only a prehistory but also something like a "pregeography." These take Americanists
far beyond the borders of the United States, to archives encompassing
the entire hemisphere: "firsthand field study of New World Negroes in
Dutch Guinea, in Trinidad," as well as in "countries of South America."[8] This two-Americas approach would, in turn, benefit from research
done on the other side of the Atlantic: "in Nigeria, the Gold Coast, and
more especially in Dahomey [where] it has been possible to study at first
hand the important ancestral civilizations."[9]

CREOLIZATION

This is what it means to give equal weight to both sides of the hyphen.
The prehistories and pregeographies that come into play generate a
broad kinship network, a "family," though not in any traditional sense.
This family is born not of the nearness of blood but of an alchemical
overcoming of distance; it multiplies not by linear descent but by the

circuitousness of shipping routes. Kinship is anything but straightforward here. It is oblique, centrifugal, laterally extended, taking the form of arcs, loops, curves of various sorts: complex paths of temporal and spatial displacement. Nonadjacency is the unexpected ground for kinship. Cross-fertilizing takes place when far-flung arcs meet at distant points.

Since this is the case, since it is these far-flung arcs that integrate the globe, that turn distant populations into distant cousins, we might want to rethink the meaning of "ancestry" itself. Rather than being land-based, patrilineal, and clannish, it is here oceanic, flotational, a large-scale and largely exogenous process of "drifting." The dynamics between the global and the local play out in such a way as to make the genetic ground itself a synthetic medium, for the "local" is not so much an indigenous given as the "nativizing" of the global within one particular site: a sequence of diffusion, osmosis, and reabsorption. Ancestry here has less to do with origins than with processes. Transmutation rather than transmission is its lifeblood.

Borrowing a term from linguists, we might speak of this oceanic process as a *creolizing* process, taking the term to describe the dynamics and consequences of cultural contact, and taking it to designate, furthermore, a primary (rather than incidental) order of phenomena. Robert Hall, in his classic study, *Pidgin and Creole Languages* (1966), distinguishes between two "contact languages," two hybrid forms born of the meeting between linguistic groups. A *pidgin* arises when the grammar and vocabulary of a natural language are drastically reduced to facilitate communication; it is a pared-down language, minimalist in its functions, used sporadically and superficially, mostly for the purposes of trade. It expressive capability is therefore limited, not adequate to the needs of any speech community, a mother tongue to no one on earth. A *creole*, on the other hand (from the Portuguese *crioulo* and the Spanish *criollo*, "native," subsequently morphing into the French *créole*), comes into being when a pidgin evolves into an autonomous tongue, with a fully developed grammar, and an ample lexicon to match. As the mother tongue for an entire speech community, it is "native" in every sense.[10]

Putting pidgins and creoles at center stage, Hall argues that these two can no longer be dismissed as crude, debased, or marginal. "[D]espite their humble social status," he says, they "must be given their rightful standing as the equals of other languages."[11] A study of these "corrupt" languages has major implications for the discipline of linguistics, for while the birth of most languages took place in the primordial past, forever unrecoverable, pidgins and creoles are recent developments, with data readily available. They are the testing ground for any genetic account of language, any theory that purports to explain how and why human beings came to speak the way they do. Furthermore, since at least two languages come into play in the making of a creole, with one serving as the "lexifier"—the host language supplying the bulk of the words in use—the question inevitably arises as to the fate of the other tongue. That one, though gradually phased out and sidelined, would nonetheless seem to have left traces of itself. Where do these traces persist? In what manner and on which level of the linguistic structure? Do they make up a "substratum" lurking beneath the surface features of the host language? Hall summaries the debate:

> One of the major problems under discussion in linguistics, for over a century, has been that of the nature and extent of substratum influence. The problem is substantially this: is it possible that a given language, when it is abandoned by its speakers in favor of a new language (as when speakers of Celtic abandoned that language for Latin in Roman Gaul) can leave traces in the new language? If the answer is affirmative, three further questions arise: (1) In what aspects of linguistic structure can substratum influence be manifest? (2) By what mechanisms are substratum features carried over into the language that replaces the earlier substratum, as Latin replaced Gaulish? (3) In what cases should we ascribe a given linguistic change to the effects of a presumed substratum? That a language can preserve traces, often numerous traces, of a previously spoken substratum in its vocabulary, is now admitted by everyone: for example, French *alouette* "lark" <Celtic *alauda*; Spanish *vega* "flat lowland" <Iberian *baika*. Concerning other levels of linguistic structure, however, there has been extensive debate. Some linguists are disposed to admit the possibility of substratum on all levels—phonological, morphological, and syntactic as well as lexical; others deny it completely.[12]

Though Hall is specifically interested in the creolization of African tongues in the New World, it soon becomes clear that "creolization" is a paradigm that touches on virtually all languages, in all historical periods. The relations between Latin and Gaulish, between French and Celtic, between Spanish and Iberian all come under this rubric. It is the most encompassing paradigm possible. It demonstrates in no uncertain terms that a history of languages is a history of global migrating, adapting, recombining. Whether or not they admit to it, most languages are creoles. They have a durational existence—and a traceable path—largely because of this long-standing, ongoing, and never-ending synthesis. The survival of a Wolof or a Fon "substratum" through standard English and into the black vernacular is analogous to the survival of a Celtic substratum through Latin and into French; the survival of an Iberian substratum through Latin and into Spanish; and (most salient example of all), the survival of an Anglo-Saxon substratum through Latin and

French and into modern English. These European and non-European languages are kin not because they stem from the same origins, but because each of them went through an analogous process of compounding: being uprooted, meandering, followed by reentry and relexification, a dialectic of endings and beginnings.

LINGUA FRANCA

The whole of linguistics can be studied under this rubric. The recent work on creolization is thus a belated tribute to the German scholar Hugo Schuchardt (1842–1927), most prescient of linguists, the first of international stature to put pidgins and creoles at the center of linguistics. Writing in the 1880s, Schuchardt brought with him knowledge of three language groups: Indo-European (in which he was trained); Hamitic (a group of African languages comprising ancient Egyptian as well as several tongues still extant, such as Berber and Cushitic, in turn related to Semitic languages such as Arabic); and Finno-Ugric (such as Hungarian).[13] Out of this knowledge of languages spoken on four continents, Schuchardt was able to single out pidgins and creoles as key players in linguistics. These were "slave languages," he pointed out. As the speech of the unfree, those who had an imperfect command of words as of their own bodies, these were humble concoctions indeed. Still, they must be linked to a larger class of phenomena, namely, the "lingua franca," for they shared with the latter an involuntary genesis: "Necessity is the sculptor of such languages, which we therefore term 'necessity languages.'"[14]

By "necessity," Schuchardt had in mind the need of the slave owners to communicate with their slaves, who often had only a rudimentary knowledge of English. He had in mind as well the linguistic gulf among the slaves themselves. Due to the multitude of tongues in Africa (prevalent even in small areas, such as Western Nigeria, from which most of the slaves were taken), those from neighboring villages often could not converse. Some lingua franca was needed, some slave *koine*, in order to convey even the most basic information. This language, hastily cobbled together, was in this case compounded of European and African languages. But Schuchardt cautioned against seeing these as fixed ingredients, for, as the very name *lingua franca* suggests, this improvised tongue was initially the product of a different linguistic environment; it was medieval and Mediterranean before it was modern and Atlantic. It first came into being as a mix of Indo-European and Arabic languages, and there is no reason why its future incarnations should not involve still other ingredients:

Lingua Franca is the communicative language formed of a Romance lexicon that arose in the Middle Ages between Romans and Arabs and subsequently Turks. . . . The Arabs termed the language of the Europeans with whom they came into contact the language of the Franks, *lisan al-farandz* (al-afrandz), or Frankish, as the Romans were called. . . . [W]e ought not therefore seek the essence of a creole in a connection between European lexicon and African or Asiatic grammar; it would be just as incorrect to say that Lingua Franca is Romance with Arabic or Turkish grammar. As speech mixture always presupposes bilingualism, it will more readily occur and further extend itself the further bilingualism is extended—that is, by broader contact between two speech communities, intimate connection between two peoples.[15]

Rather than seeing the creole form as the descendant of specific languages, Schuchardt sees it instead as a structural property of bilingualism itself: a bilingualism that, he hoped, would spread across the planet, becoming the general condition of cultural contact, the basic requirement of an educated person.[16] Anticipating in reverse the current talk about the "clash of civilizations,"[17] Schuchardt sees instead a merging of civilizations, an expanding web of words, populating the world with linguistic first and second cousins. Just to cite one example, "for ghost (i.e. departed soul, spectre, spook), we have Sranan Black English *djombi*, Trinidadian Creole French *zombi*, Santhomian Creole Dutch *ziumbi-kawai*, 'ghost horse', cf. Oldendorp (1777:117), from Mbundu (Angola) *nzumbi*, 'the peaceful spirit of a departed soul', cf. Congolese *zumbi* 'luck-bearing fetish'; Jamaican Creole *duppe*, from *dobbo* in Ewe, according to Oldenburg (1777:336), 'evil, disease-producing spirits.' "[18] Linguistic cross-fertilization is the ground of the world's oneness. These loops and clumps of words—sometimes parallel, sometimes not, but always interconnected in their mediating forms—suggest that a "family" is not just a metaphor.

PRIMACY OF SYNTAX

In chapter 4, I discussed this family as a tangle of resemblance and recoil, leading to a "fractal" kinship among literary genres. In this chapter I ask whether language itself might not benefit from this fractal analysis. What are the stakes in thinking of American dialects as creole tongues, and restoring them as such—to a coil of relations stretching across the Mediterranean, across the Atlantic? What difference does it make to think of black English, in particular, as being dotted by clumps of African languages? And, if its seemingly ungrammatical features are indeed traceable to such diasporic loops, how would that affect its pragmatic status: as legal and political instrument, educational vehicle, and medium for creative expression?

Robert Hall ends *Pidgin and Creole Languages* with a plea on behalf of such vernaculars. Focusing on Haiti, he expresses the hope that one day "Creole would be admitted on parity with French in the formal activities of the government, in Parliament, in newspapers, in the law courts . . . [and] in education."[19] The same argument for parity could, of course, be made on behalf of nonstandard speech in the United States. Should black English be seen as an ungrammatical deviation from standard English, or should it be recognized as a *coherent* departure, a law-abiding phenomenon unto itself, with a grammar of its own and a claim to political, cultural, and educational legitimacy? In a series of influential talks and essays published in the late 1960s and early 1970s, William A. Stewart made a forceful case for the latter. "It is pedagogically important," he said, "to know whether or not the majority of American Negroes make up one or more cohesive sociolinguistic speech communities and, if so, what the specific nature of these communities is."[20] Does black English have the autonomy of a linguistic subset? If so, what underwrites that autonomy: the geographical clustering of the black population, the effect of socioeconomic class, or some cognitive attribute of ethnicity?

Comparative work is needed to address these questions—a four-prong analysis, according to Stewart. In order to determine the degree of integrity of black English, it must be examined not only against standard English but also against two other vernacular forms: on the one hand, nonstandard white dialects, and, on the other hand, creole tongues elsewhere in the world with clearly established ties to Africa. This four-prong analysis will not be easy. Where does the fundamental kinship (or fundamental difference) lie, on which level of the linguistic structure? Is the primary evidence to be found in the lexicon, the system of words; in the phonology, the system of sounds; in the morphology, the derivational and inflectional rules governing nouns, verbs, and pronouns; or in the syntax, the grammatical structure of the sentence? Stewart summarizes the difficulty:

One further reason why both language teachers and dialectologists have failed to appreciate the extent to which non-standard Negro dialects may differ from non-standard white dialects (even in the Deep South) may simply be that such differences now remain mostly in syntax (i.e. grammatical patterns and categories) rather than in vocabulary or lexico-phonology (i.e. word forms), and are thus not normally uncovered by the word-comparison techniques which dialectologists and non-linguists rely on so heavily.[21]

Written in 1968, this cautionary note came at the heels of a major upheaval in modern linguistics, one that transformed the very aims and procedures of the discipline. Spearheaded by Noam Chomsky's *Syntactic Structures* (1956) and *Aspects of the Theory of Syntax* (1965), this new linguistics sets aside its traditional emphasis on taxonomy, on the cataloging of phonetic or lexical phenomena, and turns instead to a study of deep structure, a subterranean "generative grammar." This grammar, lying beneath the surface features of words, manifests itself as a set of syntactical rules, a logic that defines the relations among categories of words, making it possible for words from the same category to be substituted for one another. The number of sentences generated is infinite. Every human being can make up such sentences, and every human population has an endless supply of them. Chomsky thus puts syntax at the center of human cognition. According to him, it is syntax that allows the human mind to use words at all; it is syntax that is universal to our species.

Armed with this insight, Stewart comes up with an analytic paradigm that, while clearly indebted to Chomsky, also parts company with him in important ways. Setting aside Chomsky's ambitious use of the generative grammar to establish the *identity* of syntax in all languages, he tries to prove only the *kinship* among languages that are not obviously connected. As with Chomsky, the logical relation among categories of words is key. This is the analytic focus. And this in turn points to an evidentiary domain that is buried rather than in plain view, an object of deduction rather than an object of cataloging. Stewart thus focuses not on the "lexico-phonology"—the words and sounds residing on the surface—but on the underlying logic that gives rise to the structure of the sentence. It is on this linguistic level that he conducts his four-prong analysis, comparing four versions of a simple conjunctive sentence: in standard English (STE), in southern white nonstandard basilect (WNS), in Negro nonstandard basilect (NNS), and in Gullah Basilect (GUL):

STE: We were eating—and drinking, too.
WNS: We was eatin'—an' drinkin', too.
NNS: We was eatin'—an' we drinkin', too.
GUL: We bin duh nyam—en' we duh drink, too.

If one were to look simply at the individual words, NNS (Negro nonstandard English) would seem to be virtually identical to WNS (white nonstandard English). These individual words do not tell the full story, however, for the syntax, the underlying logic of the sentence, points to a very different set of relations, not discernible simply by cataloging words or simply by looking at the surface data. It is worth quoting Stewart at length:

> [A] comparison of the sentence structure of these dialects shows a somewhat different kind of relationship. In the foregoing equivalent sentence, this is evident in the treatment of the subject pronoun and the tense-marking auxiliary (or copula). For, although STE, WNS, NNS, and GUL can all repeat the subject pronoun and auxiliary in a conjunctive clause (e.g. STE "We were eating—and we were drinking, too"), this is not generally done in any of them. Instead, one or both will usually be omitted (provided, of course, that the subject and temporal referents remain the same). But in terms of what they omit, these dialects split along lines which are different from those indicated by word-form similarities and differences. Both STE and WNS normally omit both the subject and the auxiliary in a conjunctive clause, although the tense-marking auxiliary must be present if the subject is not omitted. But NNS, like GUL, often repeats the subject pronoun in a conjunctive clause while omitting the auxiliary—even when this indicates past tense. . . .
>
> If, in such features as the omission of a redundant auxiliary (while retaining the redundant subject pronoun) Gullah and other non-standard Negro dialects part company with standard English and non-standard white dialects (of both America and Great Britain), they do have counterparts in a number of pidgin and creole forms of English, which, though used far from the shores of the United States and in widely separated places, are all the legacy of the African slave trade. To illustrate how much these forms of English resemble Gullah and other non-standard Negro dialects with respect to auxiliary omission, the same equivalent sentences are given in Jamaican Creole (JMC); Sranan, the creole English of Surinam in South America (SRA); and West African Pidgin English (WAP):
>
> JMC: We ben a nyam—an' we a drink, too.
> SRA: We ben de nyang—en' we de dringie, too.
> WAP: We bin de eat—an' we de dring, too.
>
> In addition to the grammatical correspondences, the word-form similarities of these languages with Gullah will be apparent.[22]

West Africa, South America, the Caribbean, North America: this is what it takes to contextualize black English, for this American dialect has cousins on distant shores. Put in their midst, it regains its grammaticalness, its membership in a law-abiding family, for its seemingly aberrant syntax is in fact the norm in many languages, lexified as a creole continuum by Portuguese, Spanish, Dutch, French, as well as English. This continuum requires a world atlas to become legible. It urges upon us a research program of equal breadth.

What would the humanities look like if we were to embrace this research program, taking seriously the extension and duration of that word, "human"? Nation-based models would have to be modified, then. No longer a given, they would have to be tested by an empiricism committed to data gathering, and not deciding, ahead of time, that all the necessary data can be found within the borders of one jurisdiction. If such an empiricism were to prevail, a careful study of the world's languages would become our first order of business. Any history of the English language, in particular, must take into account the broad circumference of pidgin and creole forms. This is the circumference as well for Americanists. For, as dramatized by black English, it is worth making the effort, even when we are dealing with a seemingly American phenomenon, to go beyond the evidence supplied by a single nation, beyond a methodology that isolates a part and fancies it to be the whole.

Deleted Copula and Negative Concord

A linguistics based on syntax demands the whole, and tentatively offers it in the form of a deep structure, a cognitive foundation that can be predicated of every human being on the globe. "Globalism" of this sort is sufficiently at odds with current models to be worth exploring. Its local implications, meanwhile, are also explosive. For if syntax is the underlying logic of the sentence, if it marks the crossover point between cognitive function and linguistic usage, it seems reasonable to assume (and Chomsky has made it his central contention) that it is the same in *all* languages. Standard English does not have a monopoly here. Nonstandard dialects have sentences that are equally grammatical, and equally well formed. How, then, can we justify our usual view of these dialects as illiterate, a sign of educational (and perhaps even cognitive) deficit, to be corrected wherever they appear? For Stewart, this is a benighted view. Black English, he argues, deviates from standard English not because it has no grammar but because it has a prior history, bearing the "structural traces of a creole predecessor."[23] Acknowledging this creole predecessor restores the dialect to its rightful place. It changes the protocol of education itself:

> For the teacher, this means that such "Negro" patterns as the "zero copula," the "zero possessive," or "undifferentiated pronouns" should

not be ascribed to greater carelessness, laziness or stupidity on the part of Negroes, but rather should be treated as what they really are—language patterns which have been in existence for generations and which their present users have acquired, from parent and peer, through a perfectly normal kind of language-learning process.[24]

Does black English have a grammar of its own? Are its nonstandard features equally logical, but logical by a different route and a different set of rules? Can it claim cognitive parity with standard English, not to say political, artistic, and pedagogic legitimacy?

This is the challenge taken up by William Labov in his now classic study, *Language in the Inner City* (1972).[25] A veteran researcher in the field, funded in 1965 by the Office of Education in light of pedagogic failures in the New York City schools, Labov and his team conducted a series of taped sessions in south-central Harlem with teenage gangs—the Jets, the Cobras, and the Thunderbirds—to explore the nature of the language they spoke. The book tackles some explosive issues ("Is the Black English Vernacular a Separate System?" and "The Logic of Nonstandard English"), but there are highly technical chapters as well, devoted to the "Contraction, Deletion, and Inherent Variability of the English Copula" and "Negative Attraction and Negative Accord."

These chapters (difficult for humanists) are not just cerebral exercises. For the technicality here is entirely in the spirit of Chomsky, arguing for the grammaticalness of all spoken tongues. This is not so easily done. How does one go about proving that the following is a grammatical sentence: "He a friend"? This is a classic example of the deleted copula. The word *is* is deleted here, the present tense of the auxiliary *be*. A sentence without a verb, it seems a clear violation of a cardinal rule of English grammar.

Labov shows, however, that there are other rules at work, nonstandard rules, but rules nonetheless, demonstrable and formalizable. For it turns out that there are constraints on the *deletion* of the auxiliary *be*, constraints that are parallel, furthermore, to the constraints on the *contraction* of the auxiliary in standard English. In standard English, one cannot contract the auxiliary when it occupies the final position of the sentence: one cannot say, "He's as nice as he says he's." So too, in black English, one cannot delete the auxiliary when it occupies the final position of the sentence: one cannot say, "He's as nice as he says he." These two sets of constraints are parallel, each dictated by the word order of the sentence. They are further parallel, in that the permissibility (or not) of the deletion and contraction seems to have to do with how the sentence *sounds*: each represents a phonological contribution to a syntactic rule. It is this complex, multiplane correlation that suggests that the black vernacular is just as law-abiding as standard English. The grammar of one, while different in its surface features, is commensurate with the other in its deep structure, in the logic governing what is allowed and what is not, sharing with the other the same probability distribution of its formal variables.[26]

The rigors of syntax prove a democratic point. So too does an empirical knowledge of languages outside the Indo-European family. Labov notes in passing that the deleted copula in black English bespeaks no cognitive deficit, for "there are many languages of the world which do not have a present copula and which conjoin subject and predicate complement without a verb. Russian, Hungarian, and Arabic may be foreign, but they are not by that same token illogical."[27]

Empiricism of this sort—with a planetary database—also helps to vindicate black English on another front: the seeming illogicality of its "negative concord." Negative concord refers to the duplication of the negative in more than one syntactical position, as in the following: "It ain't no cat can't get in no coop."[28] Is this as grammatical as standard English? Labov's answer is emphatically yes. He writes: "The naive view is that the nonstandard dialects simply have too many negatives. Historically-minded linguists and dialectologists point out that multiple negation is the traditional pattern and that our standard form is a rule imposed on English by grammarians in the 18th century."[29] He goes on:

> The Anglo-Saxon authors of the Peterborough Chronicle were surely not illogical when they wrote *For ne woeren nan martyrs swa pined alse he woeron*, literally, "For never weren't no martyrs so tortured as these were." The "logical" forms of current standard English are simply the accepted conventions of our present-day formal style. Russian, Spanish, French, and Hungarian show the same negative concord as nonstandard English, and they are surely not illogical in this.[30]

"Globalizing" the syntactic form of black English, Labov restores it to a kinship network, and to cognitive legitimacy. This is exactly the sort of work that Chomsky hopes syntax would do, that adds to our understanding of the human species even as it changes the discipline of linguistics.[31] Steven Pinker, in his mainstream (and best-selling) *The Language Instinct* (1995), fully endorses this position.[32] Citing a sentence spoken by Larry, the toughest of the Jets ("In order for *that* to happen, you know it ain't no black God that's doin' that bullshit"),[33] Pinker writes: "Larry's speech uses the full inventory of grammatical paraphernalia that computer scientists struggle unsuccessfully to duplicate (relative clauses, complement structures, clause subordination, and so on), not to mention some fairly sophisticated theological argumentation."[34] He ends up repeating Labov's central point: "The great majority of sentences were grammatical, especially in casual speech, with a higher percentage of grammatical sentences in working-class speech than in middle-class speech. The highest percentage of ungrammatical sentences was found in the proceedings of learned academic conferences."[35]

Nonverbal Data

Universal grammaticalness is about as far as one can go in ontologizing democracy. Literary critics (along with legislators, educators, editors, and just about everyone else) have yet to catch up with its implications. But we have to stop and ask as well: is grammar the single most important attribute of our species? Can syntactical relations serve as the protocol for all possible relations that we might have: to ourselves, to others, to the myriad objects of the world? And, when it comes to the centuries-old legacies from Africa, does language keep a complete record, giving us all the evidence we need, or are there data to be found elsewhere? In short, is the survival of "Africanisms" first and foremost a linguistic phenomenon, or is the story better told through other records, *nonverbal* records? And how do the claims of the nonverbal affect the claims we make on behalf of literature?

These questions obviously cannot be answered with any degree of finality. But they can be tentatively explored—on two fronts. First, among neuroscientists and cognitive scientists, the competing claims of the verbal and the nonverbal are obviously of great importance. Most would probably still line up on the "verbal" side. The language-based paradigm, put forward by Chomsky, remains (in modified forms) the central paradigm for the field's leading figures: Daniel Dennett, Jerry Fodor, Gerald Edelman.[36] Even the "computational" model of the mind, seeing it as syntactical "software" driving semantic processes, seems an austere extension of Chomsky's syntactic theory.[37] The privileged relation of language to thought is in no imminent danger of collapse. Still, there has been a significant shift, a reorienting of the discipline as a whole, with a growing number of practitioners leaving behind their traditional focus and embracing an entirely new one. *Cognition* is no longer the sole player, the sole determinant of consciousness, and the unfailing ally for language. *Emotion* has entered the field as a new, undertheorized, and potentially more interesting research topic, with as yet unpredictable implications.

Antonio Damasio has been pivotal here. Beginning with *Descartes' Error* (1994), and continuing with *The Feeling of What Happens* (1999), and, most recently, *Looking for Spinoza* (2002), he makes a series of linked arguments challenging the primacy of thought in the workings of the human brain.[38] Cognition, Damasio argues, represents a higher-level neural activity, and is therefore not fundamental to our core consciousness, not the defining mark of what it means to be "human." Descartes's famous dictum, "I think therefore I am," is wrong for that reason: it has gotten things exactly backward, taking a secondary phenomenon as the determining ground. For Damasio, *being* necessarily comes before *thinking*. This priority is both evolutionary, in terms of the survival history of the species, and physiological, in terms of the neural biochemistry of the human brain. On neither count does thought have priority. While the consequences of such a claim are hard to gauge, what is of immediate interest here is its implications for the verbal/nonverbal debate. For if it turns out that human beings are emotional beings first and foremost, if cognition is something of an afterthought, that would seem to make language an afterthought as well. The close alignment of these two dislodges one along with the other. Damasio removes both of them from our core consciousness. We first register objects in a "nonlanguage form," he argues, for our core consciousness rests on a mental substrate at once precognitive and prelinguistic: a *"nonverbal, imaged* narrative"[39] that serves as the neurophysiological ground for our powerful emotions.

This challenge from neuroscientists is not likely to go away soon. Meanwhile, on another front, and in the context of a largely unrelated discipline, a parallel challenge is being voiced, most pointedly by the French linguist Robert Chaudenson. In a series of books beginning with *Les créoles français* (1979), and culminating in *Des îles, des hommes, des langues* (1992), revised in collaboration with Salikoko Mufwene as *Creolization of Language and Culture* (2001), Chaudenson casts doubt on the adequacy of verbal evidence as historical evidence, especially when it comes to the survival of African cultures. Language is not the most reliable witness, he argues, for its power of endurance (and therefore power of testimony) is weak under oppressive conditions. The large number of African languages, their mutual unintelligibility to one another, coupled with the active efforts of slave owners to stamp them out, means that English soon dominated the field as a much needed lingua franca. This lingua franca owed little to the languages of the slaves, for none had broad currency, and none had the demographic clout to survive. Language was the line of maximum pressure from the slave owners, and the line of least resistance from the slaves. Chaudenson thus returns to the earlier thesis about the eradication of African tongues—but with a difference. For him, the nonsurvival of *languages* does not mean the nonsurvival of African cultures as a whole. Quite the contrary. He cites with approval the scene in Alex Haley's television series, *Roots*, when the hero, trying to talk to the other slaves but finding no common tongue, improvised on a medium other than language: "only by drumming together on the planks of the ship can they express their common revolt."[40] The slaves survived, and something else survived with them, but in a nonlanguage form. *That* is the database we ought to be consulting; scholars who limit themselves to text-based archives are looking in the wrong place. Chaudenson writes:

> It is easy to see that the elements that have survived in material culture and music owe this survival largely to their non-verbal character. Thus it is strange that for decades some scholars have obstinately sought to identify in creoles traces of direct and positive transfers from the languages of the slaves, which are so obviously absent. Simple and rapid observation of material culture would have provided much more evidence of this non-European inheritance.[41]

Chaudenson's polemics should probably be taken with a grain of salt, but his general point remains. The cross-fertilization of cultures takes many forms, leaving behind many records, language being only one of them, and often not the primary one. Words, in and of themselves, never tell the full story. It is a small part of a larger domain of evidence. That larger domain Chaudenson calls the "creolization of cultural systems"— under which rubric he discusses music, cuisine, folk medicine and magic, and oral literature.

There is no reason to think of language as self-sufficient. Literary critics—as much as linguists—must come to terms with this. A combination of the verbal and the nonverbal might turn out to be the best strategy at once to enlarge the circumference of literature and to highlight its local inflections.[42] The methodology of Melville Herskovits has much to tell us.[43] And, since the 1940s, a rich body of material has sprung up, assembled by musicologists, anthropologists, and art historians, linking the Americas to Africa across a range of expressive media—an important alternative to text-based records.[44] I am thinking of the WPA oral histories, for instance, *Drums and Shadows* (1940), put together by the Savannah Unit of the Federal Writers' Project, with this subtitle: "Survival Studies among the Georgia Coastal Negroes." The verbal testimonies assembled here are preceded by images of material objects— masks, wooden figures, carved sticks, baskets—unmistakably stamped with the legacies of Africa and reminding us that nonstandard English might be seen as a parallel development.[45] I am thinking also of the art history of Robert Farris Thompson, dedicated to "art in motion" and celebrating a "black Atlantic visual tradition" as a supreme instance of this migrating art, bringing Africa to the Americas, with especially strong input from "Yoruba, Kongo Dahomean, Mande, and Ejagham."[46] And I am thinking, above all, of the musicology of Alan Lomax, a meticulous, monumental labor, assembling a massive archive to prove a point, namely, that "black African nonverbal performance traditions had survived intact in Africa-America, and had shaped all its distinctive rhythmic art, during both the colonial and postcolonial periods."[47]

Traveling tirelessly, and using a computerized model called cantometrics, Lomax records singing performances from every part of the world, "2500-plus songs from 233 cultures."[48] This database allows him to tabulate a list of "frequent musical behaviors," including melodic contour, melodic form, melodic range, phrase length, interval width, and so on. That tabulation, in turn, yields some striking patterns, some clustering of these musical behaviors, with one proving especially common. Spread across several continents, it typically includes these features: percussive rhythm; the predominance of one-phrase melodies (the litany form); overlapping call and response; choral integration or part-singing; polyrhythmic ("hot") accompaniments; and offbeat phrasing of melodic accents.[49] African-American music clearly conforms to this pattern. Lomax writes:

> [T]he main traditions of Afro-American song, especially the old-time congregational spiritual—are derived from the main African song style model. European song style did influence the African tradition in regard to melodic form and, of course, textual content. In most other respects Afro-American song has hewed to the main dynamic line of the principal African tradition. . . . This tradition is perhaps the most stable and the most ancient, and, in many ways, the most highly developed of the musical families of mankind.[50]

LITERARY ECOLOGIES

Students of language can only bow their heads in light of such findings. When it comes to documenting the life of humans—in its duration and variety—nonverbal records win hands down. A strictly language-based archive is incomplete at best, and misleading at worst. Art historians, musicologists, and students of material culture simply have more robust data at their disposal.

What are the implications of all of this for literary studies? I would like to think of it as an entry point rather than a closed door. For to think of language as *not* self-sufficient is to multiply its lines of filiation exponentially. It is to reorient the field in some fundamental way, giving increasing emphasis to that zone of interaction where nonverbal input combines with the verbal "lexifier" to generate a more complex geometry. Literature, in this sense, is a creole tongue not only in the commingling of languages, but equally in the commingling of expressive media. This is one way in which it differs from the logical structure of syntax. To test one against the other, and to take note of the divergence of the two, is to have a clearer sense of the peculiar ontology of literature, underscored by linguistics as a foil, by what it is as well as what it is not. The two do overlap: literature, like linguistics, works (for the most part) with logical, grammatical sentences, sentences that are law-abiding, that demonstrate the cognitive wherewithal of their authors through their syntactical rules. These rules, however, do not even begin to tell us what is compelling about these sentences. Literature is both syntax and more than syntax, both a collection of grammatical sentences and something not necessarily inferable from that grammar.

It would be interesting to speculate more about this discrepancy, and to make a claim for literature on that basis. The literary text, I suggest, is a linguistic entity whose modes of access to the world are nonetheless not strictly language-based. Its kinship network is broader than a set of grammatical rules; its input map is also broader. We can think of it as an "ecology" perhaps, a multiplane fractal environment, with looping and clumping in many different dimensions, and with irregularities robust across scales.[51] Syntax, for that reason, is no longer the sole foundation here, no longer the rule-giving and logic-bearing substrate (as linguists urge), but part of a less determinate landscape, sometimes no more than a mere lexical entry. These lines, from Derek Walcott's "A Tropical Bestiary," serve as well as any to demonstrate this difference:

> The sea crab's cunning, halting, awkward grace
> is the syntactical envy of my hand.[52]

The sentence is crystal clear as far as its grammar goes. This clarity is belied, however, by that strange phrase, "syntactical envy of my hand." The word "syntactical" is here a cipher, inserted into the poem's semantic field, and subject to ambient inflections and qualifications. In this case, an entire landscape, an entire map of the world, seems to have sprung up around it. This map first takes it to the vicinity of an emotion, envy. That emotion, in turn, is vested in a body part, the hand. And the hand, in turn, is stretched outward, gesturing toward a nonhuman creature, a sea crab, whose "cunning, halting, awkward grace" apparently enacts a human desire, a human aspiration.

Walcott's sentence is literally an ecology, in more senses than one. The human and the nonhuman are gathered together here; scripts made with words and scripts not made with words are also gathered together. This sort of ecology is infinitely vital but not exclusively verbal, for its common ground is traced not on the platform of human language, but on a very different sort of platform, a bodily register much more primitive, which is to say, much more elemental. Creatures on this planet are all united on this platform. This is where Walcott would like to put himself. Here and elsewhere, he speaks of his chosen medium as a material medium, less cerebral than manual: "language made with our hands."[53] It is the physicality of the hand that puts words on paper, and that looks enviously upon the sea crab, whose physicality produces a sinuous form of "writing" that the hand can only dream of, having only stiff and angular words at its disposal. The pairing of these two, the sea crab and the human hand, points to a world in which the somatic register of the body is the lowest and therefore most trustworthy common denominator. Derek Walcott is one with Antonio Damasio on this point. Our cognitive apparatus *is* an afterthought within the ecology of the planet. Human language must cede its primacy to scripts made by other species in the plenitude of their nonverbal lives.

African Rhythm

It is not altogether accidental that it is Derek Walcott, a poet from St. Lucia, who should make such an eloquent plea on behalf of wordless eloquence. The nonverbal has always been central to African-American poetics in general, and to Caribbean poetics in particular. Within this poetics, language and nonlanguage are not antithetical, but complementary, part of the same continuum. This is the single most important legacy of the diasporic: a synthesis of the verbal and the nonverbal, giving rise to many overlapping semantic fields on both sides of the Atlantic. Kofi Agawu, in his important study, *African Rhythm*, points to just this synthesis in Ewe music. Agawa notes "the absence of a single word for 'rhythm' in Ewe." The "semantic fields of the word are broadly distributed rather than lodged in one place," so that, while the Ewe word *vugbe* literally means "drum language" (vu = drum, gbe = language), the word can come to mean rhythm in any number of contexts.[54] Rhythm is multidimensional; it is the common thread running through music, dance, language. It enlists the physicality of the body as the unifying ground for an entire range of expressive forms, from the unscripted pace of everyday gestures to the choreographed motions of dance, from the erratic phrasing of the spoken word to the formal notations of vocal and instrumental music. J. H. Kwabena Nketia, in his study of African vocal music, also notes that "African traditions deliberately treat songs as though they were speech utterances. . . . The Yoruba, for example, exploit the overlapping elements of speech and music in their four major chants: the *rara*, *iwe*, *ifa*, and *ijala*."[55] This synthesis of language and nonlanguage extends even to percussive instruments. Akan drumming, for instance, often has a verbal basis. The drumming patterns are, literally, musical restatements of strings of words, thanks to the practice of musicians who invoke the pitch-tone configuration of words in their musical phrasing and the practice of poets who use onomatopoetic syllables to create an aural pattern analogous to the pitch contour and rhythm of the drum.[56] This verbal/nonverbal synthesis is enhanced by the fact that "almost every one of the languages spoken south of the Saraha is tonal, using pitch distinctions to differentiate words."[57]

This, then, is the most enduring input from Africa. In the United States, it transforms itself into the musical languages of blues and jazz, languages marked by the same "vocalizing" of musical instruments and the same "intrumentalizing" of the human voice—through such techniques as whooping and octave-jumping.[58] These musical languages, in turn, underwrite an entire aesthetics, informing every aspect of African-American expression. Houston Baker refers to it as a "blues matrix": "a womb, a network, a fossil-bearing rock, a rocky trace of a gemstone's removal, a principal metal in an alloy, a mat or plate for reproducing print or phonograph records."[59] Sherley Anne Williams speaks of "the blues roots of contemporary Afro-American poetry."[60] Edward Kamau Brathwaite points to a Caribbean genre he calls the "jazz novel,"[61] a fusing of words and music that he also dramatizes in a poem fittingly titled "The Making of the Drum":

> vowels of reed-
> lips, pebbles
> of consonants,
> underground dark
> of the continent.
>
> You dumb *adom* wood
> will be bent,
> will be solemnly bent, belly
> rounded with fire, wound-
> ed with tools
>
> that will shape you.
> You will bleed,
> cedar dark,
> when we cut you;
> speak, when we touch you.[62]

The sound of the drum enacts, on a percussive register, the "bleeding" of the *adom* wood; and the human vowels and consonants, reed-like and pebble-like, enact the nonverbal sounds of the nonhuman world. These phenomena are kindred and interlocking. African-American poetics enlarges upon that kinship and creates an ecology out of it, a meshing of language and more than language. This poetics is by no means limited to authors who are biologically "African-American." Wilson Harris—in tribute to Faulkner—speaks of literature in general as an endeavor that goes "beyond given verbal convention into non-verbal arts of the imagination in the womb of cultural space, as though an *unstructured force* arbitrates or mediates between articulate or verbal signs and silent or eclipsed voices of nemesis in folk religions, whose masks or sculptures subsist."[63] Unlike linguistics, literature taps into preverbal layers of consciousness; it has input from narratives generated by other bodily registers. Its fractal geometry stems from this fact, with dimensions not purely logical, and carrying a historical memory as pure grammar does not.

LIMBO DANCE

Wilson Harris himself has put forward a theory of the limbo dance as a metaphor for the multiplane ecology of literature. In the limbo, "the dancer moves under a bar which is gradually lowered until a mere slit of space, it seems, remains through which with spread-eagled limbs he passes like a spider. *Limbo* was born, it is said, on the slave ships of the Middle Passage. There was so little space that the slaves contorted themselves into human spiders."[64] But Harris argues that the limbo is not simply a measure of oppression. It is, quite literally, a countermeasure, defying measurement, for at work here

> is the curious dislocation of a chain of miles reflected in the dance so that a re-trace of the Middle Passage from Africa to the Americas and the West Indies is not to be equated with a uniform sum. . . . For *limbo* (one cannot emphasize this too much) is not the total recall of an African past, since that African past in terms of tribal sovereignty or sovereignties was modified or traumatically eclipsed with the Middle Passage and with generations of change that followed. *Limbo* was rather the renascence of a new corpus of sensibility that could translate and accommodate African and other legacies within a new architecture of culture.[65]

According to Harris, the bodily contortions of the slaves transform the very metric of space. The latitudes and longitudes of any locale cease to be a numerical given, and its distance to any other locale ceases to be a "uniform sum." Quantification breaks down. The map of the world varies with the intensity of connection, and with the nature of the kinship being traced. Africa is, ordinarily speaking, thousands of miles from the

Americas. But, on a certain emotional register, these thousands of miles can contract to zero.

I can think of no better way to theorize the ecology of literature, a set of coordinates sometimes taking in the whole world and sometimes tightening to a knot, sometimes finding adequate housing in language and sometimes haunted by what is beyond. Americanists have much to learn from this Caribbean poetics. The fact that Wilson Harris is not a familiar name to many of us only underscores the need to extend our circumference at just this point. African-American literature is infinitely richer when it is seen not as nation-based, self-contained within the United States, but as a diasporic formation, a literature of the two Americas with arcs reaching back to Africa. And American literature is infinitely richer when it takes its cue from this extended corpus, embracing a map of the world that commingles languages and cultures, just as it commingles word and sound, the verbal and the nonverbal. Such a map is, in some sense, the underside of linguistics, its penumbra, that shadowy region not reducible to our cognitive apparatus, not predicated on its logic and not simply rehearsing its grammar.

Nonstandard Mapping

Gloria Naylor's *Mama Day* gives us a map of the world mind-boggling in just this way:

> Willow Springs ain't in no state. Georgia and South Carolina done tried, though—been trying since right after the Civil War to prove that Willow Springs belong to one or the other of them. . . . So who it belong to? It belongs to us . . . who at one time all belonged to Bascombe Wade. And when they tried to trace him and how he got it, found out he wasn't even American. Was Norway-born or something, and the land had been sitting in his family over there in Europe since it got explored and claimed by the Vikings—imagine that. So thanks to the conjuring of Sapphira Wade we got it from Norway or theres about, and if taxes owed, it's owed to them. But ain't no Vikings or anybody else from over in Europe come to us with the foolishness that them folks out of Columbia and Atlanta come with—we was being un-American.[66]

Nonstandard English, nonstandard cartography. Naylor is right: there is indeed something "un-American" about African-American literature, for the weight of the hyphen is such as to produce just the sort of spatial contortion that Wilson Harris speaks of, the twisting of the United

States from a "uniform sum" into a much less recognizable shape. Like Willow Springs, *Mama Day* is stateless. It does not belong to Georgia, South Carolina, or North America; it cannot be found be on any official map. This statelessness seems to come from the ecology of literature itself: the shades of Africa are summoned, as well as the shades of Europe, and all for the benefit of something that cannot be called logic. The novel opens with a slave girl, Sapphira, flying back to Africa. It goes on to chronicle the mysterious illness of its female protagonist, victimized apparently by a conjure woman who, in turn, is punished by another conjure woman still more powerful, a "Miss Miranda." Descended from *The Tempest* and sixteenth-century England, this Miranda will make other forays into space and time: "when she's tied up the twentieth century, she'll take a little peep into the other side."[67]

Distance varies with human emotions. That is why, in Paule Marshall's *Praisesong for the Widow*, the Sea Islands legend of Ibo Landing is still a compelling legend after hundreds of years. As told by Aunt Cuney, the Ibos were able to transport themselves across the Atlantic in a peculiar fashion. Having been brought to America, and "sizing up the place real good," they just turned and walked back into the ocean: "Now you wouldna thought they'd of got very far seeing as it was water they was walking on. Besides they had all that iron on 'em. Iron on they ankles and they wrists and fastened 'round they necks like a dog collar. 'Nuff iron to sink an army. And chains hooking up the iron. But chains didn't stop those Ibos none. Neither iron."[68]

From a logical point of view, supplied by the laws of physics, or by standard cartography, the story makes no sense. But logic is not all, it seems, for the story does make sense—make sense on the strength of human emotions—for this is how water would have behaved, how physical distance would have behaved, if their operations had been governed by human desire, by the needs and impulses of the body. It speaks to the scope of literature that it is able to find housing for these needs and impulses, a dimensional plane oblique to what dismisses them and makes fun of them. If literature is an ecology, as I have tried to argue, a gathering of the cognitive and precognitive, language and more than language, its landscape would seem to be arcs of alternate geographies, alternate histories, bearing a more and more tangential relation to human rationality as we know it. Deviation from standard English is only the first of those arcs. There are others, opening steadily outward, stretching to their outermost limits, a universe at once mind-bending and emotionally necessary.

That yoking of fantasy and necessity gives another meaning to the hyphen in African-American literature, though neither pole is to be strictly correlated with either term. Unlike their ancestors, the descendants of the Ibos do not walk across the Atlantic. They are as un-African as they are un-American. At the end of *Praisesong for the Widow*, when the names of the African nations are called out, only a few old people answer. Tribal identities will not suffice, for the force of diaspora resides not in the maintenance of these names, but in the redirecting of them to a more vital, creole medium. It is a creole dance—African, Caribbean, and American—that "names" what the novel is, but names it through music and motion, on a somatic rather than linguistic register: "Even when the Big Drum reached its height in a tumult of voices, drums and the ringing iron, . . . her feet held to the restrained glide-and-stamp, the rhythmic trudge, the Carriacou Tramp, the shuffle designed to stay the course of history."[69] It is this rhythm of tramping and trudging, a rhythm born of centuries and continents, that binds us in kinship:

And for the first time since she was a girl, she felt the threads, that myriad of shiny, silken, brightly colored threads (like the kind used in embroidery) which were thin to the point of invisibility and yet as strong as the ropes at Coney Island. Looking on outside the Church in Tatem, standing waiting for the *Robert Fulton* on the crowded pier at 125th Street, she used to feel them streaming out of everyone there to enter her, making her part of what seemed a far-reaching, wide-ranging confraternity.[70]

CHAPTER EIGHT

Ecology across the Pacific:
Coyote in Sanskrit, Monkey in Chinese

WHAT WOULD ETHICS look like if its circumference were extended, its membership broadened to include not just a human population? And what would American literature look like if it were to follow suit, taking its cue from the diversity of the planet, a biosphere inhabited by more than one species, one kind of tenants?

This chapter pursues these questions through a kinship arc extending across the Pacific. The Buddhist-inflected ecology of Gary Snyder will open into a backward loop through a Sanskrit epic, the *Ramayana*, whose simian protagonist, Hanuman, would in turn take us to China, to the sixteenth-century novel *Hsi-yu-Chi* (Journey to the West). Meanwhile, the crisscrossing paths of Native American and Asian-American authors—Leslie Silko, Simon Ortiz, Gerald Vizenor, Maxine Hong Kingston—will weave in and out of this loop, turning it into a more sinuous fiber. Together, these texts not only offer relays between America and Asia, they also give us ingredients for a new ecology, for it is within these orbits that we are most likely to see animals as protagonists, and to be confronted with instances of the nonhuman that compel us to rethink the human.

BENTHAM'S ANIMAL ETHICS

I begin not with these texts, however, but with a long-standing and ongoing debate in Western philosophy, centered on the ethical claim of nonhuman animals. In a remarkable moment in his *Introduction to the Principles of Morals and Legislation* (1789), Jeremy Bentham issues a scathing attack on the English nation. Unlike the French, who were about to abolish slavery in their colonies, the English had lagged behind. This is not surprising, since they had lagged behind as well righting another wrong. This one is analogous to slavery, Bentham says, for it too draws an "insuperable line," a taxonomic bar dividing the world into two mutually exclusive classes:

> The day may come when the rest of the animal creation may acquire those rights which never could have been withholden from them but

by the hand of tyranny. The French have already discovered that the blackness of the skin is no reason why a human being should be abandoned without redress to the caprice of a tormentor. It may one day come to be recognized that the number of the legs, the villosity of the skin, or the termination of the *os sacrum*, are reasons equally insufficient for abandoning a sensitive being to the same fate. What else is it that should trace that insuperable line? Is it the faculty of reason, or perhaps the faculty of discourse? But a full-grown horse or dog is beyond comparison a more rational, as well as a more conversable animal, than an infant of a day, or a week, or even a month, old. But suppose they were otherwise, what would it avail? The question is not, Can they reason? nor Can they talk? but, *Can they suffer?*[1]

What Bentham objects to is the nonporous nature of the dividing line. Such a line cuts the biosphere into two grossly unequal halves, making a single species the default norm and turning everyone else into an inferior order. What can be done with impunity to the latter can never be extended to humans. These deeds, furthermore, are assumed to end where they begin; they do not spill over, do not reflect on those who perpetrate them. "Black slaves" were constituted as a taxonomic order in just this way, legitimizing a set of behavioral norms that could have no currency in the rest of the world. "Animals" are taxonomized by the same logic. Once again, a diverse population is put under a single yoke, sustaining action that would have been unthinkable done elsewhere; once again, they are assumed to absorb that action fully, leaving no reflexive residues in the actor.

FACTORY FARM

The analogy between "black slaves" and "animals" has lost some of its force since 1789, if only because "black slaves" is no longer a thriving taxonomic unit.[2] The same cannot be said of "animals." This taxonomic unit remains, as robust as ever, and as nonporous as it was at the end of the eighteenth century. Between animals and humans there is still an "insuperable line": unquestioned, uncrossable, and highly profitable. This line routinizes norms of conduct on one side of the divide that cannot bear thinking on the other. How else can we explain the phenomenon of the factory farm? Reporting in the *New York Times Magazine*, Michael Pollan describes this agribusiness and its CAFO (Confined Animal Feeding Operation):

[B]roiler chickens, although they do get their beaks snipped off with a hot knife to keep them from cannibalizing one another under the stress of confinement, at least don't spend their eight-week lives in cages too small to stretch a wing. That fate is reserved for the American laying hen, who passes her brief span piled together with a half-dozen other hens in a wire cage whose floor a single page of this magazine could carpet. Every natural instinct of this animal is thwarted, leading to a range of behavioral "vices" that can include cannibalizing her cage-mates and rubbing her body against the wire mesh until it is feature-less and bleeding.[3]

The Confined Animal Feeding Operation can be a guilt-free operation only if the billions of animals forced to live there from birth to death were assumed to be a separate ethical order, absolutely distinct from us, war-ranting treatment categorically different from how humans are treated. Any breakdown in that assumption would expose factory farms as what they are: mass *confinement* facilities, of unprecedented proportions, "an enterprise of degradation, cruelty, and killing which rivals anything that the Third Reich was capable of," as Elizabeth Costello, one of J. M. Coet-zee's characters, grimly reminds us.[4] What is especially mind-numbing here is not so much the killing (though the force-march to the killing floor is certainly horrifying to contemplate), but the degradation of life itself, its reduction to a suffocating fraction of a cage, unrelieved at any point and terminated only at death. And this, Coetzee further reminds us, in-flicted on "creatures least able to bear confinement," creatures with no access to language and to the mental release afforded by words, for whom freedom can only mean "the freedom of the body to move in space."[5]

SENTIENCE

The suffering of animals looms large for Coetzee as for Bentham. The ethical violation here is the violation of creatures who can feel pain. This argument—from the standpoint of sentience—has long been central to animal ethics. It is the backbone of Peter Singer's *Animal Liberation* (1975), a book that, perhaps more than any other, has succeeded in turn-ing vegetarianism from a fringe movement into an accepted practice, backed by demographics.

Singer begins with Bentham and, like Bentham, he argues that there can be no "insuperable line" between animals and humans—for one sim-ple reason. Do animals feel pain as humans do? With the help of contem-porary neuroscience, Singer answers with an emphatic yes: "the nervous systems for animals evolved as our own did, and in fact the evolutionary history of human beings and other animals, especially mammals, did not diverge until the central features of our nervous systems were already in existence."[6] Human and nonhuman animals shared the same evolutionary history for millions of years; this shared past gives us a shared present, a neurophysiology varying but little from one species to another.

This kinship among species is not limited to sentience alone. As far as our genetic program goes, humans and chimpanzees are over 98 percent identical. Rather than seeing us as an entity apart, it makes much more sense to classify humans as an animal species, a primate, the "third chimpanzee," as Jared Diamond suggests. As the third chimpanzee, we are cousin to the "pygmy chimp of Zaire and the common chimp of the rest of tropical Africa."[7] And, as a primate, we share the same capacity for pain with the rest of the mammalian family. Sentience is something that can be predicated across the species divide. It can serve as a common ground, Singer argues, a platform on which the phenomenal divisions of the world give way to something more fundamental, namely, a baseline ethical community, in which the pain of each matters as much as the pain of every other:

> If a being suffers there can be no moral justification for refusing to take that suffering into consideration. No matter what the nature of the being, the principle of equality requires that its suffering be counted equally with the like suffering—insofar as rough comparisons can be made—of any other being. If a being is not capable of suffering, or of experiencing enjoyment or happiness, there is nothing to be taken into account. So the limit of sentience (using the term as a convenient if not strictly accurate shorthand for the capacity to suffer and/or experience enjoyment) is the only defensible boundary of concern for the interests of others. To mark this boundary by some other characteristic like intelligence or rationality would be to mark it in an arbitrary manner.[8]

For Singer, a nonarbitrary ethics can be built only on the platform of sentience (rather than language or mental competence), for sentience alone grounds ethics in physiology, a common denominator that is optimally low. It is low enough to go beneath the superficial differences between humans and nonhumans, and low enough to avoid what Singer calls "speciesism," the bias, common among Homo sapiens, that "mere membership in our own biological species"[9] carries ethical weight, setting us apart from all other animals.

Singer is satisfied with this way of broadening the ethical community. And he is forthright about where he will and will not go: while his membership criteria are indeed more inclusive, they are not all inclusive. For if admission to this ethical community rests on sentience, animals outside the mammalian family—insects and fish, for instance, with vastly different nervous systems—will not be able to meet that requirement. They fall below the line, they are ethical *nonentities*—as are trees, rivers, mountains, and inanimate nature in general. As Singer says, "If a being is not capable of suffering, or of experiencing enjoyment or happiness, there is nothing to be taken into account." The "limit of sentience" is still homocentric in its mapping of the world. Its effect is to institute a series of concentric circles, centered on the human capacity to feel pain and extending that recognition to those close enough to us, those whose evolutionary histories are similar to ours and whose nervous systems are also alike, but writing off those in the outer reaches, those far removed from the human species, not feeling pain as we do.

ENVIRONMENTAL ETHICS

Rather than undoing that "insuperable line" between the human and the nonhuman, animal liberation, as envisioned by Singer, would seem only to redraw the line, acknowledging only a selective kinship with other species.[10] And yet a case can surely be made for a kinship more broadly conceived, extending beyond the mammalian family. Matt Ridley offers this account, reminding us at the same time just how dispensable the human species is at every point:

> We are apes, a group that almost went extinct fifteen million years ago in competition with the better-designed monkeys. We are primates, a group of mammals that almost went extinct forty-five million years ago in competition with the better-designed rodents. We are synapsid tetrapods, a group of reptiles that almost went extinct 200 million years ago in competition with the better-designed dinosaurs. We are descended from limbed fishes, which almost went extinct 360 million years ago in competition with the better-designed many-finned fishes. We are chordates, a phylum that survived the Cambrian era 500 million years ago by the skin of its teeth in competition with the brilliantly successful arthropods.[11]

Human beings belong to a family that can be variously defined: across many time frames, many stages of evolution. Our kinship network goes back and branches out on a scale that makes us second and third cousins to every other species on the planet. Kinship of this sort is of a piece with the planet's biodiversity; its ethics is therefore also much broader than one based on sentience. Lawrence Tribe, writing in the *Yale Law Journal* just when *Animal Liberation* was being published, proposes as much, and proposes as well a different genealogy for this revised and expanded ethics: "It is Kant, not Bentham, whose thought suggests the first step toward making us different persons from the manipulators and subjugators we are in danger of becoming."[12]

Kant rather than Bentham: the difference between these two amounts to a shift in the protocol of ethics itself, a shift in its base criterion. Kant is not primarily concerned with sentience; suffering is not an ethical category for him. Obligation is—and not obligation to others, for the most part, but rather an obligation to oneself, an internal injunction to act in such a way as to honor one's own humanity. This is a reflexive relation, to be sure, but it has important implications for how the nonhuman world is to be treated. In *Lectures on Ethics*, Kant writes that if a man shoots a dog who has served him long and faithfully, "he does not fail in his duty to the dog, for the dog cannot judge, but his act is inhuman and damages in himself that humanity which is his duty to show towards mankind."[13] Rather than drawing an "insuperable line" between humans and nonhumans, Kant makes that the line ethically porous, a membrane that takes in what it puts out. An injury to animals bounces back on us; it hardens us and empties us out; it is an injury to our own humanness. In *The Metaphysical Principles of Virtue* Kant repeats this argument, extending it to all of the inanimate world. He writes: "A propensity to the bare destruction (*spiritus destructionis*) of beautiful though lifeless things in nature is contrary to man's duty to himself."[14]

How can an external relation to the nonhuman world turn into a reflexive disfiguring of the human? Tribe glosses this Kantian paradox to mean that our humanness is affirmed only when we recognize ourselves as *merely* human, not to be equated with the multiplicity of the planet or its collective welfare. "[T]he best interests of individual persons (and even of future human generations) are not demonstrably congruent with those of the natural order as a whole."[15] Human beings cannot presume to speak for the planet and all its living and nonliving things. A truly capacious ethics must begin with the recognition that we are not the world, that our proportions are not its. Rather than being a servant to the human, the planet is a part of a solar system, a part of a galaxy, and a part of the cosmos, in all of which the human hardly matters. To be species-conscious, in this context, is to be conscious of an almost debilitating smallness. But it does not have to be debilitating, as long as we affirm our humanity negatively: affirming it by affirming what we are *not* free to do.

Kant's ethics—glossed by Lawrence Tribe—is one in which we stand with our hands freely, willingly, and respectfully tied. Since the burden is entirely on us, a burden of self-obligated restraint, it is no longer contingent on the phenomenon of pain or the ability of other creatures to feel it. Sentience is no longer a prerequisite for the ethical community. Inanimate things have standing here: we are bound in obligation to them, and they take our measure, just as animate things do. Such an ethics—making our humanity a function of the unworded and unending judgment of the world—overlaps to some extent with animal liberation,[16] but the latter is a way station rather than an end point here. For an all-encompassing ethical community (theorized by Aldo Leopold, Rachel Carson, and Arne Naess, and including anything from conservationism to "deep ecology")[17] goes beyond the sentience of individual creatures. Its baseline population is the ecosystem of the planet as a whole.

In *A Sand County Almanac* (1949), Leopold speaks of his "land ethic" as one that "enlarges the boundaries of the community to include soils, waters, plants, and animals." This enlarged community breaks down the taxonomic barrier that isolates and elevates human beings into a higher species. It names us simply as what we are: a dweller on the planet, part of a "biotic team," not the head, but a "plain member and citizen," on the same footing as the others, and owing every "respect to his fellow-members, and also respect for the community as such."[18] Rachel Carson, in the concluding pages of *Silent Spring* (1962), likewise warns us that our elevated sense of ourselves is a bias that has long outlived its usefulness, born of an ossified form "of biology and philosophy, when it was supposed that nature exists for the convenience of man."[19]

SPECIES MEMBERSHIP

Will we ever free ourselves from this artificial elevation? The concept of "species membership" is a good way to begin. As a species, we are a part of two phenomenal orders: we have one leg in the planet's biosphere, and (if Kant has his way) we have the other leg in a world-dependent and world-reflexive ethics of the human. Our species membership, in short, is both biological and philosophical. It calls us to account on both fronts. As far as biology goes, we are simply a member of the mammalian family, related to other primates, and, going further back, to reptiles, fishes, chordates, and so on. As far as philosophy goes, however, our species is quite unique, in that we alone are candidates for an ethical identity for which the jury is still out. And the eventual verdict will not be a verdict on a single person, but on all of us, an aggregate unit, defining the "human" collectively and cumulatively, across centuries and millennia. What does it mean to think of us as belonging to this unit, aggregated on such a scale? What are the consequences of choosing *this* as our baseline, an order of magnitude much greater than the ones now in use? And, when we think about it, what kind of a species is Homo sapiens, anyway? How has our membership in the biosphere panned out? Has it been for the planet's good, or the planet's ill, that we are its inhabitants?

Martin Rees, astronomer royal of Britain, argues in a recent book that it is the planet's singular misfortune to have us as tenants. It is the habit of Homo sapiens to run its home to the ground, it seems. Our planet is at its "final hour," Rees says: the human-induced threat to the biosphere is virtually irreversible, and, through the proliferation of nuclear weapons, we now have a 50 percent chance of putting it completely out of commission in the next fifty years.[20] Habitat destruction is currently the signature of this species, and it is not a signature from which we can withhold our individual names. No secession is possible from the species. Membership here is absolutely binding, an ontological given, and in that sense it is quite different from membership in a nation, a race, or a gender. We can leave the country of our birth; our racial identity is not solely determined by our skin color, nor our sexuality solely determined by our anatomy. In these three instances, the constraints of biology are loose, bending to the volition of individual actors. Species membership is different. It operates on a level much more elementary, a level where volition is more or less meaningless. It is not up to us to choose whether or not to be human: we simply *are*. We cannot switch, cannot turn into a different kind of organism, nor can we claim exemption from the handiwork of the species as a whole. As a form of aggregation, "species" represents the claim of biology at its most absolute. The extinction of the species renders each and every one of us extinct.

Ecology and Buddhism: Gary Snyder

For this, if for no other reason, this aggregate concept needs to be invoked as a counterpoint to any talk of globalization, reminding us that other species have vanished from the face of the earth, and that humans might follow suit, perhaps taking the whole biosphere with us. The earth sciences and life sciences, along with various science-advocacy groups, such as Physicians for Social Responsibility and the Union of Concerned Scientists, have provided much of the impetus for this sort of large-scale thinking. But the humanities have not been silent either. Lawrence Buell has made a compelling case for an "environmental imagination" in American literature, a mode of thinking that persistently looks beyond the merely human.[21] I would like to take this up, focusing especially on the question of *scale* urged by the authors in this tradition. These are authors steeped in non-Western cultures, whose duration is not the duration of the United States, whose dwelling place is an "earth house hold," and whose reference points are therefore not nations, but species.

"Earth house hold" is Gary Snyder's phrase, adapted from the Greek in order to link ecology to several ancient civilizations predating Christianity. The concept of the earth as a "house" is a literal rendition of the

Greek root for *ecology*: "*eco* (*oikos*) meaning "house" (c.f. "ecumeni-cal"): Housekeeping on Earth."[22] It is meant to be unidiomatic, foreign-sounding, for the prose collection published under that title is indeed a tribute to a religion not yet in the American grain, Buddhism, which Sny-der studied in Japan for twelve years, from 1956 to 1968.[23] For Snyder, ecology and Buddhism are virtually synonymous.[24] One cannot practice environmental ethics and remain a doctrinaire Christian, professing a faith that sees the natural world as a temporary home, to be left behind as heaven takes over, a heaven reserved for one species alone.[25] For Synder, the planet is a home we can never leave behind. It is our one and only. That discovery "has been forced on us," he says, in part "by the photo-graph of the earth (taken from outer space by a satellite) that shows the whole blue orb with spirals and whorls of cloud." This astronomical im-age is a "landmark for human consciousness," for "we are back again, now, in the position of our Mesolithic forebears. . . . We once more know that we live in a system that is enclosed in a certain way; that has its own kinds of limits, and that we are interdependent with it."[26]

To accept the earth as an astronomical object—which is to say, a phys-ical object, a finite object—is to embrace a religion affirming the primacy and equality of matter, a primacy and equality that cross the boundaries between species, even as they cross the boundaries between the animate and the inanimate. In his essay "Buddhism and the Coming Revolution," published in *Earth House Hold*, Snyder writes: "Avatamsaka (Kegon) Buddhist philosophy sees the world as a vast interrelated network in which all objects and creatures are necessary and illuminated."[27] Bud-dhism is, in that sense, a physical religion, as Christianity and Islam are not, and reconcilable with modern science in a way they cannot be. But it is as yet unfamiliar to the modern ear, not part of the contemporary id-iom. To recover it, we need to go back thousand of years, to the ancient civilizations. Newness can come into the world only through this oldness from other continents. Quoting his grandfather's IWW slogan, "Form-ing the new society within the shell of the old," Snyder gives the "old" an unexpected address: "it is my own view that the coming revolution will close the circle and link us in many ways with the most creative as-pects of our archaic past."[28]

SCIENCE-INSPIRED HUMANITIES

This archaic past redefines species membership itself. To accept it is to accept a much broader definition of humanity, made up of former mem-bers as well as current ones. These former members, long dead, are hu-man nonetheless, for their humanness is not something that has any defined terminus. Humanness is asymmetrical to biological life in this sense: while the latter does come to an end in each and every one of us, the former persists as long as the species persists. Humanness is the property not of an individual but of an aggregate. It is not physiological, but populational. This form of aggregation means that even those who are physiologically dead can remain populationally alive, can have a claimable and renewable input into the species, to which it still belongs.

For this reason, Snyder calls for a new, science-inspired humanities, with a long backward extension, going back 40,000 years, in order to take in this longstanding, ongoing, and never-ending input. In a remarkable essay, "Poetry and the Primitive," Synder writes:

> The human race, as it immediately concerns us, has a vertical axis of about 40,000 years and as of 1900 AD a horizontal spread of roughly 3000 different languages and 1000 different cultures. Every living culture and language is the result of countless cross-fertilizations—not a "rise and fall" of civilizations, but more like a flowerlike periodic absorbing—blooming—bursting and scattering of seed. Today we are aware as never before of the plurality of human life-styles and possibilities, while at the same time being tied, like in an silent movie, to a runaway locomotive rushing headlong toward a very singular catastrophe. Science, as far as it is capable of looking "on beauty bare," is on our side. Part of our being modern is the very fact of our awareness that we are one with our beginnings—contemporary with all periods."[29]

Taking 40,000 years as the working length, Snyder imagines a humanities with an archive to match. This archive takes the species as its subject, providing housing for its cumulative duration and extension, feeding these into what is new and emerging. This is what a science-inspired humanities would look like. Non-Western cultures would especially benefit from this elongated field: not just Buddhism, but all ancient cultures with a time frame asymmetrical to the shape of European history, and crucial to the fate of the earth if modernity is to be saved from being a runaway locomotive.

FORMER INHABITANTS

This is certainly true of Native American culture. It is probably not accidental that, like Snyder, Leslie Silko should call for a *longue durée*, much closer to the life of the species than to the history of Europeans in the New World. "Five hundred years, that is how long Europeans are in the Americas, is not a very long time. Because for 18,000 years there is evidence, and perhaps longer, of the Pueblo people being in that land."[30] This long duration, Pueblo duration, is the subject of one of Snyder's poems. "What Happened Here Before," is an attempt to bring to mind a pre-Columbian past, going even further back than Silko suggests. The poem begins with geological time, 300,000,000 years, followed by numbers only slightly more modest, 80,000,000 and 3,000,000, and then moves onward to two lengths of time within human history, 40,000 and 125:

> —300,000,000—
> First a sea: soft sands, muds, and marls
>   —loading, compressing, heating, crumpling,
>   crushing, recrytallizing, infiltrating,
> several times lifted and submerged.
> intruding molten granite magma
>   deep-cooled and speckling,
>   gold quartz fills the creaks . . .
>
> —40,000—
> And human people came with basket hats and nets
>   winter-houses underground
>   yew bows painted green,
>   feasts and dances for the boys and girls
>   songs and stories in the smoky dark.
>
> —125—
> Then came the white man: tossed up trees and
>   boulders with big hoses,
>   going after that old gravel and the gold,
> horses, apple-orchards, card-games
>   pistol-shooting, churches, county jail.[31]

The stark contrast between these two lengths of time, 40,000 and 125, speaks for itself. The United States and the California Gold Rush are mere scratches in the history of the world. But because they are the more recent scratches, they have the power to erase everything that went on before, emptying out the land along the axis of time (as they do along the axis of space), drawing the map of the new nation as on virgin soil. Anyone not consenting to this erasure must take a countermeasure, must reach back to recover a deep time wiped from the slate. This is what Leslie Silko tries to do in *Almanac of the Dead*, an almanac meant to resemble "the old Maya and Aztec almanacs." Claiming descent from them, it resurrects their form, an interconnected "spiral," to show that "time is not linear, that the past is not left behind and the past is not dead."[32] And this is what Simon Ortiz tries to do as well, when he insists that "We listen to the crickets,/cicadas, million years old sound."[33]

Snyder's own efforts to recover this deep time are reflected in the very title of his collection of poems, *Turtle Island* (1974). In his "Introductory Note," he explains why, instead of calling America by its current name, he is invoking an ancient one:

> Turtle Island—the old/new name for the continent, based on many creation myths of the peoples who have been living here for millennia, and reapplied by some of them to "North America" in recent years. Also, an idea found world-wide, of the earth, or cosmos even, sustained by a great turtle or serpent-of-eternity.
>
> A name: that we may see ourselves more accurately on this continent of watershed and life-communities—plant zones, physiographic provinces, culture areas; following natural boundaries. The "U.S.A." and its states and counties are arbitrary and inaccurate impositions on what is really here.[34]

Turtle Island: the pre-Columbian name conjures up a prenational America, a geological as well as ecological expanse. Watersheds and mesolithic dwellers remind us just how recent the nation-state is, how small a part it plays in the recorded length of the species. But Snyder is not satisfied even with a scale of 40,000 years. Beyond it, there is a time frame still more formidable, 300,000,000 years, which he is determined not to lose sight of as well.

What is the advantage of using geological time as a human measure? One effect, it seems, is that it compels us to rethink the phenomenology of race itself, seeing it retrospectively, against the history of the planet. Three hundred million years ago, there was no such thing as Homo sapiens in the world. And when this class of primates finally emerged, there was no such thing as Asians or Europeans or Americans. All of us came from Africa, the ancestral home of Homo sapiens in prehistoric times. Since this is the case, since all of us are "Africans under the skin," as Chris Stringer and Robin McKie have memorably argued,[35] racial divisions cannot be said to be fundamental in any sense. The planet did not begin with these divisions, and there is no reason why they should persist as a taxonomic bedrock, a rationale for carving up the world's populations into discrete units. There is such a thing as a preracial planet. Its reference point is geological time, at the tail end of which Homo sapiens emerged, a small, tawdry band, its survival uncertain, standing or falling as a species, and only as a species.

Nor is this solely a phenomenon of the primordial past. Time "loops" around, according to Snyder, in the form of a spiral, and so the ancient world is both a point of departure and a point of return, the undifferentiated unity of the species gesturing toward a unity yet to be born. It is in anticipation of this, and in an attempt to shape its future contours, that he would go so far as to call himself a "Native American," aligning himself with Pueblo rather than European ancestors. During a *Paris Review* interview, held as a public event at the 92nd Street Y in 1992, someone in the audience relayed to Snyder a question from his teacher, a Lakota: "Do you know that you are an Indian? A Native American." Snyder replies:

> That was very kind of her to say that. I don't know if I know I'm an Indian. However, I do know that I'm a Native American. . . . Anyone is, metaphorically speaking, a Native American who chooses, consciously and deliberately, to live on this continent, this North American continent, with a full spirit for the future, and for how to live it right, with the consciousness that says, "Yeah, my great-great-grandchildren and all will be here for thousands of years to come. . . . In this spirit, African-Americans, Euro-Americans, Asian-Americans, come together as Native Americans."[36]

Who counts as a "Native" American? The usual definition is *retrospective*, in terms of ancestry. Snyder reverses the arrow of time and makes it *prospective*. We become "Native Americans" by virtue of the descendants we can imagine, the kinds of people we would like to bequeath the world to, to see flourish in our wake. This prospective definition means that what we are is in no way a given. Our ethnicity is the least of it; it gives us no guaranteed relation to the past, and it certainly gives us no guaranteed relation to the future. *That*, to a large extent, is out of our hands, a function of what complete strangers, as yet unborn, will make of us. But at least we can try to provide the optimal condition for the emergence of these people: a planet undamaged and undepleted, a habitat robust and diverse.

COYOTE

Toward that end, we need to be "Native Americans": pre-Columbian Americans. "Turtle Island" is not just an old name for the North American continent; it is also the rallying cry for a new environmental ethics, one that looks back to the kinship between humans and animals in indigenous cultures. Ecologists have long recognized these indigenous peoples as their intellectual forebears. Native Americans, J. Baird Callicott says, regard "the two-legged," "four-legged," "the wings of the air," as well as all the plants as "children of one mother"; their bounds of community therefore extend not only to humans and animals but also to nonsentient things.[37] Hans Peter Duerr argues that Native Americans believe that "humans must become *unimportant* before the other beings of nature."[38] This self-chosen unimportance can sometimes look like self-erasure, which is what Willa Cather emphasizes in *Death Comes for the Archbishop*: "Father Latour judged that, just as it was the white man's way to assert himself in any landscape, to change it, make it over a little (at least to leave some mark of memorial of his sojourn), it was the Indian's way to pass through a country without disturbing anything; to pass and leave no trace, like fish through the water, or birds through the air."[39]

Snyder does not believe this to be the case. Rather, he admires the "Hopi and the other Pueblos" for their staying power, their "amazing resistance . . . to being worn away."[40] His essay "The Incredible Survival of Coyote" is a tribute to just that: the mythic animal stands here as an emblem of human tenacity, a stubborn refusal to disappear. Snyder's Coyote is stubborn to the core. Still, he is different from that hero in disguise celebrated in Mark Twain's *Roughing It*, a "long, slim, sick and sorry-looking skeleton" who can shed his sorry looks at a moment's notice, who, when chased, "glides along and never pants or sweats or ceases to smile," leaving the chasing dog in the dust. Twain's Coyote has a hang-dog look, but underneath he is every inch a tough guy, cool and triumphant. Snyder's never is. All he can do is to keep himself in one piece:

> He's out walking along, and he watches these beautiful little gold colored Cottonwood leaves floating down to the ground, and they go this . . . this . . . this . . . this . . . this, this, this, this, and he just watches those for the longest time. Then he goes up and he asks those leaves "Now how do you do that? That's so pretty the way you come down." And they say, "Well there's nothing to it, you just get up in a tree, and then you fall off." So he climbs up the Cottonwood tree and launches himself off, but he doesn't go all pretty like that, he just goes bonk and kills himself. But Coyote never dies, he gets killed plenty of times, but he always comes back to life again, and then he goes right on traveling.[41]

This Coyote is gullible, but luckily for him, his gullibility seems to go hand in hand with a narrative convention that undoes its harm. Things do work out in the end, but just barely. Snyder is rehearsing a time-honored sequence here: true to the Native American tradition, he is not an "originator" but a "conveyor."[42] Jarold Ramsey, who has devoted much of his writing career to the subject,[43] also notes that the basic plot is that Coyote is "unkillable." "They may suffer bad luck or just retribution in the form of starvation, poisoning, dismemberment, ingestion by monsters, incineration, drowning, fatal falls, and so on—but, as we

would have it, it is a universal convention that they revive."[44] How does
the reviving come about? In this particular essay Snyder leaves it unclear,
but we can easily fill in some of the details from the many Coyote stories
now collected, most of them about his mishaps and his ineptitude. A
bungler and a dupe, Coyote is usually in no position to revive himself.
Others have to do it for him.

It is this Coyote, sorely dependent on others, that Simon Ortiz depicts
in his poem "Telling about Coyote." Coyote is on his way to get married
but gets distracted by a gambling party. He sits in, "sure that he would
win something":

> But he lost
> everything. Everything.
> And that included his skin, his fur
> which was the subject of envy
> of all the other animals around.
>
> Coyote had the prettiest,
> the glossiest, the softest fur
> that ever was. And he lost that.
>
> So some mice
> finding him shivering in the cold
> beside a rock felt sorry for him.
> "This poor thing, beloved,"
> they said, and they got together
> just some old scraps of fur
> and glued them on Coyote with pinon pitch.
>
> And he's had the motley fur ever since.
> You know, the one that looks like
> scraps of an old coat, that one.[45]

Coyote is literally what others make of him. His stories have to be about
other animals, for *they* need to be there if these stories are to have their
customary semi-happy ending, if things are to come out all right in the
end. Deliverance by others is a narrative convention, and it is this that
Snyder puts in the foreground in one of his earliest poems, "A Berry
Feast" (1957),[46] a portrait of the mythic animal relocated to the Bay area:

> Belly stretched taut in a bulge
> Breasts swelling as you guzzle beer, who wants
>   Nirvana?
> Here is water, wine, beer

Enough books for a week
A mess of afterbirth,
A smell of hot earth, a warm mist
Steams from the crotch

"You can't be killers all your life
"The people are coming —
    —and when Magpie
Revived him, limp rag of fur in the river
Drowned and drifting, fish-food in the shallows
"Fuck you!" sang Coyote
    and ran.[47]

Coyote not only speaks English, he speaks a local, urban dialect, the English of the Beat generation, those book-reading, poetry-writing, Nirvana-dreaming creatures, whose bellies bulge with booze. His life and theirs are one, shading into each other, with no boundary to speak of. Snyder puts the two of them on exactly the same footing. And it is not a very elevated footing, because Coyote is not only a rebel, but a bungling rebel, someone who has to be fished out of the water after one of his usual peccadillos, while remaining true to form, foulmouthed and ungrateful. Bungling is the point. The Beats do not care much for glorified manhood, and Coyote is dear to them for just that reason: there is no danger he will ever be guilty on this count. Snyder says of himself: "Growing up in the fifties in Portland, Oregon; going to Reed College, associating with still struggling ex-Communist Party professors, . . . drawing on IWW lore of my grandfather, native white grass-roots political radicalism of the Northwest," he identified with Coyote as a "trickster," "an anti-hero." "The West was heroics, but as you know, in the fifties and sixties we didn't feel like heroics, we felt more like anti-heroics, and the trickster is immediately an attractive figure for the same reason."[48]

To find this antihero, the Beats have to cross the species divide. Their protagonist is an animal because he is all too human, and therefore an animal through and through, reminding us of where we began and where we still are. And, just so that we don't forget, it is Coyote's uncouth physicality that is emphasized over and over again, both in Native American literature and in literature inspired by it: his patched-together rag of fur, his landing bonk on his bottom, his various orifices, and most particularly his tail, the one body part that stamps him unmistakably as an animal. This ignoble body part is Coyote's signature. Leslie Silko highlights it in a poem, "Toe'osh: A Laguna Coyote Story," that highlights two ignoble orifices as well:

> They were after the picnic food
> that the special dancers left
> down below the cliff.
> And *Toe'osh* and his cousins hung themselves
> down over the cliff
> holding each other's tail in their mouth making a coyote
>   chain
> until someone in the middle farted
> and the guy behind him opened his
> mouth to say, "What stinks?" and they
> all went tumbling down, like that.[49]

Coyote likes human food, and, like human beings, he is not averse to stealing. His bodily functions and orifices are the same as well; the only thing that is obviously different is the tail. On this occasion, the tail is of dubious virtue, but, in what is probably the best known Coyote story—his theft of fire—it has a crucial (though still somewhat ignoble) part to play. Snyder recounts the story:

> [Coyote] found where the fire was kept. It was kept by a bunch of flies in a circle, and he couldn't get into the circle, but he was able to stick his tail in there and get his tail burning, and then off he scampered and managed to start some forest fires with his tail, and that fire kept running around the world, and people are still picking up here and there.[50]

This time, Coyote does manage to achieve what he sets out to do, and, for a change, he is actually doing it for the good of others, bringing the gift of fire to human beings. But even here, there is a limit to his heroism, since all of this is done through one ignoble body part, advertised to the exclusion of everything else. There is no better emblem for the beer-bellied radicalism of the Beats: a flabby physicality proud of itself, drawing strength from its kinship with a lowdown animal.

HANUMAN'S TAIL

Is this lowdown animal peculiar to America, found nowhere else in the world? Paul Radin, in his pioneering study, *The Trickster* (1956), notes that this Native American animal has many cognates: he can be Coyote, Raven, or Hare, and he has a great many names: "The Winnebago word for trickster is *wakdjunkaga*, which means *the tricky one*. The corresponding term for him in Ponca is *ishtinike*, in the kindred Osage, *itsike*, and in Dakota-Sioux, *ikto-mi*."[51] This multiplicity of names is not limited to the American continent. As our animal cousin, a lot like us, and just as bad as we are, the trickster is "the oldest expression of mankind," Radin says, and can be "found in clearly recognizable form among the simplest aboriginal tribes and among the most complex. We encounter it among the ancient Greeks, the Chinese, the Japanese, and in the Semitic World."[52]

Radin's book includes a short essay by Karl Kerenyi (as well as one by C. G. Jung), comparing the fire-stealing Coyote with other tricksters in antiquity: thieves of fire like Prometheus, and "Nasreddin Hodja" in Greek folktales, the "typical cunning fool or stupid rogue."[53] Are there still others, on other continents? Surprisingly, few have taken up Radin's suggestion about Chinese, Japanese, and Semitic counterparts. Yet surely there must be parallel figures in these cultures, occupying the same crossover terrain between the animal and the human. Gary Snyder is probably as good a starting point as any. The commingling of the Buddhist and the Pueblo in his work suggests, if nothing else, that there is a common ground between these two, an intercontinental kinship linking Asia to America. Snyder's friend David Padwa, pondering this kinship, puts the question most pointedly: "What's the Sanskrit word for Coyote?"[54]

Padwa himself does not have a direct answer. Since coyote is an animal native to the Americas, there would be no exact Sanskrit equivalent. The translation would have to be oblique, a different species substituted. What animal is likewise a trickster, cunning, clownish, onerous, less than human, more than human, and all too human? Silko and Snyder have already suggested an answer in giving such prominence to Coyote's tail. That body part is the signature of the beast in most animals, and most especially in one animal that would have looked human otherwise: the monkey.

The monkey is in fact the trickster par excellence in the Hindu tradition, looming large as Hanuman in the two Sanskrit epics, the *Ramayana* (300 BCE) and, to a lesser extent, the *Mahabharata* (400 CE). But he also has many other names. In the most ancient Vedic text, the *Rig-Veda*, (ca. 1500 BCE), he goes by the name of Rudravatara, since he is the eleventh incarnation of the god Rudra (the Vedic counterpart of Shiva).[55] In later puranic texts (CE 4th to 9th centuries), he is also the incarnation of a god, in this case, of Shiva himself, and goes by the name of Shiva-sunu.[56] These gods, Rudra and Shiva, have to incarnate themselves in this way, because the demon king, Ravana, has amassed great powers against Lord Rama, and they need to come down to earth to help fight him and to restore to Rama his wife, Sita, whom Ravana has abducted.

In spite of this exalted origin and equally exalted mission, Hanuman has a rocky start. He is not a comely baby, it seems, and, according to the *Bhavishya purana*, is abandoned by his mother at birth.[57] Hungry, he looks around for something to eat. Mistaking the sun for a red fruit, he leaps into the firmament to sink his teeth into it. The sun shrieks out, and the god Indra hurls his *vajra* (thunderbolt) at the little rascal (fig. 8.1). This breaks his chin. The name Hanuman comes from this episode, bearing witness to the mischievous, brutelike nature of his childhood.

Still, the baby grows up to be a musician, a dancer, and, above all, a scholar and linguist. Octavio Paz (one of the few Western writers familiar with this Sanskrit epic tradition), devotes an entire book, *The Monkey Grammarian*, to this aspect of Hanuman.[58] For ordinary Indians, though, it is not his intellectual accomplishments but his physical exploits that win them over. Being the son of the Wind god, Hanuman can fly at great speed, can cross vast stretches of ocean, can pick up the Himalayas and then put them back. These marvelous deeds, Shanti Lal Nagar says, "made him popular gradually with the masses in India who had to face the onslaught of barbaric invaders for centuries together, who had not only established their domain in the country, but also wounded the Hindu psyche to the maximum possible extent. . . . [Hanuman's] popularity, therefore, started during the late Gupta period when he was conceived to be a village god; his images were enshrined under a tree outside the villages in the belief that his divine powers would protect the residents. The Muslim rule indeed contributed massively towards the popularity of Hanuman, . . . and every Hindu household almost adored him as the only saviour from ill or dangers and the bestower of success in every walk of life."[59]

Given this mass adulation, given his godlike status, is Hanuman still a monkey? Or is he in essence a human being? It is true that for centuries and millennia he has been associated with descriptive epithets that put him firmly on the simian side: *vanara, hari, kapi, plavaga, plavamgama, sakhamrga, golangula*.[60] This is no deterrent to those who would like to claim him on the human side of the species divide. In the *Valmiki Ramayana*, for instance, Hanuman and his companions are referred to *vanaras* (monkeys). Could it be that the *vanaras* are really *va naras* (men)?[61] There are many attempts to argue along these lines, but they all flounder on one point. As Nagar says, "the tail possessed by Hanuman comes in the way." And he adds, "the tail is also not a symbolic one,"[62] for it is as a physical, fleshy (or at least furry) thing, part of the sentient body, that it will come to play a starring role, in one of the pivotal moments of the *Ramayana*, the torching of Lanka, Ravana's stronghold.

Having tracked down Sita in that citadel, Hanuman allows himself to be captured. Ravana first gives orders to have him killed, but changes his mind and settles on a modified form of punishment: "Since for monkeys the tail is the most cherished ornament," therefore this "should be singed,

Figure 8-1. Hanuman sinking his teeth into the sun (from K. C. Aryan, *Hanuman: Art, Mythology, and Folklore*).

and he should go back with that singed tail," to teach a lesson to his kinsman with "this wretched thin mutilated limb."[63] This is done. Hanuman's tail is wrapped with pieces of cotton cloth, drenched with oil and set on fire. Sita, seeing him being dragged around with his tail burning, is grief-stricken, and prays to the Fire god four times: "Please let your fire become cold on Hanuman's tail."[64] The Fire god complies, and the fire does not spread to the rest of Hanuman, but flares only "on the tip" of his tail, like a "fall of snow." This is encouraging. But Hanuman already has a plan of his own. Since he has the magical power of changing his shape and size, expanding and shrinking at will, he knows that he can easily slip off the ropes that bind him and then become "big as a mountain," squashing all of Ravana's underlings. However, he decides to save this glorious deed for Rama to perform. All he will do, in the meantime, is to use his burning tail to set the citadel on fire. Since he has not had a chance to tour the city, this torching would ensure that Lanka "should be seen properly by me at the end of the night."[65] And this is indeed what happens: Hanuman speeds across the fortress city, "with an aura of flames of his burning tail, [shining] like the sun with an aura of sun-rays."[66]

It is hard to think of a more uncouth vessel for this cloud of fire. Hanuman with his burning tail is about as far as possible from Jehovah in his burning bush. This ignoble iconography is dramatized by centuries of folk art. We see Hanuman encircling Lanka with his tail, setting it on fire (fig. 8.2); we see him about to cool that tail in the ocean, while looking back with glee at the burning Lanka (fig. 8.3); we see him tricked out with jewelry, carrying a mountain in his left hand, with a special ornament adorning his curly tail (fig. 8.4); and, even after his transformation into a Bodhisattva seated on a lotus flower atop a crocodile, his tail is still as visible as ever (fig. 8.5). Ingenuity, insatiable curiosity, and an all too palpable sense of the ridiculous—all these make him a trickster: sublime in one sense, but not too sublime, the tail reminding us that he is an animal always.

That animal comes out in force just as soon as the rescue mission is accomplished, when Hanuman is reunited with his monkey companions. Two whole "sargas" of the *Valmiki Ramayana* are devoted to the reveries and rioting of these monkeys, culminating in a raid on a sacred grove and the drinking of the honey-wine, egged on by Hanuman:

> and then all assembled monkeys, having attacked the
>   powerful forest guards in the honey forest, then
>   beat them up a hundred times.
> With their hands taking hold of the honey combs which
>   had the size of a bucket, those monkeys all together
>   threw down the combs and others were eating

Figure 8-2. Hanuman encircling Lanka with his tail. Nineteenth-century painting (from K. C. Aryan, *Hanuman: Art, Mythology, and Folklore*).

Figure 8-3. Hanuman about to cool his tail in the ocean. Courtesy of the Herbert F. Johnson Museum of Art, Cornell University.

Figure 8-4. Hanuman with an ornament on his curly tail. Eighteenth-century painting (from K. C. Aryan, *Hanuman: Art, Mythology, and Folklore*).

some of the monkeys, tawny coloured like honey, after
  drinking, started throwing the honey combs; and
  some, who were drunk, hit one another with the
  remainder of the honey
others, holding on to a branch, prevented themselves
  from falling, and very much exhausted from their
  intoxication, after spreading leaves under the
  trees, slept thereon.

Figure 8-5. Hanuman as a Bodhisattvaa with a tail. Nineteenth-century painting (from K. C. Aryan, *Hanuman: Art, Mythology, and Folklore*).

And the monkeys, drunk with honey, became very
    intoxicated, and pushed one another cheerfully,
    and others stumbled.
Some made inarticulate sounds, some uttered cries from
    pleasure, some monkeys, drunk with honey, slept
    on the ground.

                                                    (60:7–12)

The monkeys are physical creatures, bundles of uncontrollable appetite, and the *Ramayana* is nothing if not uncontrollable on this point. This is the tail end (so to speak) of the rescue mission, not a tugged-on appendix either, but a pivotal event, told in packed if ignoble detail, giving the narrative its requisite shape and sequence.

This is the heart of antiheroism, as old as any on record. It is probably not accidental that this antiheroism should be found in an ancient epic: one that both confronts and confounds the species divide, not taking the human as the measure of all things. The nonhuman here is part of the cosmos, part of the continuum of life. Reincarnation across species gives this continuum both its intellectual sinew and its anarchic force: the mortality of the human body is no longer the end, for there is a multitude of life forms folding it into their midst, loosening the burden of humanness while qualifying its absolute claim. And so it is probably not accidental either that, as this Sanskrit epic spread across Asia, migrating to China, Japan, Laos, Burma, Thailand, Malaysia, Java, and flourishing in street theater, song and dance cycles, shadow puppet shows, it was these nonhuman life forms, with their lowdown trickery, that would be amplified and dramatized, in what was to become a two-millennia-old, pan-Asian vernacular tradition.[67]

Just to take one example, the sixteenth-century Chinese novel *Hsi-yu Chi* (Journey to the West), not only features a monkey, Sun Wu-Kung, with the same shape-shifting power that Hanuman has, it also features many of his antics before he finally agrees to serve the monk Tripitika. These include the same drinking of the celestial wine, stealing of the sacred peaches, and consuming of five gourds of golden immortality tablets.[68] When pursued, Sun Wu-Kung turns himself at one point into a mud-shrine: "his wide-open mouth becomes the open door; his teeth become flapping fans; his tongue becomes the presiding Bodhisattva. He does not know what to do with his tail, though, and sticks it behind as a flag-pole."[69] His pursuer laughs out loud when he sees this, because shrines don't usually have flagpoles at the back.

ASIAN, NATIVE AMERICAN

What are we to make of these two animals, these nonhuman envoys into the human world, one Native American, the other Asian, each with a conspicuous tail, mostly useful but sometimes inconvenient? It would be foolish to claim any kind of causal relation here, any specific contact that would have allowed for the translation of this particular body part. Yet the parallel between these two cannot simply be dismissed as trivial and fanciful. How to theorize this intriguing connection? Fortunately, in dealing with this problem we have a precedent and guide, in the form of Claude Lévi-Strauss.

In *Structural Anthropology*, Lévi-Strauss links together the two continents in his chapter "The Art of Asia and America," putting deliberate emphasis on the conjunction "and." Primitive art from the "Northwest Coast of America, China, Siberia, New Zealand, and perhaps India and Persia"[70] makes up a far-flung but coherent unit of analysis, Lévi-Strauss says, for this comparative paradigm generates cross-references that allow salient patterns to emerge in each of these geographical regions. In particular, "it is impossible not to be struck by the analogies presented by Northwest Coast and ancient Chinese art."[71] Intense stylization, use of signature attributes, depiction of the body by split representation, the frontal view of one individual with two profiles—these are just some of the features found both in ancient Chinese art and in art of the Pacific Northwest.[72] These shared features are worth investigating, Lévi-Strauss says, for even though we cannot prove definitively that Chinese art has migrated across the Bering Strait, more damage is done by an intellectual inertia that "prefer[s] to deny obvious relationships because science does not yet provide an adequate method for their interpretation."[73]

Taking our cue from Lévi-Strauss, we can tentatively go forward. And, literary critics are luckier than anthropologists and archaeologists in one respect. Since the archive here is an *emerging* archive, shaped by relations that are still coming into being, we do not in fact need any airtight proof of historical causation in order to mention "Asian" and "Native American" in the same breath. Rather, taking Gary Snyder's point that "Native American" is defined by what *descends* from it, we can say that Hanuman is Native American in just this sense, in that he will be fruitful and multiply in the Americas, will leave many traces of himself. This is his newly added habitat after several millennia of flourishing life in Asia, and, by all indications, he is here to stay.

He will be seen on television in 2008, as the mascot at the Beijing Olympics. Meanwhile, there are more than 2,950,000 Hanuman entries on Google and some thirteen hundred items at Amazon.com. Arthur

Waley's translation of *Hsi-yu Chi* as *Monkey* (1943) first introduced him to the English-speaking world.[74] Henry Louis Gates's *The Signifying Monkey* (1988), without mentioning him, brought this trickster iconography to the critical foreground.[75] Maxine Hong Kingston's *Tripmaster Monkey* (1989), on the other hand, was written in explicit tribute to Hanuman, in the conviction that "the monkey spirit came to America in the 1960s."[76] "I read *Journey to the West* when I was writing *Tripmaster Monkey*," Kingston says, "to verify to myself, Am I catching the spirit of this monkey person? Am I right in seeing monkey's presence?"[77] Bringing the monkey to America, to San Francisco—home of the Beats, of the Grateful Dead—Kingston also dresses him in the local attire: " 'Tripmaster' was a word from the 1960s. People would be on acid, and there's a tripmaster who suggests trips for them and who guides them and keeps them from flipping out."[78] And there were other kinds of trips as well. "Monkey was at the Democratic Convention in Chicago, and on the march to the Pentagon."[79] To invoke an alternative species is to rethink the landscape of politics, and to hold the nation accountable on a different ontological plane.

This I take to be the burden of Gerald Vizenor's *Griever: An American Monkey King in China* (1987). With this novel—the journey of a Native American to Asia—the kinship of continents, and the kinship of the human and the nonhuman, comes full circle. Vizenor himself is something of a fateful nexus for that kinship. Part Anishinaabe (Ojibway), part Chippewa, and part French-Canadian, he is a "mixedblood on the margins,"[80] outward-looking precisely because he is native, already one leg into some other world. This other world can take the form of a physical continent, on the other side of the Pacific. At the University of Minnesota, Vizenor had done both his undergraduate and graduate work in Asian Studies and, in the 1980s, taught in Tientsin for several months with his wife, Laura Hall. This geographical distance from the United States, in turn, seems to reflect a distance from an anthropocentric world. Vizenor's collection of autobiographical sketches, *Interior Landscapes*, opens with this essay, "Families of the Crane." "The crane is one of the original five totems of the Anishinaabe," Vizenor writes. "It loves to soar among the clouds, and its cry can be heard when flying above, beyond the orbit of human vision. From this 'far sounding cry' the family who claim it as their totem derive their generic name of *passweweg*, the echo makers."[81]

An aerial view of the planet can be unsettling, as we have seen: it removes humans from center stage, erasing our records, highlighting our impermanence. This unsettling view is no doubt fed by the actual transience of life among Native Americans. "Clement William Vizenor, my father, was a crane descendant," Vizener writes. "He was born on the reservation and murdered twenty-six years later on a narrow street in Minneapolis."[82] On the night of June 30, 1938, Clement Vizenor was found in an alley, "with his head nearly cut off by an eight-inch throat slash."[83] The murderer would never be found. Horrifying as this was, it was actually a repeat performance. The *Minneapolis Journal* reported: "He was the second member of his family to die under mysterious circumstances within a month. His brother, Truman Vizenor, 649 Seventeenth Avenue Northeast, was found in the Mississippi river June 1, after he had fallen from a railroad bridge and struck his head."[84]

Gerald Vizenor was not even two years old when this happened. For him (and perhaps for Native Americans in general) death is not a remote event, something arriving in due course, after a tolerable length of time. It is abrupt, intimate, proximate, an attribute of the physical body, rooted in its injurability, its tendency to keel over and collapse. Humans are indistinguishable from animals in this respect. Cross-species kinship is not a fanciful intellectual conceit here; it is a brute fact, a physiological fact. Peter Singer could not have found a better advocate for animal liberation. *Griever* is in fact centrally about that: "I'm a frog," Griever tells his grade-school teacher when she is about to dissect one in the interest of science. He "packed the frogs on top of his lunch in a brown paper sack and liberated them one by one on the shaded cool side of the school building. There, in the gentle fiddlehead fern, he imagined that he became the king of the common green frogs."[85]

Still, animal liberation cannot remain too lyrical (or too heroic), given the combined weight of monkey and coyote. This unlyrical turn takes place when Griever travels to China, when his frog liberation morphs into something more in line with the eating habits of the locals:

> "Free the birds," said Griever. . . . "How much for the whole flock?"
>
> "*Ji wang, ji wang* . . ." The cutthroat wrapped the tether around his wrist and pushed the cock down the counter toward the foreign devil. . . .
>
> Chickens were expensive, compared to fish and pork, and most people at the counter could not afford the cost of fowl, except for special celebrations. Chicken liberation, then, was better understood as a comic opera. The audience was drawn to the trickster and his imaginative acts, not the high cost of chicken breasts. Mind monkeys, from practiced stories, would have done no less than emancipate the birds in a free market.[86]

Chicken liberation is an issue here, but it is one among others, jostled by other facts. These include the long history of Western domination and the tendency of the Chinese, even now, to call Westerners "foreign devils."

The actual presence of Chinese words—a language spoken by a quarter of the world's population, which most Americans do not understand—mocks Griever's attempt to be a *ji wang*, king of the chickens. But the most powerful ironizing force here is probably the free market itself, and the use of greenbacks as the instrument of liberation. The monkey king is wielding a capitalist weapon. Hanuman's descent, from Sanskrit through Chinese and into English, is literally a descent, sinking lower and lower into the parodic, a descent that empties out the possibility of pure heroics, just as it empties out the possibility of a pure race, a pure culture.

And so, even though on this occasion much of the comedy stems from the gulf between the English-speaking Native American and the Chinese crowd gathered around him, that dividing line turns out itself to be quite shaky. It gives way to a deeper common ground, a likeness springing up between races and species, underwritten by shared quirks of the body:

> An old woman notched through the crowd toward the counter. She carried the black hen high above her head. . . . She wore a new blue coat, too thick for the late summer weather, buttoned high to her thin wrinkled neck.
>
> "English, do you understand?" he asked. She cocked her head like a bird, and like his tribal grandmother. Both of them, he remembered, overdressed in summer. Peaches, who was born on a woodland reservation, pretended most of the time that she did not understand her trickster grandson. His urban mixedblood tongue, she snorted when he graduated from college, "wags like a mongrel, he's a wild outsider." Even at home on the reservation he was a foreigner.
>
> The old woman . . . leaned to one side, to an ancient wind, a natural pose, and then she laced her fingers behind her back and smiled.
>
> Peaches posed like that too.[87]

The angled turn of the head links a Chinese woman to a Native American woman, and links both of them to a bird. What these two women have in common is the physical fact of aging, the habit of wearing too many clothes, a sworn hostility to foreign languages, and the behind-the-back knitting and tugging away of the hands. This sort of resemblance, neither familial nor racial, but based on a random affinity of bodily gestures, is the most robust form of kinship: robust precisely because it is random, because it is a large-scale statistical effect, the effect of the world's populations converging by chance. Here, it is funny and whimsical, for Vizenor (his family history notwithstanding) thinks of chance as benign, a "spiritual balance in a comic drama."[88] But the kinship between the Asian and the Native American has other permutations as well, in contexts sometimes starkly uncomic. Leslie Silko, who has also meditated on this phenomenon, tells a very different story in *Ceremony*, about the experience of a Native American soldier in World War II, about how terrifying it can be when the Japanese and the Native American become one and the same:

> When the sergeant told them to kill all the Japanese soldiers lined up in front of the cave with their hands on their heads, Tayo could not pull the trigger. . . . [H]e saw Josiah standing there; the face was dark from the sun, and the eyes were squinting as though he were about to smile at Tayo. So Tayo stood there, stiff with nausea, while they fired at the soldiers, and he watched his uncle fall, and he *knew* it was Josiah. . . . Rocky pushed him toward the corpses and told him to look, look past the blood that was already dark like the jungle mud, with only flecks of bright red still shimmering in it. Rocky made him look at the corpse and said, "Tayo, this is a *Jap*! This is a *Jap* uniform!" And then he rolled the body over with his boot and said, "Look, Tayo, look at the face," and that was when Tayo started screaming because it wasn't a Jap, it was Josiah.[89]

Not to be able to tell friend from foe is a form of madness in one sense. In another sense it is a form of sanity, for the dividing line between these two is in fact not clear-cut, just as the dividing line between races, nationalities, and species is not. The blood from any body—human or animal, Japanese or Native American—will be bright red at first, and then it will darken, coagulating like mud. The body will grow stiff regardless of nationality. And the pain overwhelming the body also cannot distinguish between race or species. The physicality of each of us is much older than any of these recent divisions. In moments like this, when the baseline of life is extinguished and asserted at one and the same time, when the duration of an individual comes to an end, while deep time continues, we know that for all races, all nations, and all species, there is only one world.

Notes

INTRODUCTION

1. See http://web.amnesty.org/library/index/engmde 140892003.

2. For news articles from the *Independent* as well as the BBC and the Associated Press, see http://www.thememoryhole.org/history/iraq-natl-library.htm.

3. Charles Hanley, reporting for the Associated Press, April 15, 2003.

4. Benedict Anderson, *Imagined Community: Reflections on the Origin and Spread of Nationalism* (London: Verso, 1983), 28–32; Anthony Giddens, *The Consequences of Modernity* (Stanford, CA: Stanford University Press, 1990), 17-21.

5. Anderson explicitly links nationalism to two forms of seriality: the "unbound seriality" of the newspaper, and the "bound seriality" of the census. See "Nationalism, Identity, Logic of Seriality," in his *The Spectre of Comparisons: Nationalism, Southeast Asia, and the World* (London: Verso, 1998), 29–45. I try to complicate his argument by looking at chronological dates as another form of seriality.

6. Aristotle was the first to ask this question, in his *Physics*. I will discuss this genealogy more fully in chapter 6.

7. For two important discussions of non-Western challenges to standardized time, see Prasenjit Duara, "Transnationalism and the Challenge to National Histories," and Walter Johnson, "Time and Revolution in African America: Temporality and the History of Atlantic Slavery," both in *Rethinking American History in a Global Age*, ed. Thomas Bender (Berkeley and Los Angeles: University of California Press, 2002), 25–46, 148–67.

8. See, for instance, Paul Giles, *Virtual Americas: Transnational Fictions and the Transatlantic Imaginary* (Durham, NC: Duke University Press, 2002); *Multilingual America: Transnationalism, Ethnicity, and the Languages of American Literature*, ed. Werner Sollors (New York: NYU Press, 1998); *Post-National American Studies*, ed. John Carlos Rowe (Berkeley and Los Angeles: University of California Press, 2000); *Streams of Cultural Capital: Transnational Cultural Studies*, ed. David Palumbo-Liu and Hans Ulrich Gumbrecht (Stanford, CA: Stanford University Press, 1997).

9. Fernand Braudel, "Histoire et sciences sociales: La longue durée," *Annales d'histoire économique et sociale* 4 (October–December 1958): 725–53. Translated as "History and the Social Sciences: The *Longue Durée*," in *On History*, trans. Sarah Matthews (Chicago: University of Chicago Press, 1980), 25–54; quotation from 27.

10. Ibid., 33.

11. For an interesting discussion of different time frames required by world history, including a time frame of 15 billion years, see David Christian, "The Case for 'Big History,' " *Journal of World History* 2 (Fall 1991): 223–38.

12. Immanuel Wallerstein, *The Modern World-System*, 3 vols. (New York: Academic Press, 1974–1989).

13. Gayatri Chakravorty Spivak, "Planetarity," in *Death of a Discipline* (New York: Columbia University Press, 2003), 71–102, quotation from 102, 101.

14. The literature on this subject is vast. Exemplary works include Grahame Clark, *Space, Time, and Man* (Cambridge: Cambridge University Press, 1992); Stephen Jay Gould, *Time's Arrow, Time's Cycle: Myth and Metaphor in the Discovery of Geological Time* (Cambridge: Harvard University Press, 1987); Stephen W. Hawking, *A Brief History of Time: From the Big Bang to Black Holes* (New York: Bantam, 1988); Paolo Rossi, *The Dark Abyss of Time: The History of the Earth and the History of Nations from Hooke to Vico*, trans. Lydia G. Cochrane (Chicago: University of Chicago Press, 1984); Stephen Toulmin and June Goodfield, *The Discovery of Time* (Chicago: University of Chicago Press, 1965).

CHAPTER ONE: GLOBAL CIVIL SOCIETY

1. Bruce Ackerman, "The Rise of World Constitutionalism," *Virginia Law Review* 83 (May 1997): 771–97.

2. Jürgen Habermas, *Postnational Constellation*, trans. Max Pensky (Cambridge: MIT Press, 2001), 69–70. Habermas's prediction was made, of course, before the war in Iraq, a war that, as Étienne Balibar shows, has done much to *invert* Habermas's model, highlighting not a postnational constellation, but state sovereignty globally deployed. See Étienne Balibar, "What Is a War?" Public Lecture, School of Criticism and Theory, Cornell University, June 23, 2003. For Balibar's critique of nationalism and the nation-state, see "Racism and Nationalism" and "The Nation Form," in Étienne Balibar and Immanuel Wallerstein, *Race, Nation, Class: Ambiguous Identities* (London: Verso, 1991), 37–68, 86–106. While Habermas is primarily interested in the postnational constellation as democratic politics, other theorists (such as Arjun Appadurai) are more interested in it as a globalized imagination. See Appadurai, *Modernity at Large: Cultural Dimensions of Globalization* (Minneapolis: University of Minnesota Press, 1996).

3. "Global Civil Society" is a now an institutional program at the London School of Economics, with annual publications. For related works, see Mary Kaldor, *Global Civil Society: An Answer to War* (Cambridge: Polity Press, 2003). See also John Keane, *Global Civil Society?* (Cambridge: Cambridge University Press, 2003), which makes the interesting argument that the idea of a *global* civil society represents a corrective to the traditional idea of "civil society."

4. *Toward a Global Civil Society*, ed. Michael Walzer (Providence: Berghahn Books, 1995), 1.

5. Ibid., 1.

6. Ibid., 4.

7. Ibid., 9.

8. I take the term "rhizome" from Gilles Deleuze and Felix Guattari, *On the Line*, trans. John Johnston (New York: Semiotext[e]), 7–10.

9. Robert Pogue Harrison, "The Origin of Our Basic Words," chapter 5 in *The Dominion of the Dead* (Chicago: University of Chicago Press, 2003), 72–89, quotation from 85.

10. Henry David Thoreau, *Walden*, ed. J. Lyndon Shanley (1854; rpt., Princeton: Princeton University Press, 1971), 298.

11. This is true of the Concord River as well. As Lawrence Buell suggests, this American river, for Thoreau, is "as old as the Nile or Euphrates, ultimately at one with all the famous rivers of history and legend: Xanthus, Scamander, Mississippi, Ganges, Nile." See *Literary Transcendentalism: Style and Vision in the American Renaissance* (Ithaca: Cornell University Press, 1973), 209.

12. Henry David Thoreau, *A Week on the Concord and Merrimack Rivers*, ed. Carl F. Hovde et al. (1849; rpt., Princeton: Princeton University Press, 1980), 136. All other references to this edition will be included in the text as *Week*, followed by the page number.

13. For the genealogy and composition of the *Bhagavad Gita*, see the introduction, to *The Bhagavadgita, Translated with Sanskrit with an Introduction, an Argument, and a Commentary by W. Douglas P. Hill* (London: Oxford University Press, 1928), 14–18.

14. For the importance of Eastern religions not just to Thoreau but, first and foremost, to Emerson and to the contributors and readers of the *North American Review*, see Arthur Christy, *The Orient in American Transcendentalism* (New York: Columbia University Press, 1932), 23–29; Carl T. Jackson, *Oriental Religions and American Thought* (Westport, CT: Greenwood Press, 1981), 25–84. For the importance of South Asian religions to the West, see Srinivas Aravamudan, *Guru English: South Asian Religion in a Cosmopolitan Language* (Princeton: Princeton University Press, 2006).

15. The *Bhagavad Gita*, trans. Charles Wilkins, with introduction by Warren Hastings, ed. J Garrett (1784; rpt., Bangalore: Wesleyan Mission Press, 1849), 1:28–33, 36–37. Lecture 1 in the Wilkins translation is not divided into lines; I have tallied the line number against the Hill translation. All other citations to Wilkins translation will be included in parentheses in the text, the lecture number followed by the line number.

16. The *Iliad* and the *Odyssey* are both shadowed by the fact of death and by the agonized cries of mortals against their mortality. However, these agonized cries do not lead to any critical reflection on whether war is justifiable.

17. Seeing that mockery as the central fact of *A Week*, Daniel Peck argues that it leads Thoreau to write in a "decidedly elegiac tone and to cast time as the foe from whom he would have to redeem his losses." See "Killing Time," in *Thoreau's Morning Work: Memory and Perception in "A Week on the Concord and Merrimack Rivers," the Journals, and "Walden"* (New Haven: Yale University Press, 1990), 3–21, quotation from 8.

18. January 8, 1842. Henry D. Thoreau, *Journal: Volume 1, 1837–1844*, ed. Elizabeth Hall Witherell, William L. Howarth, Robert Sattelmeyer, Thomas Blanding (Princeton: Princeton University Press, 1981), 362.

19. February 21, 1842. Thoreau, *Journal*, 1:366.

20. March 12, 1842. Thoreau, *Journal*, 1:372.

21. Thoreau, "Resistance to Civil Government," in *Reform Papers*, ed. Wendell Glick (Princeton: Princeton University Press, 1973), 63–90, quotation from 65–66.

22. Thoreau, "The Last Days of John Brown," in *Reform Papers*, 145–53, quotation from 152–53.

23. Ibid., 152.

24. Thoreau, *Walden*, 325, italics in original.

25. My thanks to Dilip Gaonkar for suggesting the concept of "carrier" for the phenomenon that I am trying to describe.

26. Hannah Arendt, *The Human Condition* (Chicago: University of Chicago Press, 1958), 189. Arendt's detailed account of action is the most compelling I know of.

27. For a useful (and partisan) summary of the disagreements, see W. Douglas P. Hill's introduction to the *Bhagavad Gita*, 1–55.

28. See n. 12, above.

29. Raymond Adams, "Thoreau's Sources for 'Resistance to Civil Government,' " *Studies in Philology* 42 (July 1945): 640–53, esp. 648–49; Robert D. Richardson, Jr., *Henry Thoreau: A Life of the Mind* (Berkeley and Los Angeles: University of California Press, 1986), 176–177.

30. Adams, "Thoreau's Sources," 649–50.

31. For Garrison's relation to the Non-Resistance movement, see Henry Mayer, *All on Fire: William Llyod Garrison and the Abolition of Slavery* (New York: St. Martin's Press, 1998), 249–51, 258–64.

32. William Lloyd Garrison, "Declaration of Sentiments," in *Selections from the Writings and Speeches of William Lloyd Garrison* (Boston: R. F. Wallcut, 1852), 72–77, quotation from 72, 73–74.

33. Ibid., 72.

34. F. B. Sanborn, *The Life of Henry David Thoreau* (Boston: Houghton Mifflin, 1917), 466–69.

35. Thoreau, "The Service," in *Reform Papers*, 3–17, quotation from 14. Interestingly, the essay was rejected by Margaret Fuller. See Richardson, *Henry Thoreau*, 371.

36. Thoreau, "A Plea for Captain John Brown," in *Reform Papers*, 111–38, quotation from 132.

37. May 29, 1854. *The Journal of Henry D. Thoreau*, ed. Bradford Torrey and Francis H. Allen, 14 vols. (Boston: Houghton Mifflin, 1906), 3:315. As Sandra Petrulionis points out, quite a bit of editorializing intervened between the journal entries and Thoreau's public statements. See Sandra Harbert Petrulionis, "Editorial Savoir Faire: Thoreau Transforms His Journal into 'Slavery in Massachusetts,' " *Resources for American Literary Study* 25, no. 2 (1999): 206–31.

38. Thoreau, "Resistance to Civil Government," 134.

39. Thoreau first read the *Bhagavad Gita* in 1846. He last checked it out of the Harvard College Library in 1854, but, as Robert Sattelmeyer points out, "thereafter he seldom demonstrated an active interest in the subject—no further library withdrawls, infrequent and casual allusions in the Journal, and no extracts in the notebooks. When his English friend Thomas Cholmondeley sent him a magnificent gift of forty-four volumes of Oriental works in 1855 he responded warmly and gratefully, but he does not seem to have been inspired to read or reread the books themselves to any significant extent." See Sattelmeyer, *Thoreau's Reading: A Study in Intellectual History* (Princeton: Princeton University Press, 1988), 68.

40. Martin Luther King, "A Legacy of Creative Protest," in *Thoreau in Our Season*, ed. John H. Hicks (Amherst: University of Massachusetts Press, 1962), 13.

41. Gandhi, "Anasaktiyoga," in *The Gospel of Selfless Action, or the "Gita" According to Gandhi*, trans. Mahadev Desai (Ahmedabad: Navajivan Publishing House, 1946), 121–31, quotation from 122. Gandhi was in England from 1888 to 1891, studying law at the Inner Temple. At one point he was living in the Bayswater section of London and joined a vegetarian club, the vice president of which was Sir Edwin Arnold, who had just translated the *Bhagavad Gita* in 1885, under the title of *The Song Celestial*. See Louis Fischer, *The Life of Mahatma Gandhi* (New York: Harper, 1950), 29.

42. This is the aforementioned *The Gospel of Selfless Action, or the "Gita" According to Gandhi*, translated by Mahadev Desai back into English.

43. Fischer, *Life of Mahatma Gandhi*, 29.

44. Gandhi, "Anasaktiyoga," 130.

45. Thoreau, "Resistance to Civil Government," 75.

46. Webb Miller, *I Found No Peace* (Garden City, NY: Doubleday, 1938), 238–39. Gandhi somewhat qualified his indebtedness to Thoreau in a letter, dated September 10, 1935, to P. Kodanda Rao of the Servants of Indian Society: "The statement that I had derived my idea of Civil Disobedience from the writings of Thoreau is wrong. The resistance to authority in South Africa was well advanced before I got the essay of Thoreau on Civil Disobedience. But the movement was then known as passive resistance. As it was incomplete I had coined the word *Satyagraha* for the Gujarati readers. When I saw the title of Thoreau's great essay, I began to use his phrase to explain our struggle to the English readers. But I found that even 'Civil Disobedience' failed to convey the full meaning of the struggle. I therefore adopted the phrase Civil Resistance." See Fischer, *Life of Mahatma Gandhi*, 87–88.

47. *Indian Opinion*, October 26, 1907. For a detailed account of Gandhi's indebtedness to Thoreau, see George Hendrick, "The Influence of Thoreau's 'Civil Disobedience' on Gandhi's *Satyagraha*," *New England Quarterly* 29, no. 4 (December 1956): 462–71.

48. For an account of nonviolent resistance in South Africa, see Gandhi, *Satyagraha in South Africa*, trans. Valji Govindji Desai (Ahmedabad: Navajivan Publishing House, 1928). For his account of what he read during his three prison sentences, see "First Jail Experience," "Second Jail Experience," and "Third Experience," in *Speeches and Writings of Mahatma Gandhi*, 4th ed. (Madras: Natesan, 1933), 218, 226, 238–39.

49. M. K. Gandhi, "The Birth of Satyagraha," in *An Autobiography, or The Story of My Experiments with Truth*, trans. Mahadev Desai (Ahmedabad: Navajivan Publishing House, 1927), 389–90.

CHAPTER TWO: WORLD RELIGIONS

1. This is not true of Buddhism, and also less true of ecclesiastical structures in the twentieth and twenty-first centuries, with interfaith alliances steadily growing.

2. Thoreau quotes from the *Parables of Zoroaster*: "The oracles often give victory to our choice, and not to the order alone of the mundane periods. As, for instance, when they say that our voluntary sorrows germinate in us as the growth of the particular life we lead." See Henry David Thoreau, *A Week on the Concord and Merrimack Rivers* (1849; rpt., New York: Penguin, 1998), 101. As Daniel Peck points out, Thoreau read these parables in *The Phenix: Collection of Old and Rare Fragments* (New York: Gowan, 1835). See Peck's editorial notes to *A Week*, 324, n. 17.

3. *A Week*, 123.

4. Thoreau, "The Preaching of Buddha," *The Dial* 4 (January 1844), 391–401.

5. Thoreau, *A Week*, 58.

6. Robert Irwin, "The Emergence of the Islamic World System, 1000–1500," in *The Cambridge Illustrated History of the Islamic World*, ed. Francis Robinson (Cambridge: Cambridge University Press, 1996), 32–61.

7. William H. McNeill, *The Rise of the West: A History of the Human Community* (1963; rpt., Chicago: University of Chicago Press, 1991), 485. For Islam in Europe, in Africa, and in Asia, see Francesco Gabrieli, "Islam in the Mediterranean World"; Ioan M. Lewis, "Africa South of the Sahara"; C. E. Bosworth, "Central Asia"; Aziz Ahmad, "India"; C.A.O. Van Nieuwenhuijze, "Indonesia," in *The Legacy of Islam*, ed. Joseph Schacht with C. E. Bosworth (Oxford: Clarendon Press, 1974), 63–104, 105–15, 116–29, 130–43, 144–55.

8. Ross E. Dunn, *The Adventures of Ibn Battuta: A Muslim Traveler of the Fourteenth Century* (Berkeley and Los Angeles: University of California Press, 1989).

9. The phrase is Marshall Hodgson's. See his *Rethinking World History* (Cambridge: Cambridge University Press, 1993), 97.

10. Algebra (an Arabic word), geometry, optics, and medicine all flourished under Islam. See Martin Plessner, "The Natural Sciences and Medicine"; Juan Vernet, "Mathematics, Astronomy, Optics," both in *Legacy of Islam*, 425–60, 461–88.

11. McNeill, *The Rise of the West*, 486.

12. Ibid., 487.

13. Ibid., 488.

14. Fazlur Rahman, *Islam*, 2nd ed. (Chicago: University of Chicago Press, 1979), 153.

15. Ibid., 132. Rahman's observation is echoed by John L. Esposito, who writes: "Throughout the ninth and tenth centuries, Sufism grew in Arabia, Egypt, Syria, and Iraq. Though its origins and sources (Sufi interpretation of the Qur'an and life of the Prophet) were clearly Islamic, outside influences were absorbed from the Christian hermits of Egypt and Lebanon, Buddhist monasticism in Afghanistan, Hindu devotionalism, and Neoplatonism." See Esposito, *Islam: The Straight Path* (New York: Oxford University Press, 1991), 102.

16. Rahman, *Islam*, 154.

17. Alexander Knysh, *Islamic Mysticism* (Leiden: Brill, 2000), 7.

18. Rahman, *Islam*, 152.

19. Ibid., 85–99, 128–66, quotation from 153.

20. Ibid., 155.

21. Marshall Hodgson, *Venture of Islam, in Three Volumes*, vol. 1, *The Classical Age of Islam* (Chicago: University of Chicago Press, 1974), 57.

22. Rahman, *Islam*, 117–27.

23. Ibid., 117.

24. Al-Ghazali's *Incoherence of the Philosophers* was countered by Ibn Rushd's ringing defense, *The Incoherence of the Incoherence*. But it was Al-Ghazali who prevailed. See Esposito, *Islam*, 75.

25. Al-Ghazali's *Rebirth of the Sciences of Religion (Ihya' 'ulum al-Din)* had been burned earlier. See Roger Arnaldez, *Averroës: A Rationalist in Islam*, trans. David Streight (Notre Dame, IN: University of Notre Dame Press, 2000), 6. For the lack of influence of Ibn Rushd in the Islamic world, see Majid Fakhry, *A History of Islamic Philosophy* (New York: Columbia University Press, 1970), 302–25; Dominque Urvoy, *Ibn Rushd (Averroës)*, trans. Olivia Stewart (London: Routledge, 1991). Still, it should be pointed out that even here Islam was more tolerant than Christianity. Ibn Rushd was neither tortured nor killed, only banished.

26. NcNeill, *The Rise of the West*; Marshall G. S. Hodgson, *The Venture of Islam*, 3 vols. (Chicago: University of Chicago Press, 1974). See also Hodgson's "The Role of Islam in World History"; "Cultural Patterning in Islamdom and the Occident"; and "Modernity and the Islamic Heritage," all in his *Rethinking World History*, 97–125, 126–70, 207–46.

27. *Journal of World History* (Hawaii, Spring 1990–). An earlier version of this was published by UNESCO as the *Cahiers d'histoire mondiale* (Paris, July 1953–April 1972); this became *Cultures* in 1972.

28. For the work of Gottschalk, Stavrianos, and McNeill, see Gilbert Allardyce, "Toward World History: American Historians and the Coming of the World History Course," *Journal of World History* 1 (Spring 1990): 23–76.

29. L. S. Stavrianos, *Lifelines from Our Past: A New World History* (New York: Pantheon, 1989), 8. I thank David Palumbo-Liu for calling my attention to this work.

30. Ibid., 9.

31. Ibid., 9–10.

32. "Post-Enlightenment" is Said's word. See his *Orientalism* (New York: Vintage, 1979), 3.

33. Ibid., 3.

34. Ibid., 4.

35. Ibid., 7.

36. Ibid., 8, 7.

37. Even though Dipesh Chakrabarty does not specifically mention Edward Said, his critique of Euro-centric methodology can be usefully extended to Said's *Orientalism*. See Chakrabarty, *Provincializing Europe* (Princeton: Princeton University Press, 2000).

38. Richard Brent Turner, *Islam in the African-American Experience* (Bloomington: Indiana University Press, 1997), 11–46.

39. Allan Austin, *African Muslims in Antebellum America: A Sourcebook* (New York: Garland, 1984); Jane L. Smith, *Islam in America* (New York: Columbia University Press, 1999), 50–75.

40. Turner, *Islam in the African-American Experience*, 151.

41. Edward E. Curtis IV, *Islam in Black America: Identity, Liberation, and Difference in African-American Islamic Thought* (Albany: State University of New York Press, 2002), 75.

42. C. Eric Lincoln, *Black Muslims in America*, 3rd ed. (Trenton, NJ: Africa World Press, 1994), 130–59, quotation from 153.

43. Aminah Beverly McCloud sees this divided legacy as the tension between two Arabic words, *Ummah* and *'asabiya*, both of which define Islam. See McCloud, *African American Islam* (New York: Routledge, 1995), 3–5. See also Curtis's discussion of Islamic universalism versus black particularism, in *Islam in Black America*, passim.

44. Malcolm X with Alex Haley, *Autobiography of Malcolm X* (New York: Grove Press, 1966), 338, 339–40.

45. Holy Qur'an, trans. Abdullah Yusuf Ali (Cambridge: Murray Printing, 1946), 1407.

46. James Baldwin, *The Fire Next Time* (1962; rpt., New York: Laurel, 1988), 97–98.

47. Stanley T. Williams, *Life of Washington Irving* (New Haven: Yale University Press, 1935), 297.

48. Washington Irving, *The Alhambra*, ed. William T. Lenehan and Andrew B. Myers (Boston: Twayne, 1983), 79.

49. Ibid., 82. Akhar S. Ahmed has coined the phrase, the "Andalus Syndrome," to describe a grievance felt by many Muslims, occasioned not only by the fate of Islam in the Iberian Peninsula but also by the fate of Islam in Hyderadbad, South India. See Ahmed, *Discovering Islam: Making Sense of Muslim History and Society* (London: Routledge, 1988), 158–71.

50. For a discussion of Bronson Alcott and Theodore Parker (as well as Emerson and Thoreau) in relation to world religions, see Carl T. Jackson, *The Oriental Religions and American Throught* (Westport, CT: Greenwood, 1981), 45–84.

51. The list was given to Alcott by James Freeman Clarke, who would himself go on to write *Ten Great Religions: Essays in Comparative Theology* (Boston: Houghton Mifflin, 1871). See Arthur Christy, *The Orient in American Transcendentalism* (New York: Columbia University Press, 1932), 243.

52. Fuller had just read Firdusi's *Shah Nameh*, translated by James Atkinson (London, 1832), and was writing to Emerson about it. Fuller to Emerson, February 23, 1840, in *The Letters of Margaret Fuller*, ed. Robert N. Hudspeth, 5 vols. (Ithaca: Cornell University Press, 1983), 2:122.

53. Lydia Maria Child, *The Progress of Religious Ideas through the Ages*, 3 vols. (New York: C. S. Francis, 1855), 3:349–417.

54. Ibid., 3:417.

55. *Journals and Miscellaneous Notebooks of Ralph Waldo Emerson*, ed. William H. Gilman et al., 16 vols. (Cambridge: Harvard University Press, 1960–1982), 1:171, hereafter cited as *JMN*. The translation of the Qur'an then available in English was George Sale, *The Koran; Commonly Called the Alcoran of Muhammed; Translated into English immediately from the Original Arabic* (London: Malden, 1801).

56. Emerson mentioned Gibbon in his Journals in 1822, *JMN* 1:131.

57. In chapter 50, Gibbon writes: "In Arabia as well as in Greece, the perfection of language outstripped the refinement of manners; and her speech could diversify the fourscore names of honey, the two hundred of a serpent, the five hundred of a lion, the thousand of a sword, at a time when this copious dictionary was entrusted to the memory of an illiterate people. . . . Thirty days were employed in the exchange, not only of corn and wine, but of eloquence and poetry." *History of the Decline and Fall of the Roman Empire*, ed. J. B. Bury, 7 vols. (1788; rpt., New York: Macmillan, 1914), 346–47.

58. Frederic Ives Carpenter, *Emerson and Asia* (Cambridge: Harvard University Press, 1930), 198.

59. Carlyle said: "Our current hypothesis about Mahomet, that he was a scheming Imposter, a Falsehood incarnate, that his religion is a mere mass of quackery and fatuity, begins really to be now untenable to any one." *On Heroes, Hero-Worship and the Heroic in History*, ed. Michael K. Goldberg et al. (1841; rpt., Berkeley and Los Angeles: University of California Press, 1993), 37–66, quotation from 38.

60. For Emerson's quotations from the *Akhlak-I-Jalaly*, see *JMN*, 9:200, 263, 278, 284–88, 291, 385–86.

61. Robert E. Richardson, *The Mind on Fire* (Berkeley and Los Angeles: University of California Press, 1996), 406.

62. Mansur Ekhtiar, *Emerson and Persia* (Tehran, Iran: Tehran University Press, 1976), 22.

63. For a detailed account of Emerson's relation to the *Desatir or Sacred Writings of the Ancient Prophets; in the Original Tongue; Together with the Ancient Persian Version and Commentary* (Bombay: Courier Press, 1818), see Carpenter, *Emerson and Asia*, 217–46.

64. Emerson, "Books," in *Complete Works of Ralph Waldo Emerson*, centenary ed., 12 vols. (Boston: Houghton Mifflin, 1903): 7:218–19.

65. The importance of higher criticism to Emerson is well recognized. See, for instance, Julie Ellison, *Emerson's Romantic Style* (Princeton: Princeton University Press, 1984); John Michael, *Emerson and Skepticism* (Baltimore: Johns Hopkins University Press, 1988), 16–32; Wesley T. Mott, *"The Strains of Eloquence": Emerson and His Sermons* (University Park: Pennsylvania State University Press, 1989), 56–78; and especially Barbara Packer, "Origin and Authority: Emerson and the Higher Criticism," in *Reconstructing American Literary History*, ed. Sacvan Bercovitch (Cambridge: Harvard University Press, 1986), 67–92. Richard Grusin puts less emphasis on the higher criticism and more on Emerson's ambition to claim institutional authority. See *Transcendental Hermeneutics: Institutional Authority and the Higher Criticism of the Bible* (Durham, NC: Duke University Press, 1991), 1–54.

66. Jerry Wayne Brown, *The Rise of Biblical Criticism in America, 1800–1870: The New England Scholars* (Middletown, CT: Wesleyan University Press, 1969), 16, 23–24.

67. Ibid., 27–28.

68. In 1779 Eichhorn published his analysis of the first three chapters of Genesis, entitled *Die Urgeschichte* (Altdorf, 1790). See Hans W. Frei, *The Eclipse of Biblical Narrative: A Study in Eighteenth and Nineteenth Century Hermeneutics*

(New Haven: Yale University Press, 1974), 159. This was followed by his *Einleitung ins Alte Testament* (Leipzig, 1780).

69. Brown, *Rise of Biblical Criticism*, 16.

70. Ibid., 82.

71. Ibid., 35–44.

72. To William Emerson, November 1(?), 1824, in *Letters of Ralph Waldo Emerson*, ed. Ralph L. Rusk, 6 vols. (New York: Columbia University Press, 1939), 1:150.

73. To William Emerson, November 18, 1824, in *Letters* 1:153.

74. Emerson reported to William that he had "called on Brown at the Bookstore respecting your books. He told me that he had long ago sold all he could sell & given the proceeds to Edward with the deduction of his commission, & he was anxious to get rid of the remainder. So I bid him send them here & here they are & wait the decree of Tartary. Two books of Eichhorn's . . ." *Letters* 1:250.

75. To William Emerson, April 5, 1830, in *Letters of Ralph Waldo Emerson*, ed. Eleanor M. Tilton, expanded to 12 vols. (New York: Columbia University Press, 1990), 7:192.

76. The higher criticism of Michaelis and Eichhorn would lead logically to later iconoclastic works such as David Friedrich Strauss's *The Christ of Faith and the Jesus of History* (1865). For a detailed account, see Albert Schweitzer, *The Quest of the Historical Jesus* (1910; rpt., Baltimore: Johns Hopkins University Press, 1998).

77. As Barbara Packer points out, Emerson "cribbed shamelessly" from two sources in writing these lectures, from Marsh's "Dissertation" and Bishop Connop Thirlwall's long introduction to his translation of Friedrich Schleiermacher's *Critical Essay upon the Gospel of St. Luke*. See Packer, "Origin and Authority," 75–76.

78. Emerson, *The Vestry Lectures and a Rare Sermon*, ed. Kenneth Walter Cameron (Hartford, CT: Transcendental Books, 1984), 8.

79. Emerson, "The Divinity School Address," in *Selections from Ralph Waldo Emerson*, ed. Stephen Whicher (Boston: Houghton Mifflin, 1957), 100–116, quotations from 105, 106.

80. For William's as well as Waldo's thinking on the Lord's Supper and the input from the higher criticism, see Elisabeth Hurth, "William and Ralph Waldo Emerson and the Problem of the Lord's Supper: The Influence of German 'Historical Speculators,'" *Church History* 62 (March 1993): 190–206. Aside from the higher criticism, Emerson seems to have input as well from the Quakers. See Mary Turpie, "Quaker Source for Emerson's Lord's Supper Sermon," *New England Quarterly* 17 (1944): 95–101.

81. Emerson, sermon CLXII, "The kingdom of God is not meat and drink; but righteousness and peace and joy in the holy ghost," in *Complete Sermons of Ralph Waldo Emerson*, ed. Albert J. von Frank et al., 4 vols. (Columbia: University of Missouri Press, 1989–92), 4:186.

82. Ibid., 4:186, 187.

83. Ibid., 4:188.

84. Ibid., 4:189.

85. Ibid., 4:189.

86. Ibid., 4:191.

87. Emerson to Elizabeth Palmer Peabody, August 3, 1835. *Letters* 1:451.

88. Emerson, "The Kingdom of God Is Not Meat and Drink," *Collected Sermons* 4:192.

89. Emerson to Mary Moody Emerson, August 19, 1832. *Letters* 1:354.

90. Among the earliest books borrowed from the Boston Athenaeum was a Latin copy of Aristophanes's *Comoediae*. See Kenneth Walter Cameron, *Ralph Waldo Emerson's Reading* (Hartford, CT: Transcendental Books, 1962), 17. It is a sign of Emerson's competence in that language that he should read a translation of Aristophanes in Latin rather than English.

91. On February 17, 1825, Emerson checked out from the Harvard College Library Fenelon's *Oeuvres* and Leibniz's *Essais de Théodicée*. On November 2, 1826, Emerson checked out vol. 15 of Amyot's French translation of Plutarch and renewed the book on November 16—a good sign of his facility in French. Cameron, *Ralph Waldo Emerson's Reading*, 45, 46.

92. By July 11, 1843, Emerson seemed to be competent in Italian, as evidenced by this letter to Margaret Fuller: "Geo Bancroft gave me Dante's *Vita Nuova*, & recalling what you said, that I could not have read it, I have turned it all into English." *Letters*, 3:182–84.

93. Emerson to William Emerson, November 20, 1824, *Letters*, 1:154.

94. Cameron, *Ralph Waldo Emerson's Reading*, 47.

95. Emerson, "Goethe, or the Writer," in *Representative Men*, in *Collected Works of Ralph Waldo Emerson*, 6 vols. (Cambridge: Harvard University Press, Belknap Press, 1971), 4:156.

96. Ibid., 4:163.

97. The passage is from Goethe's *Nachgelassene Werke* (Stuttgart and Türbingen, 1832–33), 6:262.

98. Joseph von Hammer would later become Joseph von Hammer-Purgstall (1774–1856). Since his name appeared as von Hammer in the editions owned by Emerson, I refer to him simply as that.

99. Johann Wolfgang von Goethe, *West-östlicher Divan*, vol. 5 of *Werke* (Stuttgart, 1828); *Noten und Abhandlungen zu besserem Verstandnis des West-östlichen Divans* (1828–1833), vol. 6 of *Werke*.

100. Annemarie Schimmel, *A Two-Colored Brocade: The Imagery of Persian Poetry* (Chapel Hill: University of North Carolina Press, 1992), 3–9. The intensity of the outburst was also due in part to Goethe's newfound love, Marianne von Willemer. See John R. Williams, *The Life of Goethe* (Oxford: Blackwell, 1998), 111–15.

101. Goethe named Hafiz so frequently partly in deference to the convention of the *ghazal*, which requires Hafiz to include his own name in each poem.

102. "Let joy and pain / Be ours in common as twins are one!" Goethe, *West-östlicher Divan*. *West-Eastern Divan*, bilingual edition, with translations by John Whaley (New York: Peter Lang, 1998), 62, 63.

103. Ibid., 62, 63. My translation modifies Whaley's.

104. The two von Hammer anthologies owned by Emerson are at the Houghton Library: *Der Diwan von Mohammed Schemsed-din Hafis*, *AC85.Em345.Zy812h; *Geschichte der Schönen redekünste Persiens*, *AC85.Em345.Zy818h. Goethe's

Werke as well as *Sammtliche werke* (Stuttgart, 1840) are both listed by Walter Harding in *Emerson's Library* (Charlottesville: University of Virginia Press, 1967), 118. In 1862, Emerson also checked out Hafiz's *Eine Sammlung persischer Gedichte* (1856) from the Boston Athenaeum. See Cameron, *Ralph Waldo Emerson's Reading*, 34.

105. Sir William Jones, *Poeseos asiaticae commentariorum libri sex* (London, 1774). This was not listed as a book owned by Emerson in *Emerson's Library*.

106. This is a translation of "Mein Erbteil wie herrlich, weit und breit!/die Zeit ist mein Besitz, mein Acker ist die Zeit!" Whaley's translation: "Inheritance splendid, here and now!/For time is my estate, and time my field to plough." In *West-Eastern Divan. West-östlicher Divan*, 206, 207.

107. Emerson, *Complete Works*, 8:2.

108. *JMN* 8:67: "And so there are fountains all around Milton or Saadi or Menu from which they draw." Carpenter also cites a reference to Hafiz in 1841 which I have been unable to locate: "Hafiz defies you to show him or put him in a condition inopportune and ignoble." Carpenter, *Emerson and Asia*, 93.

109. Emerson, "Saadi," *The Dial* (October 1842): 265–69.

110. The first translation I am able to find is in his 1846 Journals, a translation of Hafiz's poem, "Come let us strew roses." *JMN* 9:398. For a checklist of Emerson's translations, see J. D. Yohannan, "Emerson's Translations of Persian Poetry from German Sources," *American Literature* 14 (January 1943): 407–20. See also *The Topical Notebooks of Ralph Waldo Emerson*, 3 vols., ed. Susan Sutton Smith et al. (Columbia: University of Missouri Press, 1990–94).

111. Albert J. von Frank, *An Emerson Chronology* (New York: G. K. Hall, 1994), 331, 505–6.

112. *The Gulistan, or Rose Garden of Saadi*, trans. Francis Gladwin (Boston: Ticknor and Fields, 1865), ix.

113. *Complete Works of Ralph Waldo Emerson*, 9:320–34.

114. The last entry was in 1879. *JMN* 16:527.

115. The three other drafts are in *JMN* 14:139–40.

> O Hafiz, give me thoughts,
> (If thoughts) For (&) pearls of thought thou hast;
> All (else is) beside is n(o)aught
> (Empty chatter & [noise] blast)
> All (else) is din & blast

> O Hafiz, give me thought
> (Thought) In/ golden image/ fiery fancy/ cast;
> For all beside is n(o)aught
> All else is din & blast.

> O Hafiz, give me thought(s)
> In fiery (fancies) figures cast;
> For all beside is naught,—
> All else is din & blast.

116. I should point out, however, that Hafiz was actually much honored by the rulers of Shiraz, especially Shad Abu Ishaq, a point not emphasized by Emerson.

See Edward G. Browne, *A Literary History of Persia* (1920; rpt., Bethesda, MD: Iranbooks, 1997), 3:271–93.

117. *The Topical Notebooks of Ralph Waldo Emerson*, ed. Ralph H. Orth et al., 3 vols. (Columbia: University of Missouri Press, 1990–94), 2:129. Hereafter cited in the text as *TN*.

118. *The Poetry Notebooks of Ralph Waldo Emerson* (Columbia: University of Missouri Press, 1994), 287. Hereafter cited in the text as *PN*.

119. G. M. Wickens, "Persian Literature: An Affirmation of Identity," in *Introduction to Islamic Civilization*, ed. R. M. Savory (Cambridge: Cambridge University Press, 1976), 77–88.

120. A. J. Arberry, "Persian Literature," in *The Legacy of Persia*, ed. A. J. Arberry (Oxford: Clarendon Press, 1953), 211; Reuben Levy, *An Introduction to Persian Literature* (New York: Columbia University Press, 1969), 33–35.

121. Agha Shahid Ali, introduction to *Ravishing Disunities: Real Ghazals in English* (Hanover, NH: Wesleyan University Press, 2000), 3.

122. Ibrahim Gamard, preface to *Hafiz: The Mystic Poets, Translated and with Notes by Gertrude Bell* (Woodstock, VT: SkyLight Paths, 2004), 4.

123. "Persian Poetry," in *Complete Works of Ralph Waldo Emerson*, 8:235–65, quotation from 248.

124. *The Koran. Commonly Called the Alcoran of Mohammed; Translated into English Immediately from the Original Arabic* (London: Maiden, 1801), 231.

125. Jonathan Edwards, "Sinners in the Hands of an Angry God," in *Jonathan Edwards: Representative Selections*, ed. Clarence H. Faust and Thomas H. Johnson (New York: Hill and Wang, 1962), 164.

126. "Deep Elem" refers to Elm Street, the red-light district in Dallas. Lyrics can be found at http://www3.clearlight.com/~acsa/songfile/DEEPELEM.HTM

127. Phil Lesh, longtime bass player of the Grateful Dead, gives a chilling account of the effects of cocaine, heroin, alcohol, and drugs on the band. See Lesh, *Searching for the Sound* (New York: Little, Brown, 2005).

128. Http://www.arts.ucsc.edu/gdead/agdl/allah.html. Robert Hunter was the lyricist for the Grateful Dead, working especially closely with Jerry Garcia.

CHAPTER THREE: THE PLANETARY DEAD

1. Margaret Fuller, *Woman in the Nineteenth Century* (New York: Norton, 1971), 94. Page references to this edition will be cited in parentheses in the text.

2. In a different context, Gayatri Spivak also argues for the need to "situate feminist individualism in its historical determination rather than simply to canonize it as feminism as such." See "Three Women's Texts and a Critique of Imperialism," *Critical Inquiry* 12 (Autumn 1985): 243–261, quotation from 244. Fuller's paradigm enacts Spivak's injunction through scale enlargement. In its emphasis on nonbiological reproduction, it also anticipates Judith Butler's challenge to think of kinship in nonheterosexual terms. See Butler, "Is Kinship Always Already Heterosexual?" *Differences* 13 (Spring 2002): 14–44.

3. Pierre-Simon Laplace, *Essai philosophique sur les probabilités*, 5th ed., 1825 (Christian Bourgois Editeur, 1986), 32–33: "Nous devons donc envisager l'état présent de l'univers comme l'effet de son état antérieur, et comme la cause de celui qui va suivre. Une intelligence qui pour un instant donné, connaitrait toutes les forces dont la nature est animée et la situation respective des êtres qui la composent, si d'ailleurs elle était assez vaste pour soumettre ces données a l'analyse, embrasserait dans la même formule les mouvements des plus grands corps de l'univers et ceux du plus léger atome: rien ne serait incertain pour elle, et l'avenir, comme le passé, serait présent à ses yeux. L'esprit humain offre, dans la perfection qu'il a su donner à l'Astronomie, une faible esquisse de cette intelligence." The English translation is from *A Philosophical Essay on Probabilities,* trans. Frederick Wilson Truscott and Frederick Lincoln Emory (New York: Dover, 1951), 4.

4. In a journal entry dated Sunday, October 1823, Emerson noted that "La Place has written in the mountain album of Switzerland his avowal of Atheism." *Journal and Miscellaneous Notebooks*, ed. William Gilman et al. (Cambridge: Harvard University Press, Belknap Press, 1960), 2:161.

5. Ralph Waldo Emerson, "The Relation of Man to the Globe," in *Early Lectures of Ralph Waldo Emerson*, ed. Stephen Whicher, Robert E. Spiller, and Wallace E. Williams, 3 vols. (Cambridge: Harvard University Press, 1959–72), 2:27–49, quotation from 28, 29.

6. Emerson, "The Individual," in *Early Lectures* 2:184.

7. Ibid., 185.

8. The conversations were set up with the help of Elizabeth Peabody, and a fee was charged. Those who regularly attended included Emerson, George Ripley, James Freeman Clarke, and others. See Megan Marshall, *The Peabody Sisters* (Boston: Houghton Mifflin, 2005), 386–88.

9. Caroline W. Healy [Dall], *Margaret and Her Friends; or, Ten Conversations with Margaret Fuller* (Boston: Robert's Brothers, 1895), 46.

10. See Stephen M. Stigler, *The History of Statistics: The Measurement of Uncertainty before 1900* (Cambridge: Harvard University Press, 1986), 9–220; Ian Hacking distinguishes between the numerical demonstration of the new "probability" and the old "probabilism" of the Scholastics, and argues that the new "probability" was most crucial not to physicists and astronomers but to medical practitioners and accountants computing annuities. See Ian Hacking, *The Emergence of Probability* (Cambridge: Cambridge University Press, 1975), 92–121. Lorraine Daston elaborates on this claim in *Classical Probability in the Enlightenment* (Princeton: Princeton University Press, 1988), 40–187.

11. Martin Rudwick, "Charles Lyell's Dream of a Statistical Paleontology," *Paleontology* 21 (1978): 225–44.

12. Ralph Waldo Emerson, "Fate," in *Selections from Ralph Waldo Emerson*, ed. Stephen Whicher (Boston: Houghton Mifflin, 1957), 337. For an excellent discussion of Emerson and Quetelet, see Barbara Packer, "Emerson and the Terrible Tabulations of the French," in *Transient and Permanent: The Transcendentalist Movement and Its Contexts*, ed. Charles Capper and Conrad Edick Wright (Boston: Massachusetts Historical Society, 1999), 148–67.

13. I am inspired here by Giorgio Agamben's critical terminology. See *Homo Sacer: Sovereign Power and Bare Life*, trans. Daniel Heller-Roazen (Stanford, CA: Stanford University Press, 1998).

14. Robert Pogue Harrison, *The Dominion of the Dead* (Chicago: University of Chicago Press, 2003).

15. See Michael Hardt and Antonio Negri's discussion, "Virtualities," in *Empire* (Cambridge: Harvard University Press, 2000), 353–69.

16. E. A. Wallis Budge, keeper of the Egyptian and Assyrian Antiquities in the British Museum, wrote in 1899 that "the Egyptians possessed, some six thousand years ago, a religion and a system of morality which . . . stand second to none among those which have been developed by the greatest nations of the world." See Budge, *Egyptian Ideas of the Future Life* (1899; rpt., New York: AMS Press, 1976), xii. Of course, the Egyptian care of the dead was limited to only the socially privileged, which might temper our praise somewhat.

17. The *Book of the Dead* was not the earliest of the Egyptian mortuary texts. The Pyramid Texts (dating to 2400 BCE) were the first to collect together these hymns, recitations, and instructions for the journey through the Netherworld, exclusively for the benefit of the king and his family. Later, the Coffin Texts extended this privilege to anyone who could afford a sarcophagus. By the early New Kingdom (ca.1550 BCE), the *Book of the Dead* had an even wider currency, democratizing the process further.

18. *The Egyptian Book of the Dead: The Book of Going Forth by Day, being the Papyrus of Ani*, trans. Raymond O. Faulkner, with additional translation and a commentary by Ogden Goelet (San Francisco: Chronicle Books, 1994), plate 5.

19. Ibid., plate 6.

20. E. A. Wallis Budge, *Liturgy of Funerary Offerings* (London: Kegan Paul, 1909), 2. See also Budge, *Book of Opening the Mouth*, 2 vols. (London: Kegan Paul, 1909).

21. Here I follow E. A. Wallis Budge's commentary in *The Book of the Dead* (1899; rpt., London: Arkana, 1985), 39–40.

22. Faulkner, *The Egyptian Book of the Dead*, plate 15.

23. Ibid., plate 12.

24. For a good summary of these different aspects of the soul, see Ogden Goelet's notes to Faulkner, *The Egyptian Book of the Dead*, 152.

25. I am playing here on the concept proposed by Aihwa Ong. See *Flexible Citizenship* (Durham, NC: Duke University Press, 1999).

26. Plutarchus, *Morals*, Trans. from the Greek, by Several Hands, 5th ed., rev. and corrected from the many errors of the former eds. (London: W. Taylor, 1718). See Walter Harding, *Emerson's Library* (Charlotteville: University Press of Virginia, 1967), 217.

27. "I have now of yours two vols of Milton, one of Jonson, one of Plutarch's *Morals*." Margaret Fuller to Ralph Waldo Emerson, May 30, 1837, in *The Letters of Margaret Fuller*, ed. Robert N. Hudspeth, 6 vols. (Ithaca: Cornell University Press, 1983), 1:277.

28. Bancroft had published a speech entitled "The Influence of Slavery on the Political Revolutions in Rome" in the *North American Review* 39 (October 1834): 413–37. In response, Fuller published "In Defense of Brutus" in the *Boston*

Daily Advertiser, November 27, 1834, citing Plutarch's account of Brutus. See *The Letters of Margaret Fuller*, 1: 227–28, n. 7.

29. E. A. Wallis Budge, *Egyptian Ideas of the Future Life* (1899; rpt., New York: AMS Press, 1976), 56.

30. For the date and place of composition, see J. Gwyn Griffiths, introduction to *Plutarch's "De Iside et Osiride"* (Swansea: University of Wales Press, 1970), 16–18.

31. See, for instance, William MacQuitty, *Island of Isis: Philae, Temple of the Nile* (London: Macdonald and Jane's, 1976); Louis V. Zabkar, *Hymns to Isis in Her Temple at Philae* (Hanover, NH: University Press of New England, 1988).

32. For a detailed account of this phenomenon, see R. E. Witt, *Isis in the Graeco-Roman World* (Ithaca: Cornell University Press, 1971); and Friedrich Solmsen, *Isis among the Greeks and Romans* (Cambridge: Harvard University Press, 1979).

33. Herodotus, *The Histories*, trans. Aubrey de Selincourt (Harmondsworth: Penguin, 1972), 152.

34. *Plutarch's Morals*, trans. from the Greek by Several Hands, rev. William W. Goodwin (Boston: Little, Brown, 1874), 66.

35. Ibid., 66.

36. Ibid., 78.

37. Ibid., 79.

38. Ibid., 106.

39. Ibid., 80.

40. "The Egyptian tradition points to the phallus of Osiris as one of the god's members successfully preserved as relic. Further, the myth as recorded by both Plutarch and the native sources tells of the posthumous procreation of Harpocrates by Osiris, so that his phallus is regarded as remaining intact in a specially vital sense, an idea confirmed by pictorial representations. The possibility of an intrusive Greek element must be faced. Cronus is said to have cut off the phallus of Uranus and thrown it into the sea." See Griffiths's commentary in *Plutarch's "De Iside et Osiride,"* 343.

41. *Plutarch's Morals*, 109.

42. Ibid., 110.

43. *Memoirs of Margaret Fuller Ossoli*, by R. W. Emerson, W. H. Channing, and J. F. Clarke, 2 vols. (Boston: Roberts, 1884), 1:230.

44. Drawing on Albert Torhoudt's argument in *Een Onbekend Gnostisch Systeem in Plutarchus' "De Iside et Osiride,"* J. Gwyn Griffiths traces the imperfection of Isis to a Gnostic strain in Plutarch. See *Plutarch's "De Iside et Osiride,"* 49.

45. Fuller's conversation on March 8, 1841, reported by Caroline Dall in *Margaret and Her Friends*, 41.

46. Panthea's story was recounted by Xenophon in books VI and VII of *Cyropaedia, or Institution of Cyrus*, trans. J. S. Watson and Henry Dale (London: Henry G. Bohn, 1855).

47. Xenophon, *Cyropaedia*, book 7, chap.3, 215, quoted in Fuller, *Woman in the Nineteenth Century*, 89.

48. Charles Sanders Peirce, "The Scientific Attitude and Fallibilism," in *Philosophical Writings of Peirce*, ed. Justus Buchler (New York: Dover, 1955), 42–59; Paul Ricoeur, *Fallible Man*, trans. Charles A. Kelbley (New York: Fordham University Press, 1986).

49. Thomas Taylor's notes to *The Metamorphosis; or, Golden Ass, and Philosophical Works, of Apuleius*, trans. Thomas Taylor (London: J. Moyes, 1822), 262.

50. Ibid., 262.

51. Margaret Fuller Reading Notes, BMS Am 1086 (A), Houghton Library, Harvard University.

52. For an illuminating discussion of the importance of the sistrum to Fuller, see Jeffrey Steele, *Transfiguring America: Myth, Ideology, and Mourning in Margaret Fuller's Writing* (Columbia: University of Missouri Press, 2001), 192–93.

53. Ralph Waldo Emerson, "Concord," in Emerson, Channing, and Clarke, *Memoirs of Margaret Fuller Ossoli*, 1:121.

54. Margaret Fuller, "Sistrum," in *Life Without and Life Within: Reviews, Narratives, Essays, and Poems by Margaret Fuller Ossoli*, ed. Arthur B. Fuller (Boston: Brown, Taggard and Chase, 1860), 413.

55. For the relevance of Marx to the American Renaissance in general, see Russ Castronovo, "American Literature Internationale," *ESQ* 49 (December 2004): 59–93.

56. For Marx's contributions to the *New York Tribune*, see *The American Journalism of Marx and Engels: A Selection from the New York Daily Tribune*, ed. Henry M. Christian (New York: New American Library, 1966).

57. Karl Marx, *The Eighteenth Brumaire of Louis Bonaparte* (New York: International Publishers, 1969), 15.

58. Ibid., 17.

59. Jacques Derrida points out that both the *Communist Manifesto* and the *Eighteenth Brumaire of Louis Bonaparte* deploy "something like a spectropolitics and a genealogy of ghosts, more precisely a patrimonial logic of the generations of ghosts. Marx never stops conjuring and exorcising there." See *Specters of Marx: The State of the Debt, the Work of Mourning, and the New International*, trans. Peggy Pamuf (New York: Routlege, 1994), 107.

60. For the importance of the European 1848 to American literature, see Larry J. Reynolds, *European Revolutions and the American Literary Renaissance* (New Haven: Yale University Press, 1988).

61. Fuller, dispatch to the *New York Tribune*, Rome, April 19, 1848, in *These Sad but Glorious Days: Dispatches from Europe, 1846–1850*, ed. Larry J. Reynolds and Susan Belasco Smith (New Haven: Yale University Press, 1991), 230.

62. Ibid., 238.

63. Ibid., 230.

64. Ibid., 230.

65. Ibid., 322.

66. Theodor Adorno, *Negative Dialectics*, trans. E. B. Ashton (New York: Continuum, 2003).

67. Fuller, *These Sad but Glorious Days*, 310.

68. For the importance of Fuller as a champion and translator of German literature, see Christina Zwarg, "The Storied Facts of Margaret Fuller," *New England Quarterly* 69 (1996): 128–42; Karen A, English, " 'Genuine Transcripts of Private Experience': Margaret Fuller and Translation," *American Transcendentalist Quarterly* 15 (June 2001): 131–47; and Colleen Glenney Boggs, "Margaret Fuller's American Translation," *American Literature* 76 (March 2004): 31–58.

69. Margaret Fuller, "Menzel's View of Goethe," *The Dial* 1, no. 3 (January 1841), 347.

70. Ibid., 346.

71. Ibid., 346.

72. *Conversations with Goethe, from the German of Eckermann*, trans. Margaret Fuller (Boston: Hilliard, Gray, 1839), vii–viii.

73. Fuller, "Menzel's View of Goethe," 341.

CHAPTER FOUR: GENRE AS WORLD SYSTEM

1. According to the *Oxford English Dictionary*, the earliest use of the word in English to denote a type of literary work was in 1770; in French, this sense of *genre* dates from the mid-seventeenth century.

2. Croce writes: "Every true work of art has violated some established kind and upset the ideas of the critics, who have thus been obliged to broaden the kinds, until finally even the broadened kind has proved too narrow, owing to the appearance of new works of art, naturally followed by new scandals, new upsettings, and—new broadenings." See Benedetto Croce, *Aesthetic: As Science of Expression and General Linguistic*, trans. Douglas Ainslie (Boston: Nonpareil Books, 1978), 36–37.

3. Jacques Derrida, "The Law of Genre," *Glyph* 7 (1980): 176–232; reprinted in Derrida, *Acts of Literature*, ed. Derek Attridge (New York: Routledge, 1992), 221–52, quotation from 224–25.

4. Alasdair Fowler, *Kinds of Literature: An Introduction to the Theory of Genres and Modes* (Cambridge: Harvard University Press, 1982), 37, v.

5. Gilles Deleuze and Felix Guattari, "Rhizome," in *On the Line*, trans. John Johnston (New York: Semitext[e], 1983), 1–68.

6. I am grateful to Jay Clayton for urging me to foreground this concept.

7. Ludwig Wittgenstein, *Philosophical Investigations*, trans. G.E.M. Anscombe (New York: Blackwell, 1958), no. 66, pp. 31–32.

8. Ibid., no. 67, p. 32.

9. Claude Lévi-Strauss, *Structural Anthropology*, trans. Claire Jacobson and Brooke Grundfest Schoepf (New York: Basic Books, 1963), 50.

10. Ibid., 312.

11. Ibid., 314.

12. Mandelbrot, "About the Author," in *Fractals: Form, Chance, and Dimension* (San Francisco: W. H. Freeman, 1977).

13. Mandelbrot has since left IBM and is now Sterling Professor of Mathematics at Yale University.

14. Mandelbrot, *Fractals*, 4.

15. Ibid., 1.

16. Ibid., 29.

17. Ibid., 1.

18. Ibid., 1.

19. Emmanuel Wallerstein, *The Modern World-System*, 3 vols. (New York: Academic Press, 1974); Frederic Jameson, "Magical Narratives: On the Dialectical Use of Genre Criticism," in *The Political Unconscious: Narrative as a Socially Symbolic Act* (Ithaca: Cornell University Press, 1981), 103–50.

20. Franco Moretti, "Conjectures on World Literature," *New Left Review* (January/February 2000): 54–68, quotation from 57. See also his *The Modern Epic: The World-System to Garcia Marquez* (New York: Verso, 1996); and *Graphs, Maps, Trees* (New York: Verso, 2005).

21. Moretti, "Conjectures," 57.

22. The classic statements here are Ian Watt, *The Rise of the Novel: Studies in Defoe, Richardson, and Fielding* (Berkeley and Los Angeles: University of California Press, 1957); and Michael McKeon, *The Origins of the English Novel, 1600–1740* (Baltimore: Johns Hopkins University Press, 1987).

23. While the antiquity of the epic is well established, the novel has also been shown to be of ancient origins, traceable at least to Apuleius's *Metamorphosis*, written in the 2nd century AD, and, even further back, to the *Metamorphoses* ascribed to Lucius of Patrae. See Ben Edwin Perry, *The "Metamorphoses" Ascribed to Lucius of Patrae*, Ph.D. dissertation, Princeton University, 1919. More recently, classicists have made a concerted effort to argue for the presence of the novel in ancient Greece and Rome. See, for instance, Graham Anderson, *Ancient Fiction: The Novel in the Graeco-Roman World* (Totowa, NJ: Barnes and Noble, 1984); Thomas Hagg, *The Novel in Antiquity* (Oxford: Oxford University Press, 1983); S. J. Harrison, *Oxford Readings in the Roman Novel* (Oxford: Oxford University Press, 1999); Arthur Heiserman, *The Novel before Novel* (Chicago: University of Chicago Press, 1977); P. G. Walsh, *The Roman Novel* (Cambridge: Cambridge University Press, 1970); *The Search for the Ancient Novel*, ed. James Tatum (Baltimore: Johns Hopkins University Press, 1994); John J. Winkler, *Auctor and Actor: A Narratological Reading of Apuleius' "Golden Ass"* (Berkeley and Los Angeles: University of California Press, 1985).

24. Margaret Anne Doody, *The True History of the Novel* (New Brunswick, NJ: Rutgers University Press, 1996).

25. Plato, *The Republic*, trans. Benjamin Jowett (New York: Vintage, 1991), no. 394, p. 94.

26. Aristotle, *Poetics*, trans. Gerald F. Else (Ann Arbor: University of Michigan Press, 1970), section 24, 1459b23–1459b24, pp. 63–64.

27. Ibid., section 22, 1458a20–1458a30, p. 59.

28. Ibid., 1459a9, p. 61.

29. Ibid., section 24, 1459b35, p. 64.

30. Walter Burkert, *The Orientalizing Revolution: Near Eastern Influence on Greek Culture in the Early Archaic Age*, trans. Margaret E. Pinder and Walter Burkert (Cambridge: Harvard University Press, 1992), 116.

31. Benjamin R. Foster, introduction to *The Epic of Gilgameth*, trans. Benjamin R. Foster (New York: Norton, 2001), xx.

32. William J. Jackson, *Heaven's Fractal Net: Retrieving Lost Visions in the Humanities* (Bloomington: Indiana University Press, 2004), 41.

33. Ibid., 42.

34. Dante's *De vulgari eloquentia* was written in Latin. For the transition from Latin to Italian, see Ernst Pulgram, *The Tongues of Italy: Prehistory and History* (Cambridge: Harvard University Press, 1958), 402–17; Cecil Grayson, *A Renaissance Controversy: Latin or Italian?* (Oxford: Clarendon Press, 1960), 8–28.

35. Zygmunt G. Baranski, " 'Significar per verba': Notes on Dante and Plurilingualism," *Italianist* 6 (1986): 5–18, quotation from 13.

36. Arnaut's words are as follows: "Tan m'abellis vostre cortes deman,/qu'ieu no me puese ni voill a vos cobrire./Ieu sui Arnaut, que plor e vau cantan;/consiros vei la passada folor,/e vei jausen lo joi qu'esper, denan./Ara vos prec, per aquella valor/que vos guida al som de l'escalina,/sovenha vos a temps de ma dolor!" (*Purgatorio* 26:140–47). John Sinclair's prose translation: "So much does your courteous question please me that I neither can nor would conceal myself from you. I am Arnaut, who weep and sing as I go. I see with grief past follies and see, rejoicing, the day I hope for before me. Now I beg of you, by that goodness which guides you to the summit of the stairway, to take thought in due time for my pain." See *Dante's Purgatorio*, trans. John D. Sinclair (New York: Oxford University Press, 1961), 343.

37. M. M. Bakhtin, "Epic and Novel," in *The Dialogic Imagination*, ed. Caryl Emerson and Michael Holquist (Austin: University of Texas Press, 1981), 3–40, quotation from 13.

38. Ibid., 17.

39. In his late work, Bakhtin himself seems to be moving away from his binary oppositions in "Epic and Novel" to a smaller-scale analysis, putting increasing emphasis on utterance as a "unit of speech communion." See especially his "The Problem of Speech Genres," in *Speech Genres and Other Late Essays*, trans. Vern W. McGee (Austin: University of Texas Press, 1986), 60–102.

40. Henry James, Preface, to *The Wings of the Dove* (New York: Scribner's, 1909), xix.

41. Henry James, *The Portrait of a Lady* (Boston: Houghton Mifflin, 1956), 423.

42. Benedict Anderson, *Imagined Communities: Reflections on the Origin and Spread of Nationalism* (New York: Verso, 1983), 30. For an important critique of Anderson, see Jonathan Culler, "Anderson and the Novel," *Diacritics* 29 (winter 1999): 20–39.

43. Henry James, Preface to *The Awkward Age* (New York: Scribner's, 1908), xvii.

44. *Little Review*, August 1918.

45. Ezra Pound, "Henry James," in *Literary Essays of Ezra Pound* (New York: New Directions, 1968), 296.

46. Ibid., 297, 299, 301.

47. Ibid., 302.

48. Ibid., 300.

49. W. H. Auden, "Address on Henry James," delivered October 24, 1946, published in the *Gazette of the Grolier Club*, February 1947; reprinted in Auden,

Prose, Vol. 2, 1939–1948, ed. Edward Mendelson (London: Faber, 2002), 296–303, quotation from 303.

50. ἐλανδρς and επτολις, man-destroying and city-destroying: the beauty of Helen that inaugurates the *Iliad* and the *Odyssey*. See *A Companion to the Cantos of Ezra Pound*, ed. Carroll F. Terrell (Berkeley and Los Angeles: University of California Press, 1980), 29.

51. "Si pulvis nullus," said Ovid, / "Erit, nullum tamen excute": "And if a speck of dust should fall into your lady's lap, flick it off with your fingers; if there be no speck of dust, well, flick it off anyway." From Ovid, *Ars amatoria*, 1:149–51. See *A Companion to the Cantos of Ezra Pound*, 29.

52. "y cavals armatz" (and horses in armor), a quotation from Bertran de Born, see Terrell, *A Companion to the Cantos of Ezra Pound*, 29–30.

53. "And Dante's 'ciocco,' brand struck in the game": ciocco, "log," a reference to the image of the souls rising from the fifth circle to the sixth circle in the *Paradiso*. See Terrell, *A Companion to the Cantos of Ezra Pound*, 30.

54. "Un peu moisi, plancher plus bas que le jardin" (a little musty, the floor being below garden level), a quotation from Flaubert's *Un Coeur Simple*. See Terrell, *A Companion to the Cantos of Ezra Pound*, 30.

55. Ezra Pound, canto 7, lines 24–30.

56. Pound, "Henry James," 295.

57. "Grave incessu" mixes in Virgil's line "Vera incessu patuit dea" (and from her manner of walking knew her to be a goddess), from *Aeneid*, 1:405, quoted by Pound in his "Notes on Elizabethan Classicists," in *Literary Essays of Ezra Pound*, 246. See Terrell, *Companion to the Cantos of Ezra Pound*, 31.

58. Hugh Kenner, *The Pound Era* (Berkeley and Los Angeles: University of California Press, 1971), 3–22.

59. The word "babel" is suggested to me by Jonathan Arac's important essay, "Global and Babel: Language and Planet in American Literature," forthcoming in *Shades of the Planet: American Literature as World Literature* (Princeton: Princeton University Press, 2007).

60. Lukacs is explicit about this Hegelian influence. See *Theory of the Novel: A Historico-Philosophical Essay on the Forms of Great Epic Literature*, trans. Anna Bostock (Cambridge: MIT Press, 1971), 15–19. Subsequently, with his turn to Marxism, Lukacs repudiated Hegel. In the preface to the 1962 reissue, Lukacs persisted in returning to the author of *The Theory of the Novel* in the third person.

61. Lukacs, *Theory of the Novel*, 56.

62. Rosalie Colie, *The Resources of Kind: Genre-Theory in the Renaissance*, ed. Barbara K. Lewalski (Berkeley and Los Angeles: University of California Press, 1973); Vladimir Propp, *Morphology of the Folktale*, trans. Laurence Scott, 2nd ed (Austin: University of Texas Press, 1968); Tzvetan Todorov, *Genres in Discourse*, trans. Catherine Porter (Cambridge: Cambridge University Press, 1990); Hans Robert Jauss, *Toward an Aesthetic of Reception*, trans. Timothy Bahti (Minneapolis: University of Minnesota Press, 1982), 76–109. Fowler and Moretti were discussed earlier in the chapter.

63. Henry James, *The Golden Bowl*, vol. 1 (New York: Scribner's, 1909), 3, hereafter cited by page in the text.

64. David Quint analyzes at length the shield of Aeneas, with its richly wrought, proleptic depiction of the Battle of Actium, as an emblem telescoping the rise of the Roman Empire within the narrative of the *Aeneid*. See *Epic and Empire: Politics and Generic Form from Virgil to Milton* (Princeton: Princeton University Press, 1993), 21–46.

65. Henry James, "Venice," in *Italian Hours* (New York: Ecco Press, 1909), 2–30, quotation from 18.

66. *Plutarch's Lives: The Translation called Dryden's, Corrected from the Greek and Revised by Arthur Hugh Clough* (Boston: Little, Brown, 1899), 5:184–85.

67. Plutarch describes Darius's anguish when told about the circumstances of her death and the "sumptuous funeral" Alexander gave her: "do I not lament the least of Statira's misfortunes in her captivity and death? Have I not suffered something more injurious and deplorable in her lifetime? And had I not been miserable with less dishonor, if I had met with a more severe and inhuman enemy? For how is it possible a young man as he is, should treat the wife of his opponent with so much distinction, were it not from some motive that does me disgrace?" *Plutarch's Lives*, 198.

68. *The Family of Darius before Alexander, by Paolo Veronese. A resume, some new deductions and some new facts, by Cecil Gould* (London: National Gallery Publications Department, 1978), 13.

69. Ibid., 8.

70. Ibid., 18.

71. John Ruskin, "The Turner Bequest and the National Gallery: To the Editor of the *Times*," July 7, 1857, published in the *Times* on July 9, 1857, collected in *The Works of John Ruskin*, ed. E. T. Cook and Alexander Wedderburn (New York: Longman, Green, 1905), 13:88. For Ruskin's relation to Veronese in general, see Andrew Tate, " 'Archangel' Veronese: Ruskin as Protestant Spectator," in *Ruskin's Artists*, ed. Robert Hewison (Aldershot: Ashgate, 2000), 131–46.

72. John Ruskin, *Modern Painters* (Boston: Dana Estes, 1873), 5:245.

73. Henry James, "Italy Revisited," in *Italian Hours*, 107–35, quotation from 127.

74. Henry James, "Two Old Houses and Three Young Women," in *Italian Hours*, 64–76, quotations from 73. For a fine discussion of this story in the context of the Austrian occupation of Venice, see Scott Byrd, "The Spoils of Venice: Henry James's 'Two Old Houses and Three Young Women' and *The Golden Bowl*," *American Literature* 43 (1971): 371–84.

75. James, "Two Old House." 73–74.

76. *The Adoration of Kings* was actually acquired from the Church of San Silvestro, not from a private family. See the National Gallery web site: http://www.nationalgallery_org.uk

77. Henry James, *A Small Boy and Others* (New York: Scribner's 1913), 5. James writes: ". . . mixed as such as a mixture, our Scotch with our Irish, might be, it had had still a grace to borrow from the third infusion or dimension."

78. The reminiscences of Thomas Sergeant Perry, cited in Robert C. Le Clair, *Young Henry James* (New York: Bookman Associates, 1955), 282.

79. James says of his education in Geneva: "I worried out Virgil and Tite-Live with M. Verchère." See *Notes of a Son and Brother* (New York: Scribner's, 1914), 8.

80. *Family of Darius before Alexander*, 9–10.

81. Veronese's *Family of Darius* was of course still in the Palazzo Pisani in Venice when Tiepolo was painting. Tiepolo's *Alexander and the Family of Darius* is now in a private collection.

82. Michael Levey, *Giambattista Tiepolo: His Life and Art* (New Haven: Yale University Press, 1986), 124.

83. Maria Elisa Avagnina, Fernado Rigon, and Remo Schivao, *Tiepolo: The Vicentine Villas* (Milano: Electa, 1990), 49.

84. James, *The Golden Bowl*, 2:287, hereafter cited by page in the text.

85. James, "Venice," in *Italian Hours*, 17.

86. Ruskin, "The Shrine of the Slaves," first supplement to vol. 3 of *The Stones of Venice* (New York: John Alden, 1885), 112.

87. Henry James, *The Middle Years* (New York: Scribner's, 1917), 50.

88. Ibid., 50–51.

CHAPTER FIVE: TRANSNATIONAL BEAUTY

1. See, for instance, *Revenge of the Aesthetic: The Place of Literature in Theory Today*, ed. Michael P. Clark (Berkeley and Los Angeles: University of California Press, 2000); Gérard Genette, *The Aesthetic Relation*, trans. G. M. Goshgarian (Ithaca: Cornell University Press, 1999); Elaine Scarry, *On Beauty and Being Just* (Princeton: Princeton University Press, 1999); James Soderholm, ed., *Beauty and the Critic: Aesthetics in the Age of Cultural Studies* (Tuscaloosa: University of Alabama Press, 1997). Also important is a slightly earlier volume, *Aesthetics and Ideology*, ed. George Levine (New Brunswick, NJ: Rutgers University Press, 1994).

2. Terry Eagleton, *The Ideology of the Aesthetic* (Cambridge, MA: Basil Blackwell, 1990), 3, 2.

3. As a subject-centered theory, the *Critique of Judgment* will always be of marginal interest to those who see aesthetics as object-centered. For a lucid critique of Kant from the latter standpoint, see Genette, *The Aesthetic Relation*, 61–72.

4. Immanuel Kant, "Perpetual Peace," in *Kant's Political Writings*, ed. Hans Reiss, trans. H. B. Nisbet (Cambridge: Cambridge University Press, 1970), 93–130, quotation from 129.

5. As Hans Reiss points out, Frederick William II was much offended by Kant's *Religion within the Limits of Reason Alone* (1793), and issued a Royal Command forbidding him from writing any more on religion. See Reiss, introduction to *Kant's Political Writings*, 2.

6. For a discussion of Kant's "federalist" conception of world government, see Carl Friedrich, *Inevitable Peace* (Cambridge: Harvard University Press, 1948).

7. Kant, "Perpetual Peace," 93.

8. Hannah Arendt, *Lectures on Kant's Political Philosophy*, ed. Ronald Beiner (Chicago: University of Chicago Press, 1982), 7, hereafter cited by page in the text.

9. Arendt gave these Kant lectures at the New School for Social Research during the fall semester of 1970. An earlier version of them had also been presented at the University of Chicago in 1964; she was scheduled to lecture again on Kant at the New School in 1976, but her death came in December 1975. These lectures were in preparation for "Judging," which was to have been the third and concluding part of her work, *The Life of the Mind.*

10. For a lucid and respectful dissent from Arendt, see Patrick Riley, "Hannah Arendt on Kant, Truth and Politics," in *Essays on Kant's Political Philosophy,* ed. Howard Williams (Cardiff: University of Wales Press, 1992), 305–23.

11. Arendt is not the only one to see the *Critique of Judgment* as a theory about a global humanity. In a short but suggestive volume, Dieter Henrich has also argued that the third critique grounds a theory of international human rights. Unlike Arendt, his argument proceeds by linking the *Critique of Judgment* not to "Perpetual Peace," but to the *Critique of Pure Reason.* See Henrich, *Aesthetic Judgment and the Moral Image of the World* (Stanford, CA: Stanford University Press, 1992). Relatedly, see also Mark F. Franke, *Global Limits: Immanuel Kant, International Relations, and Critique of World Politics* (Albany: State University of New York Press, 2001).

12. Immanuel Kant, *Critique of Judgment,* trans. J. H. Bernard (New York: Hafner/Macmillan, 1951), 75. Hereafter cited by section in the text.

13. Pierre Bourdieu is mistaken, I think, when, in his brief discussion of the *Critique of Judgment,* he says that Kant's aesthetics is based on "disgust at the facile" and the refusal of the "simple, primitive form of pleasure." See Bourdieu, *Distinction: A Social Critique of the Judgment of Taste,* trans. Richard Nice (Cambridge: Harvard University Press, 1984), 87–88.

14. Rita Felski has also urged us to think of aesthetics as a category running across the full spectrum of the humanities. Felski, "Aesthetics and Cultural Studies," presentation at the Americanist Colloquium, Yale University, March 2003.

15. Ernst Cassirer, "Critical Idealism as a Philosophy of Culture," in *Symbol, Myth, and Culture: Essays and Lectures of Ernst Cassirer, 1935–1945,* ed. Donald Phillip Verene (New Haven: Yale University Press, 1979), 88.

16. Paul Guyer, *Kant and the Claims of Taste* (Cambridge: Harvard University Press, 1979), 297–307.

17. Eagleton, *The Ideology of the Aesthetic,* 96.

18. Robert Hillyer, "Treason's Strange Fruit: The Case of Ezra Pound and the Bollingen Award," *Saturday Review of Literature,* June 11, 1949, 10.

19. Norman Cousins and Harrison Smith, "Ezra Pound and the Bollingen Award," *Saturday Review of Literature,* June 11, 1949, 20.

20. Eventually Pound was deemed "mentally unfit" for trial and remanded to St. Elizabeths Hospital, kept there for twelve years, 1945–58. For a full account, see Julien Cornell, *The Trial of Ezra Pound: A Documented Account of the Treason Case by the Defendant's Lawyer* (New York: John Day Co., 1966). As Conrad Rushing says, "Pound's anti-Semitism is extreme to the point of being a kind of madness, yet as disgraceful and embarrassing as his comments are, it was not the law nor is it now that a bigot is also a traitor." See Rushing, "Mere Words: The Trial of Ezra Pound," *Critical Inquiry* 14 (1987): 111–33.

21. This is the first of the two indictments against Pound. For a detailed account of this as well as of the second indictment, see Charles Norman, *The Case of Ezra Pound* (New York: Funk and Wagnalls, 1968), 62–82, quotation from 62–63.

22. The book was No. 2 on the *New York Times* bestseller list on July 20, 2003. For Coulter, treason is a long-practiced and never-acknowledged sin of the Democrats; it needs to be named, to be 'outed.' With no irony she recommends a return to McCarthyism.

23. Robert Hillyer, "Treason's Strange Fruit," 10.

24. Ibid., 28.

25. Ibid., 11.

26. Robert Hillyer, "Poetry's New Priesthood," *Saturday Review* (June 18, 1949), 7. "A Glossary of the New Criticism" was published in *Poetry: A Magazine of Verse* (November 1948–January 1949).

27. Robert Hillyer, "Poetry's New Priesthood," 8.

28. Ibid., 8.

29. The directive was announced by Senator Theodore Francis Green (D) of Rhode Island and reported in the Washington *Times-Herald* on August 20, 1949. See *The Case against the "Saturday Review of Literature"* (Chicago: Modern Poetry Association, 1949), v. Since 1949, the Bollingen Prize has been sponsored instead by Yale University.

30. Marjorie Perloff, "Fascism, Anti-Semitism, Isolationism: Contextualizing the case of EP," *Paideuma* 16, no. 3 (Winter 1987): 7–21. As Perloff shows, the intellectuals affiliated with the *Partisan Review* were almost uniformly antiwar.

31. Hillyer, "Poetry's New Priesthood," 38.

32. Walter Benjamin, epilogue to "The Work of Art in the Age of Mechanical Reproduction," in *Illuminations*, trans. Harry Zohn (New York: Schocken Books, 1969), 241.

33. Ibid., 241.

34. Russell Berman, "The Aestheticization of Politics: Walter Benjamin on Fascism and the Avant-Garde," *Stanford Italian Review* 8, no. 1–2 (1990): 35–52, especially 49.

35. See, for instance, George L. Mosse, *The Fascist Revolution* (New York: Howard Fertig, 1999), 45–54, 183–98; Mary Ann Frese Witt, *The Search for Modern Tragedy: Aesthetic Fascism in Italy and France* (Ithaca: Cornell University Press, 2001); Simonetta Falasca-Zamponi, *Fascist Spectacle: The Aesthetics of Power in Musssolini's Italy* (Berkeley and Los Angeles: University of California Press, 1993).

36. Walter Goodman, *The Committee: The Extraordinary Career of the House Committee on Un-American Activities* (New York: Farrar, Straus and Giroux, 1968), 16, 18.

37. Interestingly, the Committee on Un-American Activities actually made an appearance in the *Saturday Review* at the same time as the Bollingen controversy. John S. Wood, chair of the committee, had sent a letter to school superintendents to obtain a list of textbooks for inspection. The *Saturday Review* was firmly opposed to this. See "Speaking of Tests," *Saturday Review of Literature* (July 9, 1949), 22.

38. Library of Congress Information Office, Press Release no. 590, "Statement of the Committee of the Fellows of the Library of Congress in American Letters in Reply to Published Criticisms of the Bollingen Prize in Poetry," 10.

39. Canto 74, in *The Cantos of Ezra Pound* (New York: New Directions Books, 1996), 445.

40. Richard B. Lyttle, *Il Duce: The Rise and Fall of Benito Mussolini* (New York: Atheneum, 1987), 97–98.

41. For Mussolini's roots in Italian Socialism (specifically, the syndicalism of Georges Sorel), see A. James Gregor, *Young Mussolini and the Intellectual Origins of Fascism* (Berkeley and Los Angeles: University of California Press, 1979). Gregor draws on the monumental archival work of Renzo De Felice, the foremost Italian historian of fascism, whose eight-volume biography of Mussolini has unfortunately not been translated into English. For a short introduction to De Felice's work, see his *Fascism: An Informal Introduction to Its Theory and Practice: An Interview with Michael A. Ledeen* (New Brunswick, NJ: Transaction Books, 1976).

42. Pound wrote for A. R. Orage's *The New Age* from November 1911 to January 1921. For a detailed account of Pound's tie to British Socialism and its legacy in his admiration for Mussolini, see Wendy Stallard Flory, *The American Ezra Pound* (New Haven: Yale University Press, 1989), 42–130; Leon Surette, "Ezra Pound and British Radicalism," *English Studies in Canada* 9, no. 4 (1983): 435–51; Tim Redman, *Ezra Pound and Italian Fascism* (New York: Cambridge University Press, 1991), 17–50.

43. Pound, *Jefferson and/or Mussolini* (New York: Liveright, 1935), ix.

44. Ibid., 12.

45. I should point out, however, that Mussolini did have excellent press in America all through the 1920s. See John P. Diggins, *Musssolini and Fascism: The View from America* (Princeton: Princeton University Press, 1972), 3–73.

46. In a statement accompanying the publication of that book, Pound wrote: "The body of this Ms. was written and left my hands in February 1933. 40 publishers have refused it. No typescript of mine has been read by so many people or brought me a more interesting correspondence." *Jefferson and/or Mussolini*, iv.

47. D. H. Lawrence to Louisa Burrows, November 20, 1909. Lawrence said of Pound: "He is a well-known American poet—a good one. He is 24, like me, but his god is beauty, mine, life." *Lawrence in Love: Letters from D. H. Lawrence to Louisa Burrows*, ed. James T. Boulton (Nottingham, England: University of Nottingham Press, 1968), 46.

48. Pound, canto 74, *Cantos*, 446.

49. Philip Kuberski has also noted the importance of Mussolini as a poetic precursor for Pound. See *A Calculus of Ezra Pound* (Gainsville: University of Florida Press, 1992), 16–18. For an account of the affinity between Pound and Mussolini based on a theory of translation as well as a theory of economics, see Paul Morrison, *The Poetics of Fascism* (New York: Oxford University Press, 1996), 16–59.

50. Theodor Adorno, *Aesthetic Theory*, trans. C. Lenhardt (London: Routledge and Kegan Paul, 1984), 48, 366.

51. Pound, canto 74, *Cantos*, 450.

52. Radio Broadcast no. 6, "On Resuming" (January 29, 1942), in *Ezra Pound Speaking: Radio Speeches of World War II*, ed. Leonard W. Doob (Westport, CT: Greenwood Press, 1978), 23.

53. Ibid. As Burton Raffel points out, Pound is probably the greatest poet-translator in American literary history, translating from a dozen languages: Italian, French, Spanish, Provençal, Latin and Greek (the languages he knew best); German and Old English (which he knew reasonably well); Chinese (of which he had a smattering); and Japanese, Egyptian, and Hindi (which he knew not at all). See Raffel, *Ezra Pound: The Prime Minister of Poetry* (Hamden: Archon Books, 1984), 61–62.

54. Pound, Radio Broadcast no. 6, in *Ezra Pound Speaking*, 26.

55. Ezra Pound and Ernest Fenollosa, *The Classic Noh Theatre of Japan* (1917; rpt., New York: New Directions, 1959), introductory note. After Fenollosa's sudden death in 1908, his widow gave all his manuscripts to Pound in 1913: "eight notebooks in all, plus the volumes of notes on *Noh* drama, plus the books in which he was drafting his lectures on Chinese poetics, plus a sheaf of loose sheets." See Hugh Kenner, *The Pound Era* (Berkeley and Los Angeles: University of California Press, 1971), 198.

56. Pound, Radio Broadcast no. 6, *Ezra Pound Speaking*, 23.

CHAPTER SIX: NONSTANDARD TIME

1. Plato, *Timaeus*, trans. Benjamin Jowett (Indianapolis, IN: Bobbs-Merrill, 1949), 19–20. The full passage reads: "Now the nature of the ideal being was everlasting, but to bestow this attribute in its fullness upon a creature was impossible. Wherefore he resolved to have a moving image of eternity, and when he set in order the heaven, he made this image eternal but moving according to number, while eternity itself rests in unity; and this image we call time."

2. Aristotle, *Physics*, ed. W. D. Ross (Oxford: Clarendon Press, 1936), IV.219b.5–7, p. 386.

3. Ibid., IV.220b.7, p. 388.

4. Ibid., IV.220a.14, p. 387.

5. Ibid., IV.220a.24, p. 387.

6. Ibid., IV.218a.25, p. 385.

7. For the centrality of Newton to the Enlightenment, see Peter Gay, *The Enlightenment: The Science of Freedom* (New York: Norton, 1977), 126–87. For the importance of Newton to seventeenth- and eighteenth-century English political culture, see Margaret C. Jacob, *Newtonians and the English Revolution, 1689–1720* (Ithaca: Cornell University Press, 1976); Betty Jo Teeter Dobbs and Margaret C. Jacob, *Newton and the Culture of Newtonianism* (Atlantic Highlands, NJ: Humanities Press, 1995). For the importance of Newton to political culture in the United States, see Garry Wills, *Inventing America: Jefferson's Declaration of Independence* (New York: Vintage, 1979), 93–110; I. Bernard Cohen, *Science and the Founding Fathers* (New York: Norton, 1995).

8. Isaac Newton, *Philosophiae naturalis principia mathematica* (1686), trans. as *Mathematical Principles of Natural Philosophy*, trans. Andrew Motte, rev.

Florian Cajori (1729; Berkeley and Los Angeles: University of California Press, 1934), 6, 8.

9. It should be pointed out that this numerical regime was hardly Newton's alone. Seventeenth-century science was founded upon it. For the importance of numerical reasoning not only to the physical sciences (Kepler and Huygens) but also to the biological sciences (Harvey), see I. Bernard Cohen, *The Newtonian Revolution* (Cambridge: Cambridge University Press, 1980), 15–38.

10. For space in Newton, see Lawrence Sklar, *Space, Time, and Spacetime* (Berkeley and California: University of California Press, 1977), 182–93. For an emphatic argument about the centrality in Newton of "an absolutely immobile space, distinct from body, extending from infinity to infinity," see Robert Rynasiewicz, "By Their Properties, Causes, and Effects: Newton's Scholium on Time, Space, Place, and Motion," *Studies in History and Philosophy of Science* 26 (1995): 133–53, 295–321, quotation from 135.

11. "Simultaneity" remains an important (if thorny) concept for the physical sciences even after Newton. See Hans Reichenbach, *The Philosophy of Space and Time*, trans. Maria Reichenbach and John Freund (New York: Dover, 1958), 123–35.

12. Homi K. Bhabha, "DissemiNation: Time, Narrative, and the Margins of the Modern Nation," in *The Location of Culture* (London: Routledge, 1994), 139–70.

13. Benedict Anderson, *Imagined Communities: Reflections on the Origin and Spread of Nationalism* (London: Verso, 1983), 30.

14. Bhabha here draws on Julia Kristeva, "Women's Time," in *The Kristeva Reader*, ed. Toril Moi (Oxford: Blackwell, 1986), 187–213.

15. Bhabha, "DissemiNation," 153.

16. J. M. Coetzee, "Newton and the Ideal of a Transparent Scientific Language," *Journal of Literary Semantics* 11 (1982): 3–13; reprinted in Coetzee, *Doubling the Point: Essays and Interviews*, ed. David Attwell (Cambridge: Harvard University Press, 1992), 181–94.

17. Though Coetzee does not explicitly mention W.V.O. Quine, his position is very much compatible with Quine's rejection of any language-transcendent semantic content. See Quine, *Word and Object* (Cambridge: MIT Press, 1960), 26–79.

18. Albert Einstein, "Autobiographical Notes," in *Albert Einstein: Philosopher-Scientist*, ed. Paul Arthur Schilpp (La Salle, IL: Open Court, 1969), 33.

19. Albert Einstein, *Relativity: The Special and the General Theory*, trans. Robert W. Lawson (New York: Crown, 1961), 26.

20. Ibid., 30.

21. Ibid., 30.

22. Ibid., 31.

23. For a useful account of Einstein and non-Euclidean geometry, see Rudolf Carnap, *An Introduction to the Philosophy of Science*, ed. Martin Gardner (New York: Dover, 1995), 132–76.

24. Einstein's commitment to mathematical formalization is steadfast. See, for instance, Abraham Pais, *"Subtle is the Lord": The Science and Life of Albert Einstein* (New York: Oxford University Press, 1982), 111–291.

25. I follow Hans Robert Jauss in seeing literary history as a "dialectic" between text and reader, but whereas Jauss explores that dialectic as a history of changing "horizons of expectation," I explore it as a history of incomplete domestication. See Jauss, *Toward an Aesthetic of Reception*, trans. Timothy Bahti (Minneapolis: University of Minnesota Press, 1982).

26. Roger Chartier, *The Order of Books: Readers, Authors, and Libraries in Europe between the Fourteenth and Eighteenth Centuries*, trans. Lydia G. Cochrane (Stanford, CA: Stanford University Press, 1994), viii.

27. For theories and practices of translation, by Lowell himself and by others, see D. S. Carne-Ross, "Conversation with Robert Lowell," in *Robert Lowell: Interviews and Memoirs*, ed. Jeffrey Meyers (Ann Arbor: University of Michigan Press, 1988), 129–40.

28. Robert Lowell, introduction to *Imitations* (New York: Farrar, Straus and Giroux, 1961), xi.

29. Ibid., xi.

30. Robert Lowell, "Half a Century Gone," in *Notebook* (New York: Farrar, Straus and Giroux, 1970), 258.

31. Ibid., 259–60.

32. Helen Vendler identified Horace as a central inspiration for Lowell in her review of *Day by Day* (1977). See her "The Poetry of Autobiography," *New York Times Book Review* (August 14, 1977), 1, 24–25.

33. I am much indebted to this careful analysis. See Stephen Yenser, *Circle to Circle: The Poetry of Robert Lowell* (Berkeley and Los Angeles: University of California Press, 1975), 268–69.

34. Horace, Odes 1:37, in *Odes and Epodes, in Latin and English*, trans. Niall Rudd (Cambridge: Harvard University Press, 2004), 92.

35. Gaius Julius Caesar Germanicus (12–41), nicknamed Caligula (literally, "baby boot"), was Roman emperor from 37 to 41. His short reign, which ended with his assassination, was synonymous with tyranny.

36. Actually, "Cal" is even more complicated than that, "part Caligula and part Caliban," as Ian Hamilton points out. Hamilton quotes this interesting recollection from one of Lowell's St. Mark classmates: "He was called Caliban. He was also called Caligula—the least popular Roman emperor with all the disgusting traits, the depravity that everyone assumed Cal had." See Hamilton, *Robert Lowell: A Biography* (London: Faber and Faber, 1983), 20.

37. Lowell, "Caligula," in *For the Union Dead* (New York: Farrar, Straus and Giroux, 1964), 49.

38. Helen Vendler, *The Given and the Made: Strategies of Poetic Redefinition* (Cambridge: Harvard University Press, 1995), 20–21.

39. Lowell, "Caligula," 51.

40. This much abbreviated version in *Notebook* (New York: Farrar, Straus and Giroux 1967) reads as follows:

My sake, Little Boots, Caligula,
you disappoint me. Tell me what you saw—
Item: your body hairy, badly made,
head hairless, smoother than your marble head;

Item: eyes hollow, hollow temples, red
cheeks roughed with rouge, legs spindly, hands that leave
a clammy snail's trail on your wilting sleeve,
your hand no hand can hold . . . bald head, thin neck

you wished the Romans had a single neck.
That was no artist's bubble. Animals
ripened for your arenas suffered less
than you when slaughtered—yours the lawlessness
of something simple that has lost its law,
my namesake, not the last Caligula.
(p. 176)

41. Lowell, "Waking Early Sunday Morning," in *Near the Ocean* (New York: Farrar, Straus and Giroux, 1967), 24.

42. Hamilton, *Robert Lowell: A Biography*, 327. See also Paul Mariani, *Lost Puritan: A Life of Robert Lowell* (New York: Norton, 1994), 336. For the several drafts of "Waking Early Sunday Morning," see Alan Williamson, *Pity the Monsters: The Political Vision of Robert Lowell* (New Haven: Yale University Press, 1974), 119; and Williamson, "The Reshaping of 'Waking Early Sunday Morning,'" in his *Eloquence and Mere Life* (Ann Arbor: University of Michigan Press, 1994), 3–28.

43. George C. Herring, *America's Longest War: The United States and Vietnam, 1950–1975* (New York: Wiley, 1979), 129–35.

44. Ibid., 323.

45. As Robert von Hallberg points out, the letter went through at least five drafts. See *American Poetry and Culture, 1944–1980* (Cambridge: Harvard University Press, 1985), 170. The drafts are in the Houghton Library, Harvard University.

46. Robert Lowell to President Lyndon Johnson, *New York Times*, June 3, 1965, p. 1, collected in *Robert Lowell: Collected Prose*, ed. Robert Giroux (New York: Farrar, Straus and Giroux, 1987), 371.

47. Lowell, "Waking Early Sunday Morning," 23.

48. Ibid., 15.

49. See Yenser's excellent discussion of this passage, in *Circle to Circle*, 249–50.

50. Lowell, "The Ruins of Time," in *Near the Ocean*, 124.

51. Ibid., 120.

52. Lowell "Liberalism and Activism," *Commentary* 47, no. 4 (April 1969), 19. This was the second exchange between Lowell and Diana Trilling, starting with Trilling's long essay, "On the Steps of Low Library," *Commentary* 46, no. 5 (November 1968), 29–55.

53. Lowell, note to *Near the Ocean*.

54. Lowell's translation of Juvenal, "The Vanity of Human Wishes," in *Near the Ocean*, 98.

55. Nero Claudius Caesar (15–68), Roman emperor, 54–68. During the great fire that destroyed half of Rome in 64, he was rumored to have used the fire as

a backdrop to recite his own poem on the fall of Troy. Widespread public unrest in 68 led to his flight from Rome and to suicide.

CHAPTER SEVEN: AFRICAN, CARIBBEAN, AMERICAN

1. This important development is best exemplified by Brent Edwards's recent work, *The Practice of Diaspora* (Cambridge: Harvard University Press, 2003). While Edwards is especially interested in the transatlantic commingling of labor movements (the Anglophone and the Francophone) in this chapter I concentrate on the transatlantic commingling of languages. It is important to recognize that for some African-American authors (Ralph Ellison, for instance), diaspora is probably *not* the most vital issue.

2. R. E. Park, "The Conflict and Fusion of Cultures with Special Reference to the Negro," *Journal of Negro History* 4 (1919): 116.

3. E. F. Frazier, *The Negro Family in the United States* (Chicago: University of Chicago Press, 1939), 21.

4. Gilles Deleuze and Felix Guattari, *On the Line*, trans. John Johnston (New York: Semiotext[e], 1983), 1–68.

5. See, for instance, Philip D. Curtin, *The Atlantic Slave Trade* (Madison: University of Wisconsin Press, 1969); James Rawley, *Transatlantic Slave Trade* (New York: Norton, 1981).

6. Patricia Jones-Jackson, *When Roots Die: Endangered Traditions on the Sea Islands* (Athens: University of Georgia Press, 1987), 9.

7. Lorenzo Dow Turner, *Africanisms in the Gullah Dialect* (Chicago: University of Chicago Press, 1949), 2. Turner's work has been affirmed and extended in several recent collections. See, for instance, *The African Heritage of American English*, ed. Joseph E. Holloway and Winifred K. Vass (Bloomington: Indiana University Press, 1993); and *The Crucible of Carolina: Essays in the Development of Gullah Language and Culture*, ed. Michael Montgomery (Athens: University of Georgia Press, 1994). There have also been challenges to Turner, a debate collected in *Africanisms in Afro-American Language Varieties*, ed. Salikoko S. Mufwene (Athens: University of Georgia Press, 1993).

8. Melville J. Herskovits, *The Myth of the Negro Past* (New York: Harper Brothers, 1941), 6.

9. Ibid., 6–7.

10. Robert A. Hall, *Pidgin and Creole Languages* (Ithaca: Cornell University Press, 1966).

11. Ibid., xi.

12. Ibid., 107–8.

13. T. L. Markey, editor's note, to Hugo Schuchardt's *The Ethnography of Variation: Selected Writings on Pidgins and Creoles*, ed. and trans. T. L. Markey (Ann Arbor, MI: Karoma, 1979), xxi.

14. Hugo Schuchardt, "On Lingua Franca," in *Ethnography of Variation*, 26–47, quotation from 27. The essay is also collected in *Pidgin and Creole*

Languages: Selected Essays by Hugo Schuchardt, trans. Glenn G. Gilbert (London: Cambridge University Press, 1980), 65–88.

15. Schuchardt, "On Lingua Franca," 26, 32, 27–28.

16. For a contemporary plea in this spirit, see Doris Sommer, *Bilingual Aesthetics: A New Sentimental Education* (Durham, NC: Duke University Press, 2004).

17. I am thinking, of course, of Samuel Huntington.

18. Schuchardt, "Saramaccan," in *Ethnography of Variation*, 75–76.

19. Hall, *Pidgin and Creole Languages*, 141.

20. William A. Stewart, "Observations (1966) on the Problems of Defining Negro Dialect," postscript to remarks made in April 1966 at the Conference on the Language Component in the Training of Teachers of English and Reading, held in Washington D.C. by the Center for Applied Linguistics and the National Council of Teachers of English, reprinted in *Perspectives on Black English*, ed. J. Dillard (The Hague: Mouton, 1975), 57–64, quotation from 63.

21. William A. Stewart, "Continuity and Change in American Negro Dialects" (1968), *Florida FL Reporter*, 6, no. 1 (Spring 1968), 3–4, 14–16, 18, reprinted in *Perspectives on Black English*, 233–47, quotation from 243.

22. Ibid., 244–45.

23. Ibid., 234.

24. Ibid.

25. William Labov, *Language in the Inner City: Studies in the Black English Vernacular* (Philadelphia: University of Pennsylvania Press, 1972).

26. This is a crude summary of Labov's complex argument in "Contraction, Deletion, and Inherent Variability of the English Copula," 65–129.

27. Ibid., 68.

28. Ibid., 130.

29. Ibid., 131.

30. Ibid., 226. For a critique of a nation-based celebration of the vernacular, see Jonathan Arac, *Huckleberry Finn as Idol and Target* (Madison: University of Wisconsin Press, 1997), 154–82.

31. For a good account of Chomsky's impact on linguistics, see Howard Gardner, *The Mind's New Science: A History of the Cognitive Revolution* (New York: Basic Books, 1985).

32. Steven Pinker, *The Language Instinct: How the Mind Creates Language* (New York: HarperPerennial, 1995).

33. Labov, *Language in the Inner City*, 217; Pinker, *The Language Instinct*, 31.

34. Pinker, 31.

35. Labov, *Language in the Inner City*, 222; Pinker, *The Language Instinct*, 31.

36. See for instance, Daniel Dennett, *Consciousness Explained* (Boston: Little, Brown, 1991); Jerry Fodor, *The Language of Thought* (Cambridge: Harvard University Press, 1975); Gerald Edelman, *Bright Air, Brilliant Fire: On the Matter of the Mind* (New York: Basic Books, 1992).

37. Ned Block, "The Mind as the Software of the Brain," in *An Invitation to Cognitive Science*, 2nd ed., 4 vols. (Cambridge: MIT Press, 1995), 3: 377–426.

38. Antonio R. Damasio, *Descartes' Error: Emotion, Reason, and the Human Brain* (New York: Avon Books, 1994); Damasio, *The Feeling of What Happens* (New York: Harcourt Brace, 1999); Damasio, *Looking for Spinoza: Joy, Sorrow, and the Feeling Brain* (Orlando, FL: Harcourt, 2003).

39. Damasio, *The Feeling of What Happens*, 186.

40. Robert Chaudenson, *Creolization of Language and Culture*, rev. in collaboration with Salikoko S. Mufwene, trans. Sheri Pargman et al. (London: Routledge, 2001), 79.

41. Ibid., 309–10.

42. See, for instance, Joseph Roach, *Cities of the Dead: Circum-Atlantic Performance* (New York: Columbia University Press, 1996); and Diana Taylor, *The Archive and the Repertoire: Performing Cultural Memory in the Americas* (Durham, NC: Duke University Press, 2003).

43. Herskovits devotes almost half of *Myth of the Negro Past* to two long chapters, "Africanisms in Secular Life" and "Africanisms in Religious Life," discussing at length West African influences on family structure and magical rituals.

44. Aside from the three mentioned below, I would like to acknowledge the following: *African Roots/ American Cultures: Africa in the Creation of the Americas*, ed. Sheila S. Walker (London: Rowman and Littlefield, 2001); *Africanisms in American Culture*, ed. Joseph E. Holloway (Bloomington: Indiana University Press, 1990); Grey Gundaker, *Signs of Diaspora, Diaspora of Signs* (New York: Oxford University Press, 1998); Frederick Kaufman and John P. Guckin, *The African Roots of Jazz* (New York: Alfred Publishing Co., 1979); Betty M. Kuyk, *African Voices in the African American Heritage* (Bloomington: Indiana University Press, 2003); Sterling Stuckey, *Slave Culture* (New York: Oxford University Press, 1987), esp. 3–97; and John Vlach, *By the Work of Their Hands* (Ann Arbor: University of Michigan Press, 1991).

45. *Drums and Shadows: Survival Studies among the Georgia Coastal Negroes*, by the Savannah Unit, Georgia Writers' Project, Work Projects Administration (Athens: University of Georgia Press, 1940).

46. Thompson, *Flash of the Spirit: African and Afro-American Art and Philosophy* (New York: Random House, 1983), xiv. For related arguments, see also Thompson, *African Art in Motion* (Berkeley and Los Angeles: University of California Press, 1974).

47. Alan Lomax, *The Land Where Blues Began* (New York: Pantheon Books, 1993), xiii. Other scholars support this conclusion. See, for instance, Portia K. Maultsy, "Africanisms in African-American Music," in Holloway, *Africanisms in American Culture*, 185–210; Olly Wilson, " 'It Don' Mean a Thing If It Ain't Got That Swing': The Relation between African and African-American Music," in Walker, *African Roots/ American Cultures*, 153–68.

48. Alan Lomax, "The Homogeneity of African-Afro-American Musical Style," in *Afro-American Anthropology: Contemporary Perspectives*, ed. Norman E. Whitten, Jr., and John F. Szwed (New York: Free Press, 1970), 181–201, quotation from 181.

49. Ibid., 189.

50. Ibid., 199–200.

51. It is worth recalling that fractal geometry is the geometry of both animate and inanimate nature—of craggy coasts as well as lacy ferns—and, in this way, is a mathematics most adequate to the entire ecosystem.

52. Derek Walcott, "A Tropical Bestiary," in *The Castaway and Other Poems* (London: Jonathan Cape, 1965), 21.

53. The phrase is from the poem "The phrases of a patois rooted in this clay hillside," from Walcott, *The Bounty* (New York: Farrar, Straus, and Giroux, 1997), 38.

54. Kofi Agawu, *African Rhythm: A Northern Ewe Perspective* (Cambridge: Cambridge University Press, 1995), 6.

55. J. H. Kwabena Nketia, *The Music of Africa* (New York: Norton, 1974).

56. J. H. Kwabena Nketia, *Drumming in Akan Communities in Ghana* (London: Thomas Nelson and Sons, 1963), 32–50.

57. Jack Berry, "Language Systems and Literature," in *The African Experience*, ed. John Paden and Edward Soja (Evanston, IL: Northwestern University Press, 1970), 87.

58. Paul Oliver, Tony Russell, Robert M. M. Dixon, John Godrich, and Howard Rye, *Yonder Come the Blues: The Evolution of a Genre* (Cambridge: Cambridge University Press, 2001), 1–12, 90–105; Robert Palmer, *Deep Blues* (New York: Viking, 1981), 1–47.

59. Houston Baker, *Blues, Ideology, and Afro-American Literature: A Vernacular Theory* (Chicago: University of Chicago Press, 1984), 3. Baker's point is amply substantiated by an impressive collection of essays, *The Jazz Cadence of American Culture*, ed. Robert G. O'Meally (New York: Columbia University Press, 1998), which extends the discussion from blues to jazz.

60. Sherley Anne Williams, "The Blues Roots of Contemporary Afro-American Poetry," in *Afro-American Literature*, ed. Dexter Fisher and Robert B. Stepto (New York: Modern Language Association, 1978), 72–87.

61. Kamau Brathwaite, "Jazz and the West Indian Novel," in *Roots* (Ann Arbor: University of Michigan Press, 1993), 55–110.

62. Edward Brathwaite, "The Making of the Drum," in *Masks* (London: Oxford University Press, 1968), 7–10, quotation from 8.

63. Wilson Harris, introduction to *The Womb of Space: The Cross-Cultural Imagination* (Westport, CT: Greenwood Press, 1983), xv–xx, quotation from xix. Italics in original.

64. Wilson Harris, "History, Fable and Myth in the Caribbean and Guianas," in *Explorations* (Mundelstrup, Denmark: Dangaroo Press, 1981), 20–42.

65. Ibid., 25, 26–27.

66. Gloria Naylor, *Mama Day* (New York: Vintage, 1989), 5.

67. Ibid., 312.

68. Paule Marshall, *Praisesong for the Widow* (New York: Dutton, 1983), 38–39.

69. Ibid., 250.

70. Ibid., 249.

CHAPTER EIGHT: ECOLOGY ACROSS THE PACIFIC

1. Jeremy Bentham, *Introduction to the Principles of Moral and Legislation* (1789; rpt., Oxford: Clarendon Press, 1907) chap. 18, sec. 1, note.

2. The genocide unfolding in Sudan as I write—with perhaps a million black Africans dying in the hands of the Janjaweed militia—suggests that the ontologizing of difference is probably always looming as a destructive force.

3. Michael Pollan, "An Animal's Place," *New York Times Magazine*, November 11, 2002, at http://www.nytimes.com/2002/11/10/magazine/10ANIMAL.html

4. J. M.Coetzee, *The Lives of Animals* (Princeton: Princeton University Press, 1999), 21.

5. Ibid., 34.

6. Singer, *Animal Liberation* (New York: Random House, 1975), 11.

7. Jared Diamond, *The Third Chimpanzee: The Evolution and Future of the Human Animal* (New York: HarperPerennial, 1992), 2.

8. Ibid., 8–9.

9. Ibid., 19.

10. As Singer forthrightly admits, his aim is to "increase the importance we give to *individual animals*" as subjects of pain and bearers of interests, rather than to advance the claims of nonhuman species as such. By this criterion, living things not known for their sentience will be excluded from consideration. See Singer, "Not for Humans Only: The Place of Nonhumans in Environmental Issues," in *Environmental Ethics*, ed. Andrew Light and Holmes Rolston III (Oxford: Blackwell, 2003), 55–64, quotation from 63.

11. Matt Ridley, *Genome* (New York: HarperCollins, 2000), 5–6. Ridley's argument is further substantiated by Richard Dawkin's recent book. "All known life forms can be traced to a single ancestor which lived more than 3 billion years ago," he writes. See Dawkins, *The Ancestor's Tale* (Boston: Houghton Mifflin, 2004), 7.

12. Lawrence Tribe, "From Environmental Foundations to Constitutional Structures: Learning from Nature's Future," *Yale Law Journal* 84 (1975): 545–56, quotation from 552.

13. Immanuel Kant, "Duties towards Animals and Spirits," in *Lectures on Ethics*, trans. Louis Infield (London: Methuen, 1930), 239–41, quotation from 240.

14. Kant, *The Metaphysical Principles of Virtues*, trans. James Ellington (Indianapolis, IN: Bobbs-Merrill, 1984), 106.

15. Lawrence Tribe, "Ways Not to Think about Plastic Trees," *Yale Law Journal* 83 (1974): 1315–48, quotation from 1331.

16. The intersection between animal ethics and environmental ethics has already been suggested by several animal ethicists, notably Tom Regan and Mary Midgley, in their efforts to go beyond Peter Singer's work. Beginning with *The Case for Animal Rights* and moving on to *Earthbound*, Regan argues that the "possibility of developing an ethic *of* the environment, as distinct from an ethic *for its use*, turns on the possibility of making the case that natural objects,

though they do not meet the subject-of-a-life criterion, can nonetheless have inherent value." See Regan, *The Case for Animal Rights* (Berkeley and Los Angeles: University of California Press, 1983), 245. Midgley likewise reminds us that "two quite distinct sorts of moral claim . . . may arise on behalf of animals—social claims (on behalf of individual creatures) and ecological claims (on behalf of whole populations and species)." See *Animals and Why They Matter* (Harmondsworth: Penguin, 1983), 19. Two collections of essays have tried to link the two movements. See *Environmental Philosophy: From Animal Rights to Radical Ecology*, ed. Michael Zimmerman et al. (Englewood Cliffs, NJ: Prentice Hall, 1993); and *Earth Ethics: Environmental Ethics, Animal Rights, and Practical Applications*, ed. James P. Sterba (Englewood Cliffs, NJ: Prentice Hall, 1995). See also the section "Who Counts in Environmental Ethics—Animals? Plants? Ecosystems?" in Light and Rolston, *Environmental Ethics*, 55–128.

17. "Deep ecology" began with the Norwegian philosopher Arne Naess. I myself find this less compelling than the work of the others. But see Naess's manifesto for deep ecology, "The Shallow and the Deep, Long-Range Ecology," *Inquiry* 16 (1973): 95–100. A vast body of literature has since grown up. See, for instance, Bill Devall and George Sessions, *Deep Ecology* (Salt Lake City, UT: Peregrine Smith Books, 1985); *Deep Ecology*, ed. Michael Tobias (San Diego: Avant Books, 1985); Naess's own essays are collected in his *Ecology, Community, and Lifestyle*, trans. David Rothenberg (Cambridge: Cambridge University Press, 1990).

18. Aldo Leopold, *Sand County Almanac* (New York: Oxford University Press, 1949), 220.

19. Rachel Carson, *Silent Spring* (Boston: Houghton Mifflin, 1962), 297.

20. Martin Rees, *Our Final Hour: A Scientist's Warning* (New York: Basic Books, 2003).

21. Lawrence Buell, *The Environmental Imagination: Thoreau, Nature Writing, and the Formation of American Culture* (Cambridge: Harvard University Press, 1995); and Buell, *Writing for an Endangered World* (Cambridge: Harvard University Press, 2001).

22. Gary Snyder, "Poetry and the Primitive: Notes on Poetry as an Ecological Survival Technique," in *Earth House Hold* (New York: New Directions, 1969), 117–30, quotation from 127.

23. For much of that time he studied under the tutelage of Oda Sesso Roshi, Rinzai Zen master and head abbot of Daitoku-ji Temple, Kyoto. See Patrick Murphy, *Understanding Gary Synder* (Columbia: University of South Carolina Press, 1992), 8.

24. The connection between these two has been increasingly remarked upon. See, for instance, *Buddhism and Ecology*, ed. Mary Evelyn Tucker and Duncan Ryuken Williams (Cambridge: Harvard University Press, 1997).

25. For an important critique of the Judeo-Christian tradition as a tradition unfriendly to the environment, see Lynn White, "The Historical Root of the Ecocrisis," *Science* 155 (1967): 1203–7. Reprinted in White, *Machina Ex Deo* (Cambridge: MIT Press, 1968), 75–94.

26. Gary Snyder, "Re-inhabitation," in *The Old Ways* (San Francisco: City Light Books, 1978), 57–66, quotation from 62–63. Hannah Arendt also comments

on the 1957 launching of the satellite. See her *The Human Condition* (Chicago: University of Chicago Press, 1958), 1.

27. Gary Snyder, "Buddhism and the Coming Revolution," *Earth House Hold*, 90–93, quotation from 91–92.

28. Ibid., 93.

29. Snyder, "Poetry and the Primitive," in *Earth House Hold*, 117–30, quotation from 126.

30. Interview with Thomas Irmer and Matthias Schmidt, 1995, in *Conversations with Leslie Marmon Silko*, ed. Ellen L. Arnold (Jackson: University of Mississippi Press, 2000), 146–61, quotation from 148. I should point out, however, that Silko has also criticized Snyder for failing "to realize that although he is careful, even reverent with this land he is occupying, it is *not* 'his' land." See her "An Old-Time Indian Attack Conducted in Two Parts: Part One—Imitation 'Indian' Poems/ Part Two—Gary Snyder's *Turtle Island*," in *Nothing but the Truth: An Anthology of Native American Literature*, ed. John L. Purdy and James Ruppert (Upper Saddle River, NJ: Prentice Hall, 2001), 166–71, quotation from 171.

31. Gary Snyder, "What Happened Here Before," in *Turtle Island* (New York: New Directions, 1974), 78–81, quotation from 78, 79.

32. Leslie Silko, interview with Laura Coltelli, first published in *Native American Literature Forum* 4–5 (1992–93): 65–80; collected in Arnold, *Conversations with Leslie Marmon Silko*, 119–34, quotation from 122, 126. See also Silko, *Almanac of the Dead* (New York: Penguin, 1991).

33. Simon J. Ortiz, "Speaking," in *A Good Journey* (Berkeley: Turtle Island, 1977), 52.

34. Snyder, introduction note, in *Turtle Island*, 1.

35. Chris Stringer and Robin McKie, *African Exodus* (London: Jonathan Cape, 1996), esp. chapter 8, "Africans under the Skin," 170–83.

36. Snyder, *Paris Review* interview with Eliot Weinberger, 92nd Street Y, October 26, 1992, collected in *The Gary Snyder Reader: Prose, Poetry, Translations, 1952–1998* (Washington, DC: Counterpoint, 1999), 321–38, quotation from 336.

37. J. Baird Callicott, *The Earth's Insight: A Survey of Ecological Ethics from the Mediterranean Basin to the Australian Outback* (Berkeley and Los Angeles: University of California Press, 1994), 121. I am grateful to Ken Winkler for this reference.

38. Hans Peter Duerr, *Dreamtime: Concerning the Boundary between Wilderness and Civilization* (Oxford: Blackwell, 1985), 110–11.

39. Willa Cather, *Death Comes for the Archbishop* (New York: Vintage, 1971), 233.

40. Snyder, interview with the *East West Journal*, collected in *The Real Work: Interviews and Talks, 1964–1979* (New York: New Directions, 1980), 92–137, quotation from 115.

41. Snyder, "The Incredible Survival of Coyote," in *The Real Work*, 70–71.

42. For the "anonymity" of Native American literature, see Arnold Krupat, in *Recovering the Word*, ed. Brian Swann and Arnold Krupat (Berkeley and Los Angeles: University of California Press, 1987).

43. Ramsey's work on Coyote includes *Love in an Earthquake* (Seattle: University of Washington Press, 1973); *Coyote Was Going There: Indian Literature of the Oregon Country* (Seattle: University of Washington Press, 1977); "Coyote Goes Upriver: A Cycle for Story-Theater and Mime," *Georgia Review* 35 (1981): 524–51; *Reading the Fire: Essays in the Traditional Indian Literatures of the Far West* (Lincoln: University of Nebraska Press, 1983).

44. Ramsey, *Reading the Fire*.

45. Simon Ortiz, "Telling about Coyote," in *A Good Journey*, 15–18, quotation from 16.

46. "A Berry Feast" was first published in *Evergreen Review* 2 (1957): 110–14, reprinted in Snyder, *Back Country* (New York: New Directions, 1968), 13–16.

47. Snyder, "A Berry Feast," *Back Country*, 15.

48. Snyder, "The Incredible Survival of Coyote," 84.

49. Leslie Silko, "Toe'esh: A Laguna Coyote Story," in *Storyteller* (New York: Seaver Books, 1981), 236–39, quotation from 239.

50. Ibid., 69.

51. Paul Radin, *The Trickster: A Study in American Indian Mythology, with Commentaries by Karl Kerenyi and C. G. Jung* (London: Routledge and Kegan Paul, 1956), 132.

52. Ibid., ix.

53. Karl Kerenyi, "The Trickster in Relation to Greek Mythology," in Radin, *The Trickster*, 171–91, quotation from 180.

54. David Padwa, "What's the Sanskrit Word for Coyote?" in *Gary Snyder: Dimensions of a Life*, ed. John Halper (San Francisco: Sierra Club Books, 1991), 302–11.

55. A. R. Aryan, *Hanuman: Art, Mythology, and Folklore*, 2nd ed. (New Delhi: Rekha Prakashan, 1994), 13.

56. Ibid., 13.

57. Ibid., 16.

58. Octavio Paz, *El Mono Gramatico*, translated as *The Monkey Grammarian*, trans. Helen R. Lane (New York: Seaver Books, 1981). My thanks to Doris Sommer for alerting me to this text.

59. Shanti Lal Nagar, *Hanuman: In Art, Culture, Thought and Literature* (New Delhi: Intellectual Publishing House, 1995), xv.

60. These names refer to the forest-dwelling *vanara*, the reddish-brown or yellow *hari*, the trembling *kapi*, the leaping *plavaga*, the branch gazelle *sakhamrga* and the cow-tailed *golangula*. See Catherine Ludvik, *Hanuman in the Ramayana of Valmiki and the Ramacaritamanasa of Tulasi Dasa* (Delhi: Motilal Banarsidass Publishers, 1994), 2, 15 n. 5.

61. For an interesting account of the debate, see Ludvik, *Hanuman*, 2.

62. Shanti Lal Nagar, *Hanuman in Art, Culture, Thought and Literature* (New Delhi: Intellectual Publishing House, 1995), x.

63. *Ramayana*, 51:3–4. I take the translation from *Hanuman in Valmiki's Ramayana: Sanskrit Text of Selected Chapters with Word-by-Word translation into English*, trans. Irma Schotsman (Delhi: NAG Publishers, 2002), since it

emphasizes the syntax and the repetitive nature of the Sanskrit original, in a way that is lost in Richard P. Goldman's standard translation.

64. *Ramayana*, 51:24–27.

65. *Ramayana*, 51:13.

66. *Ramayana*, 51:39.

67. See, for instance, Srinivasa Iyengar, *Asian Variations in Ramayana* (New Delhi: Sahitya Akademi, 1983); V. Raghavan, *The Ramayana Traditions in Asia* (New Delhi: Sahitya Akademi, 1980); *Many Ramayanas*, ed. Paula Richman (Berkeley and Los Angeles: University of California Press, 1991). See especially Rich Freeman, "Thereupon Hangs a Tail: The Deification of Vali in the Teyyam Worship of Malabar," in *Questioning Ramayanas*, ed. Paula Richman (Berkeley and Los Angeles: University of California Press, 2001), 187–220.

68. The non-Chinese input into this, the most celebrated of Chinese novels, is a matter of fierce debate, begun in the early-twentieth century by two prominent scholars, Hu Shih and Lu Hsun. See Hu Shih, "Hsi-yu chi k'ao-cheng" (1923), reprinted in *Hu Shih wen-ts'un* (Hong Kong: Commercial Press, 1962), 354–99; Lu Hsun, "Kuan yu San-tsang ch'u ching chi teng" (1927), reprinted in *Lu Hsun ch'uen-chi* 20 (1948), 372–77. See also Glen Dudbridge, *The Hsi-yu chi: A Study of Antecedents to the Sixteenth-Century Chinese Novel* (Cambridge: Cambridge University Press, 1970).

69. *Hsi-yu Chi*, chap. 6, my translation. For a standard translation, see *Monkey: Folk Novel of China by We Ch'eng-En*, trans. Arthur Waley (1943; rpt., New York: Grove Press, 1958), 68.

70. Claude Levi-Strauss, *Structural Anthropology*, trans. Claire Jacobson and Brooke Grundfest Schoef (New York: Basic Books, 1963), 246.

71. Ibid., 248.

72. Ibid. 245–48. Levi-Strauss is partly drawing on the work of Leonhard Adam, "Northwest American Indian Art and Its Early Chinese Parallels," *Man* 36, no. 3 (1936).

73. Lévi-Strauss, *Structural Anthropology*, 248.

74. *Monkey: Folk Novel of China by Wu Ch'eng-en*.

75. Gates focuses on the African trickster, Esu-Elegbara. See *The Signifying Monkey: A Theory of Afro-American Literary Criticism* (New York: Oxford University Press, 1988).

76. Neila C. Seshachari, "Reinventing Peace: Conversations with Tripmaster Maxine Hong Kingston," in *Conversations with Maxine Hong Kingston*, ed. Paul Skenazy and Tera Martin (Jackson: University of Mississippi Press, 1998), 192–214, quotation from 204.

77. Ibid., 205.

78. Ibid., 204.

79. Ibid., 204.

80. Gerald Vizenor, "December 1946: Saturnalia at Dayton's," in *Interior Landscapes* (Minneapolis: University of Minnesota Press, 1990), 50–56, quotation from 50.

81. Vizenor, "Families of the Crane," in *Interior Landscapes*, 3–20, quotation from 4–5.

82. Ibid., 3.

83. Vizenor, "June 1936: Measuring My Blood," in *Interior Landscapes*, 26–33, quotation from 27.

84. Ibid., 27.

85. Gerald Vizenor, *Griever: An American Monkey King in China* (Normal: Illinois State University Fiction Collective, 1987), 51.

86. Ibid., 37, 40.

87. Ibid., 41–42.

88. Vizenor, "June 1936: Measuring My Blood," 26.

89. Leslie Marmon Silko, *Ceremony* (New York: Penguin, 1977), 7–8.

Index